The world's children thank you for your fine support.

Judith Spiegelman

We Are the Children

We Are the Children

A celebration of UNICEF's first forty years

by Judith M. Spiegelman and UNICEF

The Atlantic Monthly Press
Boston/New York

Dedication

Carl Sandburg once wrote, "There is only one
child in the world; and the child's name is
ALL CHILDREN."

This book is dedicated to ALL CHILDREN.

FIRST EDITION

Copyright acknowledgments appear on page 224.

LIBRARY OF CONGRESS CATALOGING-IN-PUBLICATION DATA

Spiegelman, Judith M.
  We are the children.

  1. UNICEF – History.   2. Child welfare – Developing
countries – History.   I. UNICEF.   II. Title.
HV703.U4766S67   1986   341.7'6   86-25922
ISBN 0-87113-105-6

Published simultaneously in Canada

PRINTED IN THE UNITED STATES OF AMERICA

Contents

Prologue

On our fortieth birthday

This is a story of children in trouble. In pictures and words it records the suffering of children in war, children in hunger, children in natural disasters and, most poignant of all, children in neglect. It also tells us what people who care have been doing about it and what can be done to stop, or at least reduce drastically, the needless dying of fifteen million children every year, the needless mental and physical maiming of many other millions.

This is not a one-dimensional story of gloom and doom and horror but a rich and complex one of human courage, generosity, and kindness. To be kind, in its original sense, means "to treat like kin." And there have been many instances in the past forty years of how people and their institutions have treated children of other parents and other lands like their own kin. This is the history of UNICEF—the world's children's agency. It is a rounded account of how UNICEF acquired the reputation of being a nonpolitical United Nations agency; of how political skill is required to be politically uninvolved; and of how people's support of an institution is the ultimate measure of the value of the work being done. Wherever children are in trouble, people expect UNICEF to be there, doing what needs doing.

Yet UNICEF is only a handful of people with a handful of money, deployed across 110 developing countries. How can 500 professional men and women convey the impression of being ubiquitous? By linking hands with other people— private groups of citizens banded into national committees for UNICEF, private voluntary organizations, business corporations, religious bodies, trade unions, professional associations and people's movements and school groups that, year by year, tend to the needs of children, set out to raise funds for them, raise the level of awareness of their needs everywhere, and put private pressure on governments to be generous to UNICEF. The latter is essential, because UNICEF is a voluntary agency to which governments are not required by international law to contribute, as they are to the United Nations and its big specialized agencies.

But governments are also people, and government leaders relate to UNICEF as a humane institution, concerned with their own children and their neighbors'. Children are their future. I learned that truth forty years ago in my own country.

In 1947, during the months preceding independence, the Board of Ministers of Sri Lanka talked to themselves: What does self-government mean? It means we will be free people in the future. What is that future? The future is our children. What do our children need to make that future a good future? Education. Right! All children will be educated free. What else do our children need? Health. Right! There will be free health care for every family. And soon, cottage hospitals and health clinics in every district and township. What else do our children need? Food. Right! No child will go hungry in independent Sri Lanka. There will be subsidized rice for everyone and free rice for the poorest. And they made a mnemonic out of the Sinhalese word for a child, to prod themselves into remembering these needs: LA–MA–YA. On posters and banners in the streets they decoded this mnemonic: LA = Lankavay (Sri Lanka's); MA = Matudiyunuwa (Better Future); YA = Yatura (Key). The child is the key to Sri Lanka's future.

When the wiseacres asked cost-efficiency questions such as, Can you afford all this? the ministers answered: What we *cannot* afford is to neglect our children's needs—because they are the future. And they naively and resolutely held on to this faith under fire from a barrage of foreign-aid experts who tried to dismantle this apparatus of human caring.

Many years later, Arthur Lewis, the brilliant West Indian economist, enunciated what the naive leaders of the first government of Sri Lanka had known without the benefit of book knowledge: Unless people at the top care about human growth and set out resolutely to translate that caring into practice, "development" will fail.

Sri Lanka's experience taught the world other important

lessons. Within a few years of the granting of free education to all children, their parents—even the illiterate ones—recognized the value of education and health for the future of their families. Fewer and fewer of their children were dying in their infancy and early years. The statisticians noticed that infant and child mortality rates were falling. Parents, realizing that they no longer needed to have insurance-size families to be certain that some of their children would survive, began to have fewer children. Then the statisticians saw that the birth rate and the rate of population growth were also falling. They said they had no "proof" that fewer child deaths were the cause of fewer child births, but there was little doubt that parents were beginning to correlate the two. The fallacy of the "scientific" mind that regards the absence of proof as proof of absence had been exploded by common experience. If the indicators of the statisticians showed that the GNP per capita was under three hundred dollars, it did not mean underdevelopment. It meant that Sri Lanka had spent its material wealth on developing its people's lives, a process the economists have now begun to call human resource development. My country's investment in children had yielded rich dividends and produced a population in which fewer children were dying from preventable causes; the average family size had been halved in twenty to thirty years; most people—90 percent—could read and write letters and numbers; the female population had been brought into the mainstream of national life through equal access to schooling and training, and though people were materially poor, unemployment rife, and malnutrition common, children were no longer dropping dead from hunger.

It is a story, by and large, of successful development. And, measured by the human development indicators designed by UNICEF's executive director, Jim Grant, and his associates—the PQLI, or Physical Quality of Life Index—Sri Lanka is an example of how rich a nation can be in the quality of its people when its leaders care about their children, the key to the future.

Can the lessons of this story be translated into all the world's languages? Can the world's leaders summon the political will and hold fast to it against political whim and the fads of the economic theorists?

It does not take much, in money terms, to enable poor countries to provide the basic services children need: food, fresh water, some household energy for cooking, a house, a school, a community health clinic, a playground, clothes, shoes, and loving care. Just 1 percent of the $900 billion the world's governments spend on making weapons of war would make the difference. The world need never again be treated to the obscene spectacle of children with bulging eyes, bellies bloated from marasmus, and limbs rickety from hunger, if the world's leaders would resolve to put children at the center of their political agenda and in national budgets.

The history of the past forty years has shown that people do care about the suffering of other people's children; that is why UNICEF exists, to give substance to that feeling. Governments have shown that they can and will respond to that popular concern when they are confronted by photographs of the *loud* emergencies of famine, war, and natural disasters. But in the next fourteen years, those preceding the year 2000, this will to care needs to be transformed into a concern for the daily needs of children, for the needless, quiet dying of forty thousand children every day, for the sadness of forty thousand families carrying a child's coffin to the graveyard, with no headlines or television to record their grief. Can they learn from Sri Lanka's experience that to resolve and sustain the will to care about that *silent* emergency is the measure of civilized governance?

Tarzie Vittachi, UNICEF's Deputy Executive Director, External Relations

I: Survivors of World War II

The rescue of a new generation

Somewhere, the place it matters not—somewhere
I saw a child hungry and thin of face,
Eyes in whose pool life's joy no longer stirred
Lips that were dead to laughter's eager kiss,
Yet parted fiercely to a crust of bread.
And since that time I walk in ceaseless dread,
Fear that the child I saw, and all the hosts
Of children of a world at play with death
May die, or living, live in bitterness. . . .
O God, today, above the cries of war,
Hear then thy children's prayer, and grant to us
Thy peace—God's peace
And bread for starving children!

— from *Prayer for Children,*
    Francis Cardinal Spellman,
    December 1944

"All wars are a war against children." The perception was by Eglantyne Jebb, the British social reformer, who was moved by seeing the impact of World War I on the young. It was mild compared to merely the chance casualties of battle, though those deaths and maimings were legion. In World War II, children were deliberately sought out as victims. They saw their parents taken away, and they themselves were taken to camps where numbers were tattooed on their small wrists in readiness for slave labor or execution. World War II robbed eleven million children of mothers and fathers. It broke up millions of families who were never together again. From England to the Soviet Union, across China and Japan, children hid from enemy bombs and shells. Their homes, their teachers, their playgrounds, their nurses, and their churches and synagogues were destroyed. Millions became refugees or were displaced inside their own countries. A handful survived the dropping of the first atomic bombs. In the end, all children suffered—the children of the victors as well as the vanquished.

The church bells began to ring in May 1945. People gathered in the streets, singing and dancing, kissing each other, weeping for joy. There were big parades. The war in Europe was over. Three months later, in August, the war in the Pacific was over. It was the end of the most massive destruction in human history.

The children who had survived the war had now to survive the peace. Millions of them had no homes; millions were orphans, and many whose parents were still alive had no idea where they were. In Europe children roamed the streets and countryside in "wolf packs." They begged or stole the food they ate, the sticks to make a fire, old rags for clothes. Some of them were blinded and crippled. They sought shelter in the ruins of bombed-out buildings, in caves and basements. Milk was almost unknown to them. If it could be found, they had not the money to buy it. So, too, with soap and medical supplies. Children were collected and brought to centers, where officials faced the dilemma of what to do with them. Orphanages could not hold them; nowhere was the supply of food, clothing, medicine remotely adequate.

Tuberculosis struck many of these children. So did rickets, bending legs that would never be straight again. There also began to appear an age-old scourge linked to war but not thought of in relation to children: syphilis. Great numbers of newborns and small children were affected.

The victors were not oblivious to all this. Even before the first Allied soldiers landed on the beaches of France, plans were made to ship supplies inside Fortress Europe. After towns and villages were liberated, a remarkable international organization created by the wartime Allies came to the rescue. It was the United Nations Relief and Rehabilitation Administration (UNRRA). It helped rebuild shattered nations and fed millions of their youngsters with daily food shipments. From 1943 through 1946, and even for months afterward, UNRRA staved off famine and epidemic.

But the postwar world had turbulence, too, in civil war, in the mass migration of people, and most of all, in the start of the cold war between East and West. It was this that led to the winding down of UNRRA's work. It was a premature conclusion to a great humanitarian operation. Its demise threatened the new generation most of all, and a handful of caring individuals asked the rest of the world: Are the children who have survived now to be abandoned? Is the spark of conscience felt for these children by people everywhere strong enough to rekindle a sense of common cause and purpose—the spirit that won the war?

The answer the world gave to its children is documented in these pages. It begins in the ruins of war.

Above: Orphaned: In 1949, after four years in refugee camps, brother and sister are on their way to a new home, all their worldly possessions in their hands.

Right: Haunted: David Seymour's famous photograph epitomizing the damage to a child's psyche. Tereska, age four, was asked to draw a picture of her home; she filled the blackboard with scribbles. Tereska was born in 1944, after Poland had been under the Nazis for five years.

Left: Scavenger: For this boy in China's Hunan province in 1946, survival means a few beans salvaged from a filthy Hengyang gutter—his first meal in three days.

Below: Survivor: A year after the first atomic bomb was dropped, a two-year-old sits sobbing alone amid the ruins of Hiroshima.

In a lighter moment, *Seeds of Destiny* producer-director Captain David Miller (seated center) and five of the ten-member crew pose outside Hitler headquarters ("Reichs Kansel") in Berlin in 1945. Standing left to right are cameramen Lt. Jean C. Barrere, P.F.C. Angelo M. Tempesta, Tec 4 George F. Jensen, and Lt. Robert C. Scrivner. To Miller's left is scriptwriter P.F.C. Arthur Arthur. The remaining four crew—Lt. Andrew C. Burt, Jr., Top Sgt. John E. Muth, Tec 4 David B. Mott, and Tec 5 William A. Ashworth—are behind the camera.

A seed of destiny

Soon after peace was declared, eight Americans—cameramen who had spent the war in an elite U.S. Army Signal Corps film unit under Hollywood film director George Stevens—were asked if they would stay on in Europe. Their mission: to participate in the making of a documentary for the U.S. Army and UNRRA. They had already filmed some of the most momentous events of the war, including the Allied landing on the beaches of Normandy, the liberation of the Nazi death camps, and the German surrender at Reims. Now they were being asked to delay their homecoming in order to record the impact of the war on children.

Captain David Miller, a filmmaker and Signal Corps member now living in Los Angeles, remembers what he said that day: "When I asked for volunteers, I told the men: 'The shooting war is over, but the war itself is not. Now we have to go out there and save all the children.' We were in Paris at the time. I promised to get the men home in time for Christmas. So they agreed to come along."

With special orders from General Dwight D. Eisenhower giving them access everywhere, producer-director Miller and his camera crew set out across Europe in jeeps and trucks, through war-stricken Belgium, Germany, Italy, Yugoslavia, and Greece. For over four months they focused their hand-held cameras on children wherever they found them: warming themselves over fires in bombed-out buildings; languishing in hospitals and orphanages; foraging for scraps in garbage cans; living in ruins, caves, even in sheds that had been used for cattle. Many begged, stole, or sold black-market cigarettes to stay alive.

"We went into an improvised hospital somewhere in Italy," Miller recalls, "where ill children were being treated. The stench was so terrible in the children's ward that we had to cover our mouths and noses with wet handkerchiefs while we filmed. We took turns going outside to vomit. During the two to three hours it took us to shoot a hundred feet of film, three children died. We found conditions like this in many countries. This was a heartbreaking film to make."

STILLS FROM FILM SEEDS OF DESTINY

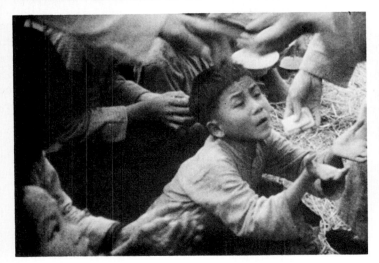

The film's first screening was held at the White House in the spring of 1946. Among those in attendance was Fiorello La Guardia, newly appointed director of UNRRA. "It will be a tragedy," La Guardia wrote a few weeks after viewing the film, "if *Seeds of Destiny* is not shown in every moving picture theater in this country."

But it never was. Only nineteen minutes long, *Seeds of Destiny* revealed too much of the stark horror of war. Both La Guardia and Miller tried to persuade Spiros Skouras and other top Hollywood moguls to get movie-theater owners to show the film. In June 1946, the reviewing committee of the American Theaters Association vetoed *Seeds of Destiny*. Yes, they said, it had a "sock message," but it was "entirely too gruesome, not a fit subject to show children . . . and not even a fit subject for theaters generally."

Since the documentary couldn't "go public," it had to go private. Screenings were held by parent-teacher associations, churches, unions, service clubs, and other private groups. Within three years, some eleven million people saw *Seeds of Destiny* across Canada, the United States, Britain, France, and Australia. Everywhere, people were stunned. Many audiences sat silent through the entire film. But when it was over, they were moved to give more than $200 million to children's welfare, making *Seeds of Destiny* the biggest money-maker for charity of its day. In 1947, at the Academy Awards ceremony, it became the first documentary to receive an Oscar.

The film was sent to Geneva in August 1946, where Lord Philip Noel-Baker, U.K. delegate to UNRRA, arranged for it to be shown daily during the UNRRA governing council's last meeting. UNRRA was winding down. Its council had voted unanimously to propose to the United Nations that an international children's emergency fund—UNICEF—be created out of UNRRA's unspent funds, and the film, many thought, made the importance of such an organization clear. When the Marshall Plan came before Congress in 1947, a special showing of *Seeds of Destiny* also helped gain support for its passage. The film had become perhaps "the most powerful editorial ever written."

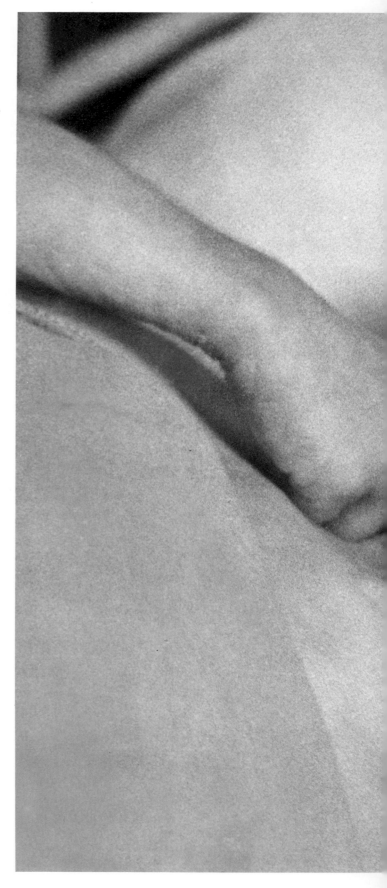

The lolling head of a listless child. Captured onscreen, it caused millions to weep and donations to flow.

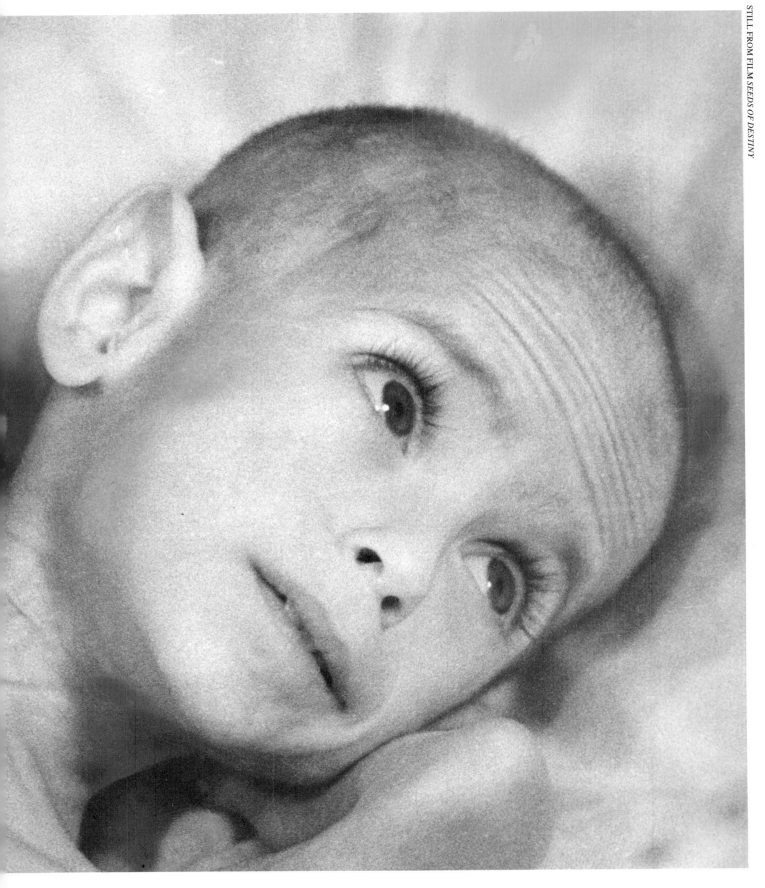

Above: Childhood prevails. Two little ones in Italy play with what was once a doll.

Opposite: A few minutes of fun help them to forget. This group dances near the ruins of their former orphanage in Monte Cassino, Italy. To the left, but not visible, is their new home built by the Pope's fund.

What I saw

by David Seymour
August 1948

As a photographer, I don't know much about words. I speak the language of pictures. I look around and try to record what I see. In the first six months of 1948, I saw plenty. I went to Poland, Hungary, Greece, Italy, and Austria with my eyes and camera open to the faces of children. The key picture to the series of photos I shot shows a bunch of kids who, in the midst of the ruins of their bombed-out cities, are playing with bricks. It illustrates their direct response to the destruction that surrounded them; they wanted a school to replace their lost homes—a place to play as well as learn. They wanted a doctor to protect and build up their frail health. All over the five countries I witnessed the same terrible need and the great challenge—in youngsters sitting on the steps of bombed-out, naked houses, where through the smashed-in stairways you could see the sky; among Italian boys playing with empty shells in the rubble of Monte Cassino; and in little girls selling black-market cigarettes and soap on the streets of Naples.

But I also saw the beginnings, the wonderful beginnings of the recovery effort. In Poland, amid the desert of the Warsaw ghetto, I saw the genesis of a garden school for handicapped and backward children—orphans, kids born in concentration camps, war-scarred victims of all sorts. At the Villagio del Fanciullo in Italy, an entire children's community was equipped with adequate medical, educational, and recreational facilities.

Near the Acropolis in Athens, Danish nurses and doctors vaccinated Greek children against tuberculosis. This project was being carried out jointly by UNICEF and the Scandinavian Red Cross Societies, with cooperation from the World Health Organization. Together with the local governments, these agencies aimed at reaching, in the next five years, fifty million children the world over. I watched fifty doctor-nurse teams operate in Poland and Hungary. They had already tested and treated close to three million children in those two countries alone. And I became aware that UNICEF-distributed milk was helping troubled children sleep better, as it was improving their dietary balance.

Wherever I went, I saw children playing out their dreams of a full and peaceful life amid the ruins of their parents' world. But the reality of giving that world back to them—making sense of their different experiences, working out psychological treatments and other appropriate methods of healing, rehabilitating, and educating—presented a greater challenge than ever before.

Barefoot boys simulate war in Vienna's Favoriten district.
MAGNUM PHOTOS / DAVID SEYMOUR

Born amid the rubble

"There is a time to be born . . ." says the Old Testament. But no one could say that the years 1945–1950 in continental Europe were such a time. More than thirty-one million babies started their lives amid the rubble of World War II, when almost everything they needed to survive and flourish—milk, fat, other foods, medicine, diapers, blankets, fuel, and housing—was scarce, or so expensive that only a few lucky mothers could provide the basic necessities. The world was ill-prepared for new life. Many hospitals had been destroyed. Others had barely enough doctors and nurses, medical equipment, and drugs to function. In some famine areas in the winter of 1946–1947, one out of two babies died before its first birthday.

Of greatest concern was the sudden birth of many premature and underweight infants to malnourished mothers. Their numbers soared. Under the best prewar conditions, their hold on life would have been precarious. What chance did they have of surviving in postwar circumstances? In addition, thousands of newborn babies in countries on the main paths of invading armies were found to have syphilis and gonorrhea. The diseases had apparently been contracted from their infected mothers during pregnancy.

Out of the war effort came two medical innovations that saved many babies' lives. One was the modern-day incubator, inside of which a premature infant could not only survive but could continue growing. The other was mass-production of the twentieth century's first "miracle" drug: penicillin.

"It's twins."

Above: Born during battle: Cartoonist Bill Mauldin shows how Allied army medics took the place of destroyed local health services during the last days of World War II.

Opposite: Grandma finds relief from grim surroundings in the child she wheels, 1947, Essen, Germany. The city, home of Krupp munitions works, was heavily bombed during the war and occupied by the British soon after.

"It's twins."

Above: Born during battle: Cartoonist Bill Mauldin shows how Allied army medics took the place of destroyed local health services during the last days of World War II.

Opposite: Grandma finds relief from grim surroundings in the child she wheels, 1947, Essen, Germany. The city, home of Krupp munitions works, was heavily bombed during the war and occupied by the British soon after.

Born amid the rubble

"There is a time to be born . . ." says the Old Testament. But no one could say that the years 1945–1950 in continental Europe were such a time. More than thirty-one million babies started their lives amid the rubble of World War II, when almost everything they needed to survive and flourish—milk, fat, other foods, medicine, diapers, blankets, fuel, and housing—was scarce, or so expensive that only a few lucky mothers could provide the basic necessities. The world was ill-prepared for new life. Many hospitals had been destroyed. Others had barely enough doctors and nurses, medical equipment, and drugs to function. In some famine areas in the winter of 1946–1947, one out of two babies died before its first birthday.

Of greatest concern was the sudden birth of many premature and underweight infants to malnourished mothers. Their numbers soared. Under the best prewar conditions, their hold on life would have been precarious. What chance did they have of surviving in postwar circumstances? In addition, thousands of newborn babies in countries on the main paths of invading armies were found to have syphilis and gonorrhea. The diseases had apparently been contracted from their infected mothers during pregnancy.

Out of the war effort came two medical innovations that saved many babies' lives. One was the modern-day incubator, inside of which a premature infant could not only survive but could continue growing. The other was mass-production of the twentieth century's first "miracle" drug: penicillin.

Barefoot boys simulate war in
Vienna's Favoriten district.

First in line to be cured of
endemic syphilis were foundlings
in Naples. Penicillin provided by
UNICEF in great doses made
them well.

The new bulletproof, acrylic-plastic cockpit of the B-25 bomber (below) helped protect bombardiers from death. After the war, this same plastic was a lifesaver for premature babies. Margaret Wynn (bottom) uses a doll to demonstrate how the incubator kept out germs and made possible the maintenance of a constant temperature and oxygen supply—optimum conditions for the survival of a premature baby.

UPI

The incubator was made possible by a marvelous new material, acrylic plastic, which had come off the drawing boards during the war. The bulletproof plastic was used for cockpits of fighter-bombers; it wrapped a protective shield around bombardiers, saving many of their lives. After the war, the same plastic formed a protective shield for the fragile premature infant, making possible an even flow of oxygen and a constant temperature. The infant's new home was the closest artificial equivalent to a mother's womb yet devised. The incubator increased a premature baby's chances of survival many times over the crude "hot boxes" used before its discovery.

UNICEF provided incubators to Europe, but its role didn't end there. Doctors and nurses in countries receiving the incubators needed training to handle fragile newborns properly inside the new equipment. Working closely with pediatricians and other experts from the World Health Organization (WHO), and with medical authorities in each coun-

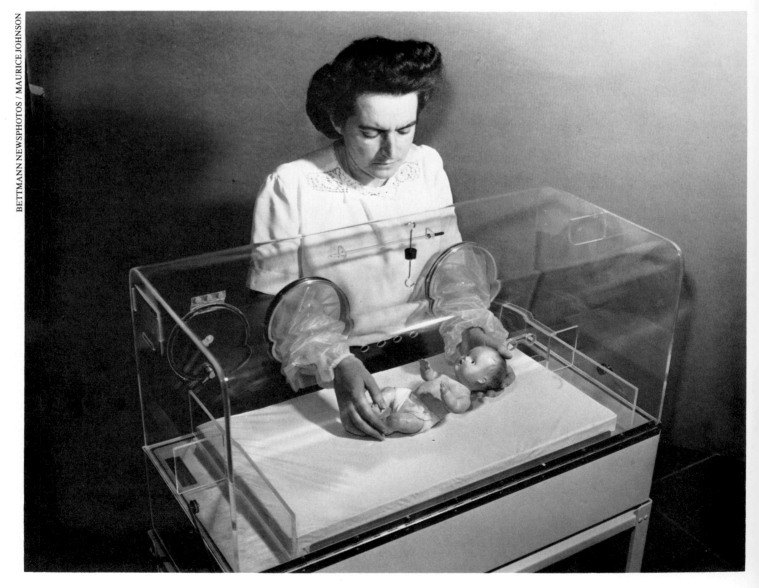

BETTMANN NEWSPHOTOS / MAURICE JOHNSON

try, UNICEF made possible such instruction.

In France, UNICEF provided over five hundred incubators and other supplies for premature-baby centers throughout the country. Nineteen provincial centers in Italy were similarly equipped, and their medical personnel trained. Premature babies born in Finland, Poland, and Czechoslovakia benefited from the new invention and the improved care it brought.

Penicillin had been discovered in the United Kingdom by Sir Alexander Fleming in 1928, and the first human subjects had been treated with it in 1941. But mass-producing the drug seemed a near-impossibility until 1943 and 1944, when the U.S. government gave it utmost priority. Enough penicillin was produced so that all forty thousand Allied soldiers wounded in the Normandy invasion could be treated with the miracle drug. Injections of it were also found to be a modern-day "magic bullet," curing syphilis, an age-old scourge, especially among soldiers.

The very war that inflicted the horror of social disease on newborn babies thus provided a cure. Although the postwar cost of the drug was high, UNICEF became the supplier of penicillin to nations organizing massive syphilis-eradication programs, as well as those attempting smaller-scale action.

Thousands of newborns were protected against syphilis when, during pregnancy, their mothers were screened for the disease and treated with penicillin UNICEF provided. In the spring of 1948 Poland took the lead, mounting the world's first national campaign against syphilis. Less than a year later, 18,000 mothers and 5,600 children with syphilis were treated. Two other countries, Yugoslavia and Czechoslovakia, also mounted nationwide campaigns. In Yugoslavia, in 1949, nearly two million people were screened for syphilis, and those infected were treated. An existing penicillin plant in Zemun was modernized with UNICEF equipment, strengthening Yugoslavia's ability to fight syphilis as well as other diseases threatening children's lives. In Slovakia, Bohemia, and Moravia, penicillin and laboratory equipment supplied by UNICEF enabled those Czechoslovakian districts to give 1.5 million blood tests in 1950. Bulgaria, Greece, Finland, Italy, and Hungary also received help in battling the disease. UNICEF supplies were used exclusively for the treatment of children and mothers, while the governments themselves paid the cost of diagnosing and treating the disease in the rest of the population.

Maurice Pate, founding executive director of UNICEF, was nicknamed the "Nappie King" by an Australian journalist after UNICEF gave enough cotton cloth for the making of more than a million diapers for Europe's babies.

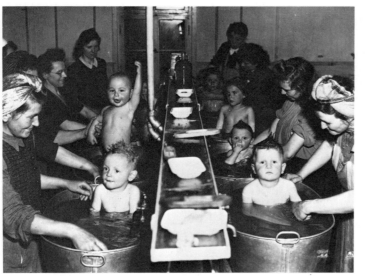

A million diapers

"Just ship us bolts of cloth, and we will make up the diapers ourselves," one hospital's medical director pleaded with Dr. Martha Eliot, UNICEF's chief medical consultant. Dr. Eliot, who had been sent in 1947 to investigate children's institutions in seven war-torn countries, found the diaper shortage was so acute that mothers had to use rags, dishcloths, even newspapers.

She recommended that UNICEF provide massive amounts of cotton cloth—8,500,000 pounds' worth—to European governments, which would then pay to have it made mainly into layettes, blankets, and other necessities for babies. Local workers cut the cloth into diapers, baby shirts, and dresses.

In Poland alone, four hundred thousand layettes were made from UNICEF cotton and wool. These were distributed through maternity clinics to new mothers, who otherwise would not have had the means to clothe their babies. Nearly half the layettes distributed under Poland's national program were produced from UNICEF's materials.

In Finland, 73,374 new mothers received supplies in wooden "baby boxes." The container was almost as important as the diapers, infant shirts, and creepers inside, for it was used as the baby's crib.

Over 661,000 diapers were made and handed out to Czech mothers through the end of April 1950. Each Czech baby got a set of ten wrapped in a band, which was marked "UNICEF." Across Europe, over a million babies received diapers, infant clothing, and blankets made from the cotton and wool UNICEF provided.

Above:
Surmounting the soap shortage: Karlsdorf, Germany, opened free bathhouses for babies, with plenty of soap and hot water. UNICEF shipped three million bars, courtesy of Australia, to new European mothers.

Opposite: Diapers:
A postwar European priority. Here, a farm woman outside Rouen, France, cares for foundlings.

A Greek dock worker unloads a cod-liver oil shipment in Piraeus. Coming through UNICEF from Norway and Canada, it relieved postwar victims of rickets.

The oil crisis

Dr. Martha Eliot was no ordinary pediatrician. A first cousin to poet T. S. Eliot, she was a pioneer in combating rickets in the United States. She was also known internationally as an expert in children's and mothers' health, and in her own country as assistant chief, U.S. Children's Bureau. UNICEF recognized this when they called upon her to become their chief medical consultant. They needed her keen eyes and experience to help structure a recovery program for Europe's most seriously deprived children and infants.

In the spring of 1947, Dr. Eliot visited Austria, Czechoslovakia, France, Greece, Italy, Poland, and Yugoslavia—countries whose children she had seen just ten years earlier, in 1937, just before the war engulfed Europe. "There were great numbers of children, thin, pale, stunted in growth," she reported back to civic and welfare leaders in Washington, D.C., and to UNICEF's Executive Board in New York. "Children appeared to be four or five, but were actually six or seven years old. Others I judged to be six or seven years old were known to be eight, nine, even ten and eleven years old. Some were so weak from lack of food that they remained absolutely motionless as we examined them."

If there was anyone who understood what was wrong, it was Dr. Eliot. Six years of occupation, war, and postwar food deprivation had stunted children's growth from two to four years. Out of every three infants or small children, one, she learned, had rickets. She saw children with legs bowed like parentheses, a telltale sign of the advanced stages of the malady. While their legs could never be straight again, they needed instant protection from further growth damage.

Dr. Eliot knew how to stop the slow but steady decline of these children. Her research in the United States had proven that rickets could be cured by delivering daily doses of cod-liver oil and sunlight to each victim on a community-wide basis. Eliot was instrumental in preventing rickets, having helped the disease all but disappear among U.S. children. In Europe, she prescribed a daily dose, for infants under age one, of three to five milligrams of cod-liver oil, and for children one to six years old and pregnant women, five milligrams.

Filling Dr. Eliot's prescription for such a vast quantity of cod-liver oil was a tall order. Inside the devastated countries there was little or none available and no possibility, she reported, of manufacturing it soon. Unfortunately, 1947 was a poor year for cod fishing in the icy waters of the Atlantic. The size of the catch was down, so there was an actual shortage of the fish oil on the world market.

Norway, Canada, and New Zealand—the biggest producers of cod-liver oil at that time—came to the rescue. They supplied huge metal drums of the precious oil as part of their governments' generous contribution to UNICEF. This enabled UNICEF to supply a daily dose of cod-liver oil to three

Smiles notwithstanding, these Czech children hated the taste of cod-liver oil, just like children everywhere else. That's why their teacher had to set a good example and swallow the stuff himself.

Gunter Schossig's pen-and-ink sketch (below) was one of
the many thank-you's for cod-liver oil UNICEF received.
Rupert Hochrainer's card depicting boats flying the
UNICEF flag across the sea with shipments of oil for an
eager Austrian child (bottom) was another.

children for about three months' time for only one dollar—the cost of shipping it.

Shipping companies cooperated by reducing cargo costs to UNICEF. Flagships of eleven nations carried drums of cod-liver oil across the seven seas to key European ports. From there they were distributed to feeding centers, schools, and children's institutions.

With the help of UNICEF program officers, from December 1948 through the end of 1950, UNICEF got cod-liver oil into the mouths of more than one million German children. Some called it "golden sunshine." The German word was "*Lebertran.*" Thank-you letters and drawings from the grateful children of Chemnitz were addressed "*Liebe UNICEF . . . danke für den Lebertran.*" Some youngsters even praised its smell ("*Euer Lebertran schmeckt sehr gut*").

On the other side of the border, nearly one-third of Poland's children under age seven suffered from rickets. In a stepped-up effort to control the disease, UNICEF supplied, and Polish health officials distributed, cod-liver oil to 1,400,000 young children in 1949–1950. In Greece, the oil, with milk and food, went to 280,000 infants, children under age six, and pregnant and nursing women. Most of these recipients were in refugee camps created by the Greek civil war.

English-born Fred Hamilton, an old UNICEF hand, delivered cod-liver oil to postwar Czechoslovakia. "I remember very well that the cod-liver oil came in big metal drums. The liquid had to be bottled by a special firm in order to ship it to the schools. The average teacher had to coax and cajole children to swallow daily spoonfuls. Some even had to swallow the oil themselves before the children would be persuaded to do it. Some youngsters were on the point of spitting it up. . . . We saw something rare in Slovakia: children prepared to swallow cod-liver oil by the cupful. Then came the action of the New Zealand government to make child-size capsules. That was very good. No problem to ship it, easy for children to swallow, nothing to land on the floor."

Even though great amounts were shipped, the demands of children still could not be met. There simply wasn't enough of the fish oil to make an across-the-board distribution to all those who needed it.

Deciding who got the cod-liver oil was poignant and sometimes heartbreaking. In some communities, it was regarded as medicine, and doctors decided which child needed it most. In other areas, infants and pregnant women got priority.

Most cod-liver oil was passed out during the winter months to offset children's poorer diets at a time when sunrays, crucial for the production of vitamin D, were weaker.

By January 1949, studies showed that children living in institutions were getting more aid than those living with their families. School-age children were getting less than younger brothers and sisters, who had priority in local milk and infant-health programs. Accordingly, distributors shifted the focus to school-age children. After all, they were "the war's children," having endured the ravages of a subsistence diet the longest.

"I want to be some kind of a social doctor," Martha May Eliot wrote in 1915 while still a medical student at Johns Hopkins University. As medical consultant to UNICEF in 1947– 1948, Dr. Eliot shaped UNICEF's recovery program for Europe's children, pregnant women, and nursing mothers.

In 1953, the New Zealand government took big strides to alleviate the "oil crisis." It contributed shark-liver oil extract, a much richer source of vitamins A and D, which was produced from sharks fished in the waters of the South Pacific. Canadian and U.K. firms turned the shark oil into millions of child-size capsules, which were shipped all over Europe and Asia. Children swallowed them without a fuss, much to the relief of many a weary health worker.

But what was easy to swallow in most places didn't go down well at all in the newborn state of Israel. On the docks of Tel Aviv in 1948, large amounts of shark-liver oil capsules sent to stave off rickets among both Israeli and Palestinian children sat in the holds of ships and were not permitted to be unloaded. Had the ships carried cod rather than shark oil, their cargo would have immediately been off-loaded. But under Jewish religious law, the shark, because it has no scales, is considered non-kosher. After some consideration, Israeli officials finally did make an exception: they could not put religion before the desperate needs of their own young.

Whether via capsule or liquid, by July 1951, UNICEF had filled Dr. Eliot's prescription to the brim with a staggering 8,500,000 pounds of cod-liver oil and 700,000,000 shark-liver oil capsules worth $5,000,000. Today, many a European adult in his forties and fifties who has straight legs, a straight back and strong teeth, and who has reached a normal height can be grateful to the partnership of people at all levels of government, industry, shipping, and public health, who made this particular road to recovery possible.

Mountains of milk

The casualty lists of war conventionally omit the farm animals—on whom humans depend. In World War II, no one knows how many cattle were the accidental victims of battle. But in addition, the occupying power claimed the beasts for their own citizens, so that at war's end Europe's young cried for milk and suffered from stunted growth and listless spirits. The little milk that was produced by the shattered dairy industry was sometimes itself a carrier of disease.

Shipping fresh milk from overseas was out of the question. There was not enough. It cost too much. Neither UNICEF nor the governments that would receive milk could afford to refrigerate it in liquid form. The answer was the newfangled dried milk. During the war, dried-milk technology had reached a level of competence at which it was able to supply American soldiers with millions of gallons of the stuff, reconstituted with water, in far-flung army camps and fighting units. It was still a mystery to the average consumer.

Where to find the powder quickly? Everyone in the world wanted milk. "We had to beg to buy milk," one UNICEF supply officer remembers. Fiorello La Guardia, ex-mayor of New York and UNRRA's second director, was one of the heroes of this story. He had faithfully guarded $550,000 from an emergency food collection, and turned it over to UNICEF so that the great detective hunt could begin. In mid-1947, vast quantities began to be shipped to Europe.

Milk powder came from U.S., Canadian, and Australian stockpiles: from the dairy heartlands of America—Wisconsin and Minnesota; from farms in faraway Victoria and New South Wales, Australia; from northern Quebec and Ontario. By rail, truck, boat, and then by horse-drawn cart or muleback, drums of the dried milk powder reached their destinations: hungry children in towns and remote mountain villages where there was little or no milk at all.

When the milk powder reached feeding centers in schools and hospitals, churches or day-care centers, the stuff was strange and new to almost everyone concerned. "What is it and what do we do with it?" asked one UNICEF worker when a drumful appeared at his office in Vienna. In time, UNICEF staff became experts in the care and mixing of dried milk.

Concern over the taste of the powder started with Maurice Pate, UNICEF's founding director. Dr. Katherine Lenroot, U.S. delegate to UNICEF's Executive Board in 1947 and chief of the U.S. Children's Bureau, remembers, "Maurice and I were talking about what might be done to powdered milk, whether there ought to be efforts to improve its palatability. So he came up to my apartment one evening, and, thinking that maybe cocoa would do the trick, we cooked a mess of powdered milk cocoa in my kitchen to test it out."

Since both cocoa and sugar were scarce and expensive, UNICEF could afford to supply only small amounts on its tight budget. Children's Fund officers asked governments for

Above: August 27, 1947: Milk powder hits the docks. Four hundred fifty emergency tons were loaded aboard the S.S. *Mark Hanna* in New York and bound for Poland. When the freighter reached Gdynia, on the Baltic Sea, eight hundred children sang at the pier.

Opposite: Months of UNICEF effort, dollars, and ingenuity made possible a long swallow of milk— for many others besides this Greek boy.

The Prince and the Pauper.

Above: A common scene across Europe: Youngsters begging for what seemed princely U.S. Army rations. Cartoonist Bill Mauldin dramatized this and other situations in the life of GI Joe.

Opposite: Saved: Cows in Cherbourg during the American advance, July 4, 1944. GI's gave them right-of-way while Nazis shelled the road. More often, cows were victims.

contributions "in kind." By 1948, Poland, which had been Europe's most devastated nation immediately after the war, was able to donate one thousand tons of beet sugar to UNICEF to be used in Austria. War-torn Italy and Czechoslovakia also sweetened the milk pots of hungry children in other nations by donating sugar to UNICEF.

In Greece, where there was no tradition of children drinking milk at all, it was only the addition of sugar that made the drink palatable to children, and the feeding program a success. There were other typical problems to overcome. According to photojournalist Ann Parsons, "In Greece, at first

people were skeptical about the powdered milk and didn't know how to prepare it. In 1948, Dr. Roger P. Stewart, a well-known British pediatrician and UNICEF's field representative in Epirus, went out with his interpreter and mixed up the stuff himself to show people how to do the job. After that, the feeding program was carried out all over northern Greece by volunteers or workers paid by PIKPA, the Greek government-sponsored children's fund. By Christmas 1949, the program was so successful that nearly 650,000 youngsters and nearly 11,000 pregnant women were being fed in towns, villages, and refugee camps."

In some Greek villages, destruction of homes and churches was so widespread that the only place available for feeding was the tiny village square. Most children brought their own cup—an empty beer can or cocoa tin.

In Italy, milk bars were set up in corners of churches and warehouses—in any available interior space large enough to hold a stove, a table, and the children. At 7:30 A.M., women volunteers heated the milk and put things in order. At 7:45, mothers, fathers, older brothers and sisters began arriving with small children and infants. Promptly at eight o'clock the doors opened. Each child received a generous ladleful of hot

milk, and often a piece of bread.

In most places, getting a feeding center under way was largely a labor of love on the part of the volunteers—mothers, teachers, nurses. Each day they mixed up mounds of fresh milk powder, adding cold water to it. In some areas, this meant getting up before dawn to gather fuel for a fire. The milk tasted much better hot than cold. Using big vats, they experimented with recipes from UNICEF, adding noodles or macaroni to perk up the liquid. Hungry children were no different from other children; they drank only what tasted good to them. Cooking made the milk powder taste better, smoothing out the lumps, and a few spoonfuls of flavoring made it more appealing.

Whatever the difficulties to overcome in the beginning, more than thirty-five thousand feeding centers—including those in schools, hospitals and orphanages—were set up. Children received more than milk through the feeding centers. Daily doses of cod-liver oil extract, butter and margarine, meats and fish, and grains, potatoes, and vegetables provided locally, were consumed on the spot. The children thus got a balanced supplementary meal in addition to what they had at home.

About three million undernourished and tubercular-prone youngsters in all benefiting European countries were specially fed in the summer of 1948—a critical period after the drought and food shortages of the previous two years. Most youngsters came from orphanages and special institutions in towns, cities, and industrial or mining centers. They were selected because of their poor physical condition or bad housing conditions. In some countries, children at camp got double UNICEF rations of everything—that is, six hundred calories instead of three hundred, made up of milk, fats, meat paste, canned meat and fish—to build them up quickly. By the time summer camp ended, children had gained anywhere from one to eight pounds.

Of the twenty to thirty million children estimated in 1946 to be nutritionally needy, UNICEF reached a substantial number: over five million. Despite milk shortages, strikes, droughts, and civil wars, UNICEF and its partner-governments had mounted the greatest relief operation for children ever conducted. Between 1947 and mid-1951, UNICEF shipped upward of four hundred million pounds of milk powder—enough to make 6,400,000,000 cups of milk. Nearly seven million infants and children had been fed.

UNICEF became known as "the cup of milk" organization, earning the nickname "milkman to the world's children." It aided the recovery of Europe's dairy industry by reequipping and modernizing plants all over the continent. So when UNICEF's "milk train" stopped, countries continued to produce a stream of safe, pasteurized milk for their children. The silhouette of a child holding a cup of milk up to its lips became UNICEF's first symbol. Some children even asked for a glass of "UNICEF," thinking that it was another word for milk.

UNICEF PHOTO

Opposite: Italian orphans enjoy a UNICEF meal, their fullest plate in months.

Above: Little more than a toddler herself, a Greek girl waits protectively by her brother for their share of the milk. They have found a safe haven in this refugee camp in Ioannina, one of the many camps through which UNICEF sent supplementary foods for some two hundred thousand Greek refugee children during the civil war.

UNICEF PHOTO

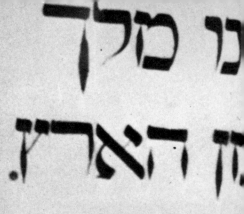

Italian Jewish girls thank God and UNICEF for noodle soup with milk and bread. The traditional Hebrew blessing over bread is mounted above them.

UNICEF PHOTO

ברוך אתה ה' אל
העולם המוציא לחם

UNICEF PHOTO

Above: An old shoe was better than no shoe at all when you had to take turns wearing a single pair.

Opposite: A moment of ecstasy in a sad young life: Werfel, orphaned at six, receives a new pair of shoes on the steps of his Viennese shelter.

Barefoot in Europe

Little feet of children
blue with cold,
how can they see you and not cover you—
dear God!

Little wounded feet
cut by every stone
hurt by snow
and mire. . . .

Little feet of children,
two tiny suffering jewels,
how can people pass
and not see you!

—Gabriela Mistral

In an era of designer shoes, it's hard to imagine children having to scamper unshod through war-strewn cities and rugged rural terrain in zero-degree temperatures. But in the early years after World War II, there were many who went barefoot. The destruction of factories and continuing shortage of cowhide made shoes a genuine luxury. In some areas of Europe, reported Dr. Martha Eliot, the need for shoes surpassed all others.

There was much more to a child's going barefoot than met the eye. For want of a pair of shoes, children stayed home from school in the winter, missing not only the teacher's lessons but the daily hot cup of milk and piece of bread spread with butter, jam, meat paste, or fish.

If there was one pair of children's shoes in a family, children took turns wearing them to school. Rips and holes grew bigger, faster. More than a few children who ran barefoot through rubble, rain, or snow in the bitter winters of 1945, 1946, 1947, and 1948 contracted tetanus or respiratory infections. Some developed pneumonia and died.

Although there were some outright gifts of shoes made through UNICEF, it simply wasn't possible to give finished pairs of shoes to all the millions of children who needed them. So UNICEF, following Dr. Eliot's advice, took another tack. Two of the world's biggest leather producers, England and Australia, stood ready to ship quantities of precious hides as part of their contribution to UNICEF. It worked out a plan with individual governments to process that leather into shoes and boots and then distribute them free to the poorest children in each country.

In Finland, in the winter of 1947, many children wore wooden shoes and paper clothes in subzero weather. The following winter, UNICEF sent enough leather to Finland for fifty thousand pairs of boots. Each youngster who received a pair of boots shared it with four others. That way, each could go to school one day a week. The arrival of the shoes and boots in villages was such an occasion that schools held parties to celebrate. At Pohjolan, Finland, only the leather arrived. The boys fabricated their own footwear in the school workshop.

AMERICAN RED CROSS PHOTO

Greek schoolchildren giggle and grin after abandoning their worn-out shoes for new pairs from UNICEF.

One youngster from Finland's frozen north sent UNICEF the following letter, dated April 1948: "UNICEF, I send my warmest spring greetings to all you good people. Yet here in the north we still have winter. . . . I am ten years old and this is my fourth year at school. Our home, clothing, and other necessities were destroyed during the war. . . . I have four brothers and three sisters. We are very poor since there are so many of us. Still, I am happy to have both my parents alive. Many, many thanks for the warm nice shoes which I received through my school. And thank you for remembering us children in the north. With best regards, Raskel Enguske."

In Italy, over 830,000 pairs of children's shoes were produced, with UNICEF supplying the leather at eighty-eight cents a pair. Italian workers manufactured them; the government bore the cost. But when allotments were made for each town or village, they were found to be not nearly enough, posing a thorny problem for local officials. The mayor of one village told UNICEF officials he'd been notified that a gift of fifty pairs of shoes would soon be arriving. Knowing that three hundred poor youngsters were in equal need of shoes, he reluctantly refused to accept any.

As with the cod-liver oil distribution system, in some villages mayors set up committees to determine who ought to receive shoes. Children were listed in two categories: shoeless and badly shod. Those without shoes, of course, got priority. Hard-pressed officials in other towns used lotteries, so that random chance selected the lucky recipients.

For many children, the shoes or overcoats provided by UNICEF were the first they had received in their young lives. They felt intense happiness and a new sense of self-worth.

In the end, over two million pairs of shoes and boots were produced and distributed across the continent to refugee children, particularly in Germany and Greece; to orphans in institutions; and to poor schoolchildren. One of these was Werfel, an Austrian orphan pictured here. Another was a four-year-old Greek girl whose village was in the middle of civil war territory. On the day in 1948 when Elefteria Tranopoulos received her first leather shoes, she hugged and kissed their sides, then the heels and soles, before she dared to put them on.

UNICEF PHOTO

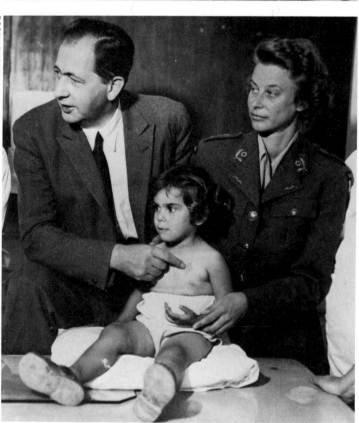

Top: Equipped with vaccines, Dr. Johannes Holm traveled to eastern Europe in 1946 in the de Havilland Rapide biplane, at the start of what became the International Tuberculosis Campaign (ITC).

Above: ITC director Holm shares techniques for tuberculin testing and vaccinating with colleagues at Athens' Patissia Polyclinic, circa 1949.

Scandinavia's crusade

Armed only with leather vaccination kits, strong constitutions, good nerves, and suitcases, ninety-nine Danish nurses and doctors in gray Red Cross uniforms set out in the spring of 1947 for Poland, Germany, and Yugoslavia, determined to protect millions of children, with the cooperation of national and local health authorities, against Public Enemy Number One: tuberculosis. In the wake of war, the disease reached near-epidemic proportions among the young.

"The tubercule bacillus doesn't discriminate politically, and so we must operate without politics," said Dr. Johannes Holm, the internationally recognized TB specialist who played a leading role in what became the International Tuberculosis Campaign and who acted as its director from 1948 to 1951.

On a scale never before attempted, Danish teams injected tuberculin as a test into all children, toddlers as well as adolescents, to find which youngsters did not already harbor the tubercule bacillus. They were the ones who could be and were inoculated with the only known anti-TB vaccine: Bacillus Calmette-Guerin, or BCG, which confers between three and five years of protection.

In a recent telephone interview, Dr. Holm, now eighty-four and living outside Copenhagen, reminisced about those hectic years.

"For the first six months, when we started out with the Danish Red Cross, we flew in a little biplane, the de Havilland Rapide, delivering vaccine to our local headquarters in Berlin, Budapest, and Warsaw. The little English-made machine had only one pilot: Simonsen. I don't remember his first name. Telephone connections were very difficult in 1947, so when we were over Warsaw, for example, Simonsen flew down low, buzzing the headquarters so that people would go pick up the vaccines right away at the airport. We never had an accident with that plane—not one. Later on, when UNICEF got behind the campaign, we were lent a DC-3 by the U.S. Army, which Simonsen also flew.

"It was very hard work," Holm recalls, "but we all considered it a pioneering activity. We had to accept tough living conditions. In Warsaw, we couldn't find any place for the vaccinating teams to sleep, so we got one house, and ten people slept in one room. We had to bring in food from Denmark because there was such a food shortage. The medical teams were kept very, very strictly. They received practically no pocket money. We arranged for uniforms, for everything from housing to food for them."

By early 1948, the Swedish Red Cross and Norwegian Relief for Europe had joined forces with the Danes in what became Scandinavia's greatest contribution to the postwar recovery of Europe's children. Using jeeps, trucks, needles, vaccines, and syringes from UNICEF, teams from all over Scandinavia fanned out across the continent, vaccinating children against tuberculosis.

The baby is Bohemian—and too young to know the shot Danish nurse Helen Hvidberg administers will protect him from TB for three to five years.

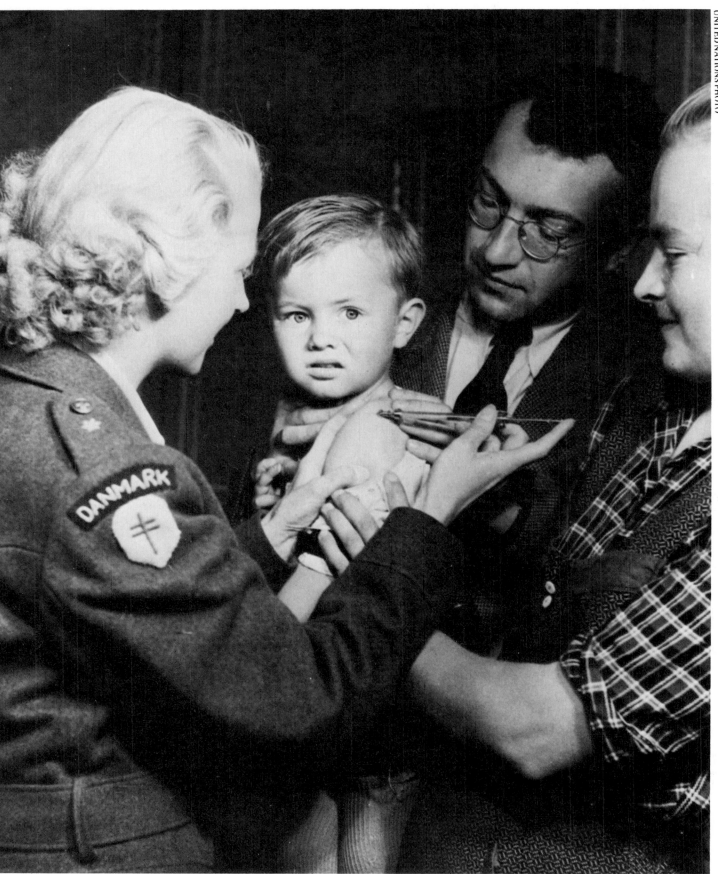

Dr. Holm remembers that applicants were screened for the right human qualities above and beyond the capacity to skillfully inject a syringe. "Even in the field we closely observed our staff to make sure they were not looking down on the local people—as soon as they didn't behave well, we put them on the next plane home."

The word went out that applicants should be "old enough to work independently and young enough to adjust to strange and, at times, primitive conditions." There were more applicants for the job of nurse-vaccinator than there were posts. The majority of those chosen were about thirty years old.

According to Dr. Holm, each team usually consisted of three people: one doctor and two nurses. "Two vaccinators could easily reach one thousand to two thousand children a day. If they were sitting in one place, they could do many more." Teams traveled by jeep, horse and buggy, canoe, raft, and on foot.

One prominent figure in the TB campaign was Dr. Ludwik Rajchman, a Polish-born international public health specialist elected chairman of UNICEF's first Executive Board in 1947. "It was really Rajchman's idea to train young people for the practical work in different countries," Holm says. "Tuberculosis specialists had trouble adapting to the conditions. Young doctors were needed not only for diagnosis and treatment but for other preventive work. A 'College for Tuberculosis' in Denmark offered special training to doctors from all over. In addition, I insisted that the young doctors engaged for the International Tuberculosis Campaign should first spend two weeks under the supervision of a nurse to learn how to inject tuberculin properly and to vaccinate those free of the TB germ. The doctors didn't like this much, but it was important that everyone in the campaign know how to vaccinate properly. The nurses were the experts at this."

It was Dr. Rajchman who spurred UNICEF into partnership with the Scandinavian Red Cross organizations. By providing sorely needed supplies, UNICEF not only enabled the campaign to branch out into almost every European country, but also across North Africa and much of Asia, sub-Saharan Africa, and Latin America. UNICEF's missions and offices supported each national campaign.

"One of the biggest problems," Dr. Holm continues, "was keeping vaccine cold and protecting it against light until it was injected into the child. The team were taught never to allow vaccine to sit in the open, for light weakens its potency. They had to do their work in 'good shadows.' Each ampule was hand-wrapped in black paper to protect the vaccine."

Under Dr. Holm's direction, the vaccine and tuberculin were mass-produced, at the State Serum Institute in Copenhagen, for all European campaigns. Luckily the Institute, Denmark's control center for infectious diseases and the country's main vaccine-production plant, had come through the war intact. Later on, UNICEF would help equip local plants for production in Ecuador, Mexico, Egypt, Israel, India, and Pakistan, but meanwhile, since vaccine was potent for only two weeks' time, a fresh supply had to be produced and flown directly into each country where a national vaccination campaign was under way. Vaccine was packed in special boxes with ice to keep it cold.

In Yugoslavia, the quickest and most efficient way to transfer vaccine from airport to local district was to hand it over to conductors of sleeping-car trains. At key stations along their route they were met by special couriers from the Ministries of Health, who delivered the vaccine to Scandinavian teams in the field.

"It was one interesting period in my life," Holm says. "The campaigns were organized by a number of people. . . . I got help from many sides. . . . But I had complete responsibility for the financial side, for BCG vaccine and tuberculin production at the State Serum Institute for twenty-two countries, and for training medical personnel from other countries. Half the time I had to travel around to see that everything was organized, to demonstrate, to negotiate with governments, doctors, and health officials."

What made the campaign such a challenge was that in every country touched by the war, health services, hospitals, medical laboratories, and their sources of supply had been almost totally disrupted or destroyed. Many doctors and nurses had died or left, and those who survived had been cut off for some years from the mainstream of science.

While some countries had had prewar experience with BCG vaccinations for children, in most, doctors, nurses, and the public at large required continuing education to convince them of the safety and effectiveness of the procedures, not to mention the BCG vaccine itself. Good press, movies, lectures, posters, and leaflets helped raise support for the campaign, community by community.

"When it was all over, I was pretty tired," Holm admits. And well he might have been. By June 1951, when the International Tuberculosis Campaign as such had officially ended, it had tested some thirty million and vaccinated fourteen million children in twenty-three countries, and trained over one thousand vaccinators. Today, children all over the developing world continue to receive BCG vaccinations to protect them against TB, as nations push forward—with help from the World Health Organization and UNICEF—to immunize all children against the six main child-killing and disabling diseases.

Where are they now?

by Tsutomo Mizota and Sharon Meager

More people than we can count owe their lives to UNICEF—among them today's fathers and mothers who were themselves children a generation ago. For the most part they live among us anonymously. The pictures in this book are UNICEF's best record of its beneficiaries, and they remain, in most cases, unidentified. In 1985, in preparation for this book, UNICEF decided to try and find a child from the Japanese nursery-school class (right) that received milk in the years 1948 to 1951.

We began with an advertisement in the *Asahi* weekly. The response was instantaneous and gratifying. The same day it appeared, a Miss Yoshiko Ishii rang UNICEF's Tokyo office to identify the photo as having been taken at the Kanda Nursery School, where she once taught. She recognized the toy giraffe and elephant that the teachers, facing postwar shortages, had made from vegetable baskets to brighten the small assembly hall.

The next caller, Mr. Kazuo Segawa, confirmed the setting. He had served as the government's contact with the UNICEF-assisted nursery-school milk program from 1948 until 1958. The Kanda school, he explained, had been one of two "model" nursery schools in Tokyo to receive UNICEF dried skim milk for three daily feedings at 10:00 A.M., noon, and 3:00 P.M. The children's height, weight, and chest measurements were recorded monthly for comparison with statistics from control schools that received no milk supplies. "This sort of scientific survey was new to Japan and a good innovation," Mr. Segawa said. "There was a notable difference between the two sets of statistics."

Through information supplied by these two respondents to the *Asahi Marion* newspaper ad, UNICEF was able to contact Miss Aya Noji, the teacher photographed above. "This picture must have been taken in 1950," Miss Noji said. "It shows two classes combined, probably the two upper levels, the five- and six-year-olds. . . . We had such a terrible time getting the children to drink their milk. They objected to both the smell and the taste. Sometimes before feeding time we would prolong the outdoor play period, hoping the children would work up a thirst. Occasionally, we even skipped a feeding or two. We made wonderful playthings from the milk drums when they were empty."

Miss Noji, who is today the principal of the Honchō Nursery School in Tokyo, provided names and addresses of three people in the photograph who are still living in the Tokyo area: Mr. Minoru Kaneda (second from the right, second-to-last row) and twins, Mr. Hideo Kuboshima (far right, first row) and Mrs. Noriko Ōwa (third from the right, fourth row). Mr. Kaneda (born 1945) is officer in charge of the Survey Section in the Tokyo Municipal Government Department of Town Planning. Mr. Kuboshima (born 1946) is a

Top: The Kaneda family poses in their Tokyo apartment. From left to right: Tomoko Kaneda, daughter Reiko, six, son Masao, eight, and Minoru Kaneda, officer in charge of town planning for the city of Tokyo.

Above: Twins Noriko Ōwa (left, center) and Hideo Kuboshima (right, center), flanked by their parents— mother Hana and father Yasuo— outside Mr. Kuboshima's barbershop "Nippon," in the same Kanda district where the twins went to nursery school in 1948– 1950.

Opposite: "We were poor and hungry, but we were *all* equally poor and hungry. It was a shared experience," remembers Minoru Kaneda. In this class photo from 1950, Kaneda, age five, is seated in the next to last row, second from the right. In the first row sits four-year-old Hideo Kuboshima. His twin sister Noriko is in the fourth row, third from the right. Kanda was one of two "model" nursery schools in Tokyo to receive UNICEF dried skim milk.

barber in the Nippon Barbershop owned by his father. His twin, Mrs. Ōwa, is a mother of two, a mountain climber and jogger who competes in Japan's most famous marathon—the thirty-kilometer Ōmé Marathon. Although none of the three could remember the day the picture was taken, all have vivid recollections of the UNICEF-supplied milk, and realize the important part it played in improving their health.

Today, they know of UNICEF's work through their own children, who bring home news of UNICEF classroom activities carried out under the school program of the Japan Committee for UNICEF. They speak proudly of their children. That same pride echoes in the voice of Mrs. Ōwa's father as he says, "Look at Noriko. She was so weak, always sick. UNICEF milk helped her survive. It makes us so happy to see how she has grown up into a good mother with children of her own. We are grateful for UNICEF's contribution."

Tokyo, 1950: According to the message on the blackboard, UNICEF milk made the difference. The six- or seven-year-olds at left drank it three times daily in nursery school, in 1949–1951. Those at right did not.

Above: New York City mayor Fiorello H. La Guardia, drawn from life by Oscar Berger.

Opposite: "The people are crying for bread, not advice," La Guardia said in accepting the job as UNRRA director-general, March 29, 1946. "I want plows, not typewriters . . . I want fast-moving ships, not slow-reading resolutions."

II. UNICEF's Hall of Fame

Fiorello La Guardia: his last hurrah

New York City mayor Fiorello H. La Guardia was an original, one of the most dynamic and colorful political leaders of his time. In 1945—his last year as reform mayor—La Guardia did something the city's children never forgot. Every Sunday afternoon during the citywide newspaper strike, he read the "funnies"—the comic strips published in the city's tabloids—out loud over the radio, so children wouldn't miss what had happened in the lives of their favorite characters that week. With typical La Guardia gusto, he acted out all the parts—Blondie, Dagwood, Dick Tracy—raising his voice to a little squeak to play "Little Orphan Annie." He was a sensation.

What few people know or remember is that a year later, in March 1946, after La Guardia had stepped down as mayor, he received an important telephone call from Harry S Truman. The president urged him to accept the position of director-general of the United Nations Relief and Rehabilitation Administration, succeeding Herbert H. Lehman, who had just resigned. La Guardia's appointment catapulted him into the center of an international drama. In his new role, he had profound effect upon the lives of millions of war-stricken children.

Although only those closest to him knew it, La Guardia was already ill with cancer when he became the UNRRA head. His sense of responsibility to the children under his care never waned. In early May, he attended a White House screening of *Seeds of Destiny*. As producer-director David Miller recalls: "La Guardia wept during the film. When it was over, he jumped up and pointed his finger at me, saying: 'I thought I was dealing in statistics of life. Now I realize we're dealing in statistics of death. Get this film into every theater in America.'"

Helping millions of children wasn't going to be easy, for La Guardia had been assigned an unusual balancing act. UNRRA's days were already numbered. The United States, its main contributor, was planning to withdraw funding by the end of 1946. Down the line the United States would create the Marshall Plan. But in the meantime, La Guardia was called on to find enough food and other supplies to keep the relief program going through the end of the year, while helping it to wind down smoothly.

In mid-August, La Guardia took center stage when the UNRRA Governing Council met for the last time in Geneva. With winter fast approaching, La Guardia and the Council made plans to reduce, as much as possible, the hardships of those who depended on UNRRA's food for sheer survival. La Guardia pleaded with the delegates on behalf of the displaced persons, whom he called "this great stockpile of human misery." Asking for the authorization to continue UNRRA's DP activities for sixty days, he said: "I am going to ask you not to abandon these people until the International Organization of the United Nations can take over—Do not abandon them! We will find the money some way. What the world needs is a spiritual UNRRA. We can provide the food, but only God can give these people their souls and their willingness to understand, their willingness to cooperate. Let this be the message of UNRRA: 'We have done it! We have done it!'"

At that fateful meeting, Poland's representative, Dr. Ludwik Rajchman, raised the question: What will become of UNRRA's children? UNRRA had been helping countries feed and care for over five million youngsters throughout Europe and China. Rajchman proposed that funds left over after UNRRA's liquidation be used to launch an international children's emergency feeding program under the auspices of the United Nations. With constant showings of *Seeds of Destiny* keeping children's needs uppermost in the delegates' minds, and with Rajchman shepherding the proposal through the UNRRA Council, the child-feeding resolution was passed unanimously.

Fiorello La Guardia's legendary eloquence came to the fore in the fall of 1946, when the United Nations considered that resolution for the first time. According to a close colleague, "La Guardia became an irresistible force in the Economic and Social Council and in the General Assembly. What he was doing was completing the selling of an imaginative and humanitarian concept that had been conceived by a few people in UNRRA. . . . His great contribution was his oratory. He was also a very brave man who was in pain much of the time from his illness."

Pain dimmed neither his energy nor his characteristic frankness. ". . . I have set aside an initial $550,000—as a first installment—for this organization, assuming that it is approved by your Council [the Economic and Social Council] and the Assembly [General Assembly]. The money is tied up. I will see to it that no one is able to touch it," La Guardia promised. "The prompt adoption of this plan will encourage people all over the world and give new hope to the usefulness and effectiveness of this new world organization. Here we start with the children, with the infants, and we give them, for the first time in the history of the world, an equal chance to benefit from the progress of science and medicine."

He was indeed persuasive. The plan to use UNRRA money for an international children's fund was endorsed by the General Assembly on December 11, when it created UNICEF. That same day, President Truman accepted La Guardia's resignation as UNRRA director, saying, "Your valiant and strenuous efforts to overcome this crisis have earned the admiration of us all and the gratitude of many millions of people in the world . . . threatened with hunger."

Nine months later, by September 1946, Fiorello La Guardia was dead, but ships were already on the high seas, bringing milk and medicine to Europe's sick and hungry children. That help was his last hurrah.

**Herbert Hoover, by
Emilio Angelo, from
the *Philadelphia
Inquirer*, 1940.**

Herbert Hoover:
the return of "the Chief"

At the age of seventy-two, when most men are content to play with grandchildren or pursue hobbies, Herbert Hoover answered the call to serve humanity once again. It was March 1946, and President Truman was proposing that Hoover fly around the world on a rapid country-by-country fact- and food-finding survey. The goal: to identify which European and Asian countries had the most severe food shortages, and to aid them whenever and however possible.

Despite his age, Hoover had the physical vitality and drive of a much younger man. His Quaker upbringing had given him a strong desire to relieve human suffering. He saw this as a chance to redeem his good name, which had been tarnished ever since the Great Depression struck during his term in the White House.

Truman chose the former president for this crucial assignment because Hoover was experienced in handling food relief on a vast scale, having demonstrated great skill in delivering twenty-three million tons of food to near-starving people during and after World War I. His name was revered in almost every European country.

Before leaving on his whirlwind mission, Hoover appealed to the American people for funds over coast-to-coast radio. He asked every American family to take to their table "an invisible guest" from a starving nation and provide food for that guest, as they would not hesitate to give bread to hungry neighbors.

The white-haired elder statesman took off in a U.S. C-54 transport plane, which carried him fifty thousand miles around the world to thirty-eight countries in eighty-two days. Four hand-picked veterans from Hoover's World War I relief work accompanied him. Among them was Maurice Pate, whom Hoover had appointed director of Polish relief in 1918. About Pate Hoover wrote: "I recruited the invaluable Maurice Pate for the specific duty of investigating the conditions of the children in each of the thirty-eight countries we visited." To join the new Hoover convoy, Pate had left his job as director of the multimillion-dollar American Red Cross prisoner-of-war package service. Like all those close to Hoover, Pate called him "the Chief."

Throughout that trip, Hoover took every opportunity he could to dramatize the plight of children—in speeches, short-wave broadcasts and press conferences from Prague, Warsaw, Helsinki, Bangalore. "The rehabilitation of children cannot wait," he cautioned Londoners. "It cannot be postponed until some other day. They are not like a bridge or a factory. They lose ground every day that is lost. Already a year has been lost. The world cannot hate children, even of the enemy. Our children must live in the same world with them."

PATE INSTITUTE FOR HUMAN SURVIVAL

Hoover's recurring theme was that *all* children, including those of the "ex-enemies"—Germany and Japan—must be assisted. This was a humanitarian principle he had also championed during and after World War I. At that time, he had proposed that the United States feed "ex-enemy" children and adults in both Austria and Germany. When the Senate rejected that idea, Hoover turned to President Wilson, convincing him to allocate five million dollars from funds at his disposal for the purpose of starting a child-feeding program in starving Austria.

Witnessing the impact of World War II on Europe's children firsthand sobered and saddened both Hoover and Pate. They found that children's needs were three times greater than they had been in 1918. In his final report, made to the Canadian Parliament and broadcast from Ottawa on June 28, 1946, Hoover conveyed that stark reality. "Millions of mothers are today watching their children wilt before their eyes. . . . There are somewhere between twenty to thirty million physically subnormal children on the continent of Europe. There are millions of others in Asia. . . . The redemption of these children should be organized at once. . . . I deplore the fact that special aid for children through a widespread organization has not been set up after this war. . . . Civilization marches forward on the feet of healthy children. It is not too late to stop this costly retreat."

Hoover's strong stance came at a critical time. In August, the U.S. government, UNRRA's major contributor, announced it was withdrawing funding. Other important contributors were ready to follow suit. Hoover's survey confirmed that unless special child-feeding plans were put into effect immediately, UNRRA's phase-out could prove devastating to millions. He pressed friends in the Canadian, British, Polish, Belgian, French, and other delegations to the UN General Assembly to vote "yes" to the resolution that would create UNICEF. Hoover also influenced his friends in the U.S. Congress, and a first U.S. government contribution of forty million dollars was approved in June 1947, enabling UNICEF to start operations.

One source of Hoover's enthusiasm for the new organization was his confidence in Maurice Pate, named its director. Of his lifelong friend and colleague, Hoover said: "He is an unusual soul . . . a great administrator as well as a persuasive evangelist for children."

In 1953, UNICEF's future came up for review by the UN General Assembly. The support of the U.S. government, UNICEF's principal contributor, was essential. Hoover's statements brought UNICEF's accomplishments to the attention of the incoming Eisenhower administration, who gave the organization its vote of confidence, thereby setting a precedent for all subsequent administrations.

Ludwik Rajchman: persuasive patriarch

Ludwik Rajchman was a great man. Everyone who met him, said his friend and colleague Lord Philip Noel-Baker, sensed his marvelous brain and character, that he was a man who knew what he wanted and how to get it. Rajchman, a public health expert, wanted one thing, and he did indeed get it: UNICEF—a children's agency within the United Nations.

Rajchman was one of the first practitioners of social medicine to exchange information about disease regularly with foreign countries, thus checking the spread of epidemic diseases. For eighteen years he headed the League of Nations' Health Organization, one of its most successful groups. When it was clear that UNRRA was on its way out, "Rajchman introduced the resolution in the Council of the United Nations Relief and Rehabilitation Administration to create a fund for mothers and children," recalled Lord Noel-Baker. "He had great influence because of his record with the League, because of his whole personality. As the British delegate, I seconded the resolution, pledging His Majesty's Government's warmest support. This made it very difficult for any others to say they were against it."

"He did a tremendous lobbying job," said an inside observer. A delegate recalled, "It was almost entirely due to Rajchman's obstinate, stubborn persistence and the human, common sense of his plea that the countries finally agreed on the creation of UNICEF."

It was a happy Ludwik Rajchman who was unanimously elected chairman of UNICEF's board shortly thereafter. Under his leadership, UNICEF became partners with the Danish and other Scandinavian Red Cross societies in the successful International Tuberculosis Campaign.

Rajchman insisted that UNICEF aid should promote self-help. That philosophy, which continues to prevail, was perhaps Rajchman's greatest contribution to UNICEF.

Dr. Ludwik Rajchman, in Emery Kelén's cartoon, reprinted by permission of Betty Kelén.

Polish-born Dr. Rajchman worked as lab assistant at the Royal Institute of Health in London early in his career. He escaped to England from Poland (then under Russian rule) to avoid imprisonment for anti-czarist activities before World War I.

Maurice Pate: Mr. UNICEF

Opposite: UNICEF and children were Pate's obsession and, some said, his only hobby. The founding director of the United Nations Children's Fund had no children of his own; he was godfather to them all, as here, in Stockholm.

One Sunday morning just before the turn of the century, a shy four-year-old boy attending church with his family in Denver listened to the minister say there were needy children in their own neighborhood. This youngster knew every comfort. His father was a successful businessman. This was the first time he'd heard that children went to bed hungry, and he was profoundly moved. Despite his painful shyness and a serious stammer that he overcame in later life, the child knocked on every door, collecting more money for the needy children than anyone else.

That child was Maurice Pate. He grew up to become founding director of the United Nations Children's Fund. The desire to ease children's suffering, which had surfaced when he was four, became the motivating force of his whole life. Although childless himself, Pate was godfather to millions of poor, forgotten children the world over. He spent almost twenty years of his life in the corridors of world power doing exactly what he had done that Sunday morning in Denver: knocking on every possible door to make a passionate appeal to people's consciences.

Pate had an unusual mix of credentials for this work. After graduating from Princeton, he volunteered, during World War I, to work for Herbert Hoover's Commission for Relief in Belgium, and soon became one of Hoover's right-hand men. A lifelong friendship developed between the two of them. After the armistice in 1919, Hoover named Pate to head up a major child-relief feeding program in Poland under the American Relief Administration, a privately funded U.S. effort. Pate proved adept at cutting through red tape to get food to 1,300,000 hungry Polish children. When the Russian Revolution shook czarist Russia, and civil war, famine, and a typhus epidemic brought great suffering and want, Pate's skill in negotiating with the Soviets made it possible to bring in children's food and medicine as relief measures, thus saving many young lives.

Because of his expertise, Pate was chosen by Hoover in 1946 to join in a World Food Survey. During a stopover at a children's soup kitchen in Berlin, Pate mused: "To see the eagerness with which small girls and boys, amid the wreckage of war, devour a thin cereal soup of two hundred calories gives cause for reflection. That they were born in an ex-enemy country is a fact over which they have no control. These little children cannot be held responsible for the actions of their parents." Some months later, in December 1946, when asked to head the new UNICEF, Pate posed a single condition: He would take on the post only if *all* needy children, including those in ex-enemy countries, could be helped by the agency. That meant children in Japan, Italy, Finland, and Germany. By winning acceptance of that condition, Pate held aloft the banner of a new humanitarian ideal

which UNICEF has followed ever since: that children's needs must be kept above politics.

Pate's background both as an investment banker and as director of the American Red Cross Prisoner of War operation during World War II inspired confidence among world leaders. They reasoned that if he could move $170,000,000 worth of relief supplies to Allied prisoners of war, then UNICEF, under his leadership, could help millions of children efficiently and frugally. In him they recognized that special breed of American idealist with a peculiar knack for getting things done in a big way.

Pate won over notoriously stubborn people to UNICEF's cause, among them the late Ernest Bevin. In 1950, as Secretary of State for Foreign Affairs of the United Kingdom, Bevin had decided not to increase his government's modest contribution to UNICEF. It took Pate just fifteen minutes to change the secretary's mind. And he was successful in winning strong support for UNICEF's cause from widely diverse leaders, including Lübke, Nehru, Tito, and Popes Paul VI, Pius XII, and John XXIII.

Pate's admirers say contradictory personality traits accounted for his success. During complicated negotiations, at first he appeared to be conciliatory and easy to deal with, but sometimes he displayed typical Yankee acumen and hard-headedness. He bewildered and then persuaded others to his cause. "He had this extraordinary capacity for getting his way by his honesty even under very strong opposition," remembers Alfred Katzin, who served as UNICEF's fund-raising coordinator in 1949. Another colleague remarked, "He was one of the most dedicated, stubborn, quiet men I have ever met."

Pate proved his courage in two well-publicized crises. Within days of the Hungarian uprising in 1956, against all advice, he flew to Vienna, hitching a ride to Budapest with a Red Cross relief convoy. He reached Budapest at noon, just as the fighting stopped, and walked alone through bombed-out streets filled with the wounded. There he saw for himself that small children without blankets were freezing to death. Speedily he drew up plans to distribute $750,000 worth of UNICEF food, clothes, and blankets through the newly reconstructed Hungarian Red Cross.

Again, immediately following the Congo crisis in July 1960, Pate flew to Leopoldville at the request of Dag Hammarskjöld (then UN secretary-general), to arrange for emergency food relief. With the assistance of hundreds of eager helpers, most of them Congolese teenagers, he set up milk distribution points in Leopoldville and half a dozen other cities. A few days after the first shipments of skim milk powder arrived at the airport, tens of thousands of hungry children all over the Congo were having their first cup of milk. Pate's remarkable performance won new support for UNICEF and enhanced the prestige of the United Nations.

Pate practiced what he preached. He was the UN's most traveled executive, visiting ninety-three countries and terri-

tories during his leadership years. He wanted to see for himself how UNICEF aid was being used. Invariably, he crammed his six-foot three-inch frame into a tourist-class seat to save every possible penny for children.

UNICEF and children were his obsession and, some said, his only hobby. When Pate married in 1961, his wife Martha chose their wedding date very carefully. She was sure Pate would remember their anniversary since that day—October 31—was Halloween, when droves of children went out Trick-or-Treating for UNICEF. Helenka Pantaleoni, president of the U.S. Committee for UNICEF for more than thirty-five

Prime Minister Jawaharlal Nehru (right) receives Maurice Pate in New Delhi on December 11, 1958, while Sam Keeny, UNICEF regional director for Asia, looks on.

ears and Pate's close friend, remembers well that "No detail was too small or unimportant to concern Maurice. He had that training under Hoover."

Several times admirers wanted to nominate Pate for the Nobel Peace Prize. He would reply: "No, not for myself alone. It's UNICEF—our whole dedicated team, whom I'd like to see get the award." Nine months after Pate's death, on October 25, 1965, a telegram with an Oslo dateline arrived in UNICEF's New York headquarters. "Urgent," it read; "the Nobel Committee of the Norwegian Parliament has today awarded UNICEF the Nobel Peace Prize for 1965."

Roosevelt and Bokhari: colleagues in collision

They were strange and unlikely adversaries. She was the First Lady of the whole world; the most popular and admired delegate at the UN, the symbol of compassion and concern for human rights and social justice. He was an ambassador to the UN, a Cambridge-educated literature professor, a Shakespearean producer-actor with a flair for the dramatic. She represented the world's richest and most powerful country—he, one of the world's poorest. She was Eleanor Roosevelt of the United States. He was Ahmed Shah Bokhari of Pakistan. At issue in the dramatic debate between them on Friday afternoon, October 6, 1950, was UNICEF's future.

Europe's children seemed well on the road to recovery, and UNICEF had already started to help children in a limited way in Asia and Latin America, when these two spokesmen confronted each other before the UN's Social, Cultural and Humanitarian Committee. Should UN work for children now be parceled out to WHO, FAO, and other UN technical-assistance agencies, as the United States, represented by Eleanor Roosevelt, proposed? Or should UNICEF continue, and give large-scale material help to children outside Europe, where hunger, disease, and poverty were age-old problems, as Ahmed Bokhari insisted?

Eyewitnesses say it was an unforgettable day. They remember the scene this way:

> Bokhari was vice-chairman of the committee, so he opened the meeting at Lake Success that morning. Then he gave the floor to Mrs. Roosevelt. She read a speech prepared for her by the U.S. State Department. True, she said, UNICEF had done marvelous work feeding the children in Europe, but the postwar emergency was over. UNICEF was supposed to be a temporary agency. Its main supporter, the U.S. government, was signaling, "Cut out massive food aid." When she had finished, Bokhari said he would like to step down from presiding over the committee and speak extemporaneously as the delegate from Pakistan.
>
> "I have the greatest respect for my distinguished colleague, Mrs. Roosevelt," he began, "but in listening to her, I felt as though I was at the funeral of the International Children's Emergency Fund." In an intense, husky voice, he continued: "Pakistan as well as other countries in Asia have been shocked to see UNICEF photographs of emaciated European children, victims of the war. They have been even more shocked, however, to realize that those European children still appear to be in no worse state than millions of children living so-called 'normal lives' in underdeveloped countries. You were willing to help postwar needy children in Europe," Bokhari concluded, "but now you're not willing to come through for equally needy children of the developing world?"

Above: Mrs. Eleanor Roosevelt, as drawn from life by Oscar Berger.

Opposite: Mrs. Roosevelt, champion of human rights, represented the United States at the United Nations in 1950, when UNICEF's future hung in the balance.

"It was a brilliant speech," remembers Helenka Pantaleoni. "When it was over, the Asian countries, the Latin American and Middle Eastern countries, one after the other, spoke in favor of UNICEF continuing to give their children the same kind of help. Mrs. Roosevelt dropped her head and all the blood seemed to flow out of her. She became very white. I don't think she ever in her whole experience had had such a reaction to one of her speeches."

In her book, *On My Own,* Mrs. Roosevelt wrote: "The feelings aroused were so great that no other nation dared join the United States in making the changes [in UNICEF's work], although I responded to Mr. Bokhari as best I could. This was one of the few times when I could find no way to 'get through' the barrier of misunderstanding among the delegates of many nations . . . although I tried in various ways to talk calmly and informally with Mr. Bokhari."

On December 1, 1950, the General Assembly unanimously extended UNICEF's work for three more years. They gave their blessing to its efforts to help children caught in the silent emergency of poverty, disease, and hunger in Asia, Africa, Latin America, and the Middle East. Ahmed Shah Bokhari had led a kind of revolution for those children and won a great moral victory. His eloquence and courage had turned around the thinking of the entire United Nations. The outpouring of support for UNICEF's work showed that in only four short years it had come into its own. As it had from the start, the United States continued to provide the lion's share—about two-thirds—of UNICEF's funding.

Soon after the General Assembly decision, the ever-gracious First Lady invited Ambassador Bokhari to Hyde Park for an evening of square-dancing. Until her death in 1962, she continued to be an active UNICEF supporter. She praised its work for children in her speeches and articles, contributing some book royalties to its cause. In 1953, when the General Assembly once again considered UNICEF's future, she came to UNICEF's defense with these widely quoted words: "There are about nine hundred million children under fifteen on earth today. More than half—about five hundred million—live and die in want . . . they are familiar with hunger, cold, and disease. The only organization that even begins to answer their needs is UNICEF. Yet its total expenditure has been less than half the cost of a single aircraft-carrier. . . . My hope—and the only practical salvation for these five hundred million children—is that UNICEF will be made permanent."

Unlikely adversaries: Eleanor Roosevelt and Ahmed Shah Bokhari of Pakistan met first on the UN committee floor in 1950, where they disputed the future of UNICEF.

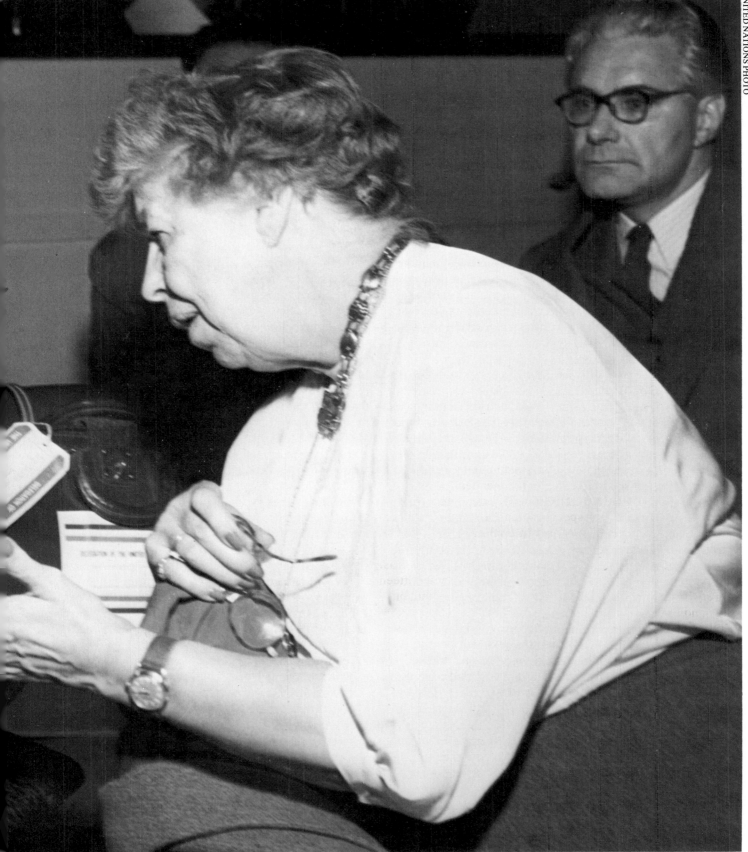

III. The Silent Killers

Gifts of life

There was optimism and a spirit of adventure in the air. The time was the early fifties. Medical science had just produced "miracle" cures for age-old diseases—yaws, syphilis, trachoma, leprosy—and a potent insecticide against malaria-bearing mosquitoes. Penicillin, aureomycin, streptomycin, and DDT prices were dropping. Huge amounts were now within UNICEF's modest budget. So UNICEF, in partnership with WHO, set out to do what no one had ever done before: to help countries on a mass scale attack the "Silent Emergency," and lift the burden of communicable diseases afflicting millions of children. The means: a series of nationwide campaigns in newly independent Asian countries, in Latin America, the Middle East, and Africa.

According to Swiss-born Dr. Otto Lehner, UNICEF's representative for West Africa in the mid-fifties, "Leprosy control was carried out by the French army's sanitary service. We had some success with malaria in Africa. Yaws control was organized like a military campaign. I must say the French and British did what they could at the time. They went from village to village, giving penicillin injections to everyone. Without that kind of effort, control of the disease would have been impossible. The mass campaigns were a great success, paving the way for health centers, where modern medical care could begin to reach the people."

Health ministers, campaign organizers, and UNICEF staff were improvisational geniuses when it came to places like Haiti, where illiteracy, mountainous terrain, and extreme poverty predominated. Despite the difficult conditions, one of the world's first mass campaigns against yaws met with great success. Instead of relying on people to come where teams were stationed, Haiti's campaign used a house-to-house visiting system. From 1950 on, jeep drivers doubled as lay vaccinators. The rationale for this was, if drivers had enough skill and intelligence to man a jeep, why couldn't they be trained by a doctor to give injections? After learning how to do so at the General Hospital in Port-au-Prince, they were sent out for a ten-day field test. Based on their performance, supervisors would choose among them for workers on the countrywide campaign. Driver-vaccinators were also sent to a "Statistics School" to master the techniques of keeping records, without which the disease could not be stamped out. In a mountainous country like Haiti, training jeep drivers was

An enlarged spleen is an almost-sure sign that this Senegalese child suffers from malaria, the number-one killer of children, primarily infants, in the 1950s. Mass campaigns to control the disease were just being initiated.

an inspired idea. UNICEF contributed the necessary penicillin, needles, and the jeeps themselves. More than two million cases were treated, and yaws was virtually eliminated from children's lives.

About the same time, Morocco, still a French protectorate, became the first country to receive UNICEF help for a far different drive—against a highly contagious eye sickness, trachoma. Called "the disease of dirty hands," trachoma often led to blindness, especially among children.

Southeast of Fez, Dr. François Rémy, then a young public health officer and later a UNICEF staff member, organized a three-year program to prevent trachoma among those living in the desert valley of Moulouya. His artist wife, Hélène Valentin, helped by painting canvases with huge eyes—healthy and diseased—which Rémy and his helpers then carried from village to village. In each place they set up the paintings as audiovisual attractions. People gathered around, as if for a spectacle. Rémy recounts, "We showed them how to apply the antibiotic ointment from UNICEF and we told them to do it twice a day, that it was very easy, and that they didn't need doctors for that."

Educating people in suburbs outside Fez required another tack. Valentin's canvases alone were not enough. Dr. Rémy knew that people love a good story. So he assigned two nurses who were very gifted storytellers to dress up in costume. He coached them carefully on how to weave basic eye-health messages into their tales. Then he sent them out into the bazaars, armed only with eyedrops, ointment, and Valentin's canvases. Between the stalls, with gestures, antics, and the paintings, the two men drew crowds. They began telling their audience the story of trachoma. "These miraculous eye lotions," they cried, pulling the ointments out from under their robes, "are as powerful as doctors." And then, throwing back their heads so all could see, the two costumed nurses promptly put ointment into their own eyes while the crowd applauded.

"All this was perfectly illegal," Dr. Rémy freely admits. "The public health service has no right to sell anything. We were supposed to distribute the drugs free. But we knew that sometimes only what is paid for arouses people's curiosity." The income from the sale of these drugs went back into a fund to buy more drugs, so that the storytelling nurses could teach more residents of Fez suburbs how to prevent trachoma from blinding their children and themselves.

The mass campaigns were only the most visible and tangible part of UNICEF's health work. The equipping of rural health posts where there were none before, the training of nurses, doctors, midwives, nutrition volunteers, and village leaders, all began in the 1950s. So did one of the most important kinds of training that UNICEF has continued to underwrite: the effort to bring traditional birth attendants—illiterate "grannies," in many countries—into contact with modern medicine.

Deformed lips, and sores on this Haitian child's elbow,
show she has yaws, once one of the world's most painful,
contagious diseases. In 1949, it crippled half the Haitian
population; after a nine-year UNICEF-assisted government
campaign, it was virtually eliminated in that country.

UNICEF PHOTO

*No one knows more about UNICEF's early work than Sam (Spur-
geon) Keeny. "Tough" to some, "lovable" to others, "effective at
the highest levels"—no one could ignore the Pennsylvania farm boy
with an Oxford education. As UNICEF's first regional director, he
traveled nearly half a million miles through Asia's cities and
villages—the right man in the right place at the right time. In one
hand, Keeny held UNICEF's freshly minted mandate to help
governments tackle age-old threats to children's lives. In the other,
he offered medical supplies, jeeps, and a batch of new weapons—
penicillin, DDT, aureomycin ointment, BCG vaccine—to fight those
threats.*

*Some say Sam Keeny "made a greater contribution to UNICEF's
practical work than any other single person in its history." Alive and
well and living in Washington, D.C., Keeny, now in his early
nineties, reminisces about his Asian years.*

Sam Keeny's story

When I first went to Asia in March 1950, I wanted to see for
myself what life was like in its villages. I ended up visiting all
twenty-two countries in the region—from Afghanistan in the
West to the Pacific Islands: home to half the world's children.
They were twenty-two countries with twenty-two different
kinds of problems.

Between 1950 and 1963 (my years of service to UNICEF in
Asia), I visited about two thousand villages. I tried, wherever
possible, to spend a day in each. I drove endless miles in
jeeps, rode in oxcarts or on muleback to see how the TB
program or the yaws program or a combination of programs
was working.

I spent a lot of time fishing around for the right interpreter.
This made some people impatient, but it meant an awful lot.
You needed men when you went to speak with men, and
women when you went to speak with women. You needed
someone who was outgoing and sympathetic, who spoke the
dialect, and who came from that neighborhood. There are
fifteen or so states in India and about that many languages
officially recognized. There are actually hundreds of dialects
within that system. Even in Indonesia, where officially all
speak Bahasa, there are at least a half-dozen distinct dialects.

You learned much more by spending a whole day at a
particular place than by visiting ten villages in ten hours. In
the first hour, you got the usual ritual hospitality—everything
from coconuts to any other local fruits that are growing. After
two or three hours, people began to tell you what they really
thought. One Thai countryman once said, "Odd people these
'farang' [foreigners]. Some of them scratch where we don't
itch." And that comes close to the heart of the matter.

However, I don't think anybody would say that about our
first big adventure fighting a communicable disease called
yaws. Yaws is a disease, as they say in Indonesia, that is
found "at the end of the road." It's a disease of the rural areas
where there is great poverty, often a scarcity of water, where
there have been no medical services, where all children go
barefoot, and where the chances of transmitting the disease
are usually good.

Globally, there were about forty to fifty million overt cases,
with perhaps another 150 million at risk. Our region had more
than fifteen million of them. Yaws spreads wildly; it persists;
it's recurrent. Yaws cripples but seldom kills. In its advanced
states it merely makes people wish they were dead. Grown-
ups catch the infection mostly from children, or in their own
childhood. During play, one kid usually spreads it to another
who has scratches on his legs caused by running about
barefoot, which everybody did.

Most North Americans have never seen a case of yaws.
Imagine having a boil, and then another, until you have
dozens of them—and keep on having them for years. Imagine
having them on the soles of your feet so that you can't walk,
and on the palms of your hands so that you can't work. Many
a case I've seen too late for Nature to repair the damage.
Victims had to be carried in a bamboo chair. They could not
walk or even stand alone.

Experiments in Haiti showed that long-acting penicillin
could cure this disease with two injections. This was in the
early days of penicillin, which, you remember, was discovered by Fleming on a bit of mold in a saucer in an English
university. Two doctors named Chain and Florey had helped

mass-produce it. But no one had ever tried to cure millions of cases of yaws with it before.

At the first world conference on yaws held in Bangkok in the early fifties, the experts were cautious, except for one young doctor who expressed different views. I took him aside and asked: "What's the *real* line we ought to take?" His answer: "Go after this straight. Get the penicillin into these people—as many as you can as quickly as you can, and you can break up the disease."

We got approval and technical advice from our partner, the World Health Organization (WHO). Indonesia's health authorities were ready to begin a mass attack, ready to match the cost of UNICEF penicillin, jeeps, needles, and syringes more than two times over, ready to train teams to go into every village, administer mass injections, and rout out yaws.

Everybody should be treated, WHO advised, because the number of hidden infected cases was probably three times as many as those with open sores. Unless everybody with yaws was found, treated, and cured, children could be reinfected in short order.

Luckily, the price of penicillin came down rapidly. At first it cost a dollar per person. UNICEF bought large quantities. I think we were the biggest buyers of penicillin on the market. As the price came down, it was also discovered that a much smaller dose than previously thought necessary was enough. By the time several million cases a year were being treated, the cost of penicillin per person had dropped to about five cents. The total campaign costs amounted to less than a dollar a person cured.

If you had suffered from yaws for months or years and learned that you could be cured by a single shot of penicillin, wouldn't you get that shot the first chance you had? And if you were a field man for UNICEF who had seen thousands of cases of yaws and knew that you could get results like that, wouldn't you try to reach more and more cases every day as fast as possible until the disease was totally wiped out? Wouldn't you be impatient to get penicillin into millions of buttocks as rapidly as you could train the injectors? If we pressed our headquarters for more action and they asked for more money from governments and from UNICEF supporters, can you blame us?

From 1949 through 1969, UNICEF and WHO cooperated with governments of fifty countries in a series of campaigns to eliminate yaws and related diseases of endemic syphilis and pinta. About 160 million were examined and penicillin treatment given to nearly sixty million found to be infected or in contact with those who were.

How the job was done varied. Here, from my diary, is a picture of how the work was organized in Nigeria. (Africa had perhaps half of all the yaws cases in the world.)

A Moroccan primary-school teacher explains the danger of trachoma—total or partial blindness—to his students. Children have long been the chief sufferers of this communicable eye disease.

WHO PHOTO

About an hour's drive from Enugu (eastern Nigeria), we saw in action a veritable jumbo team of thirty workers busy with two long lines of Ibo villagers—more than a thousand in each line. Because the clearing was small, the lines were doubled back and forth, each moving forward through an amazing bamboo labyrinth built (no doubt with more care than usual) for this special demonstration. The whole process was as well arranged as an automobile assembly line in Detroit. The villagers were grouped in the line by "kindreds" so that they helped one another with the children and largely organized themselves.

The examiner inspected each person carefully—including the palms of the hands and the soles of the feet, where yaws often starts. Even for the adults this was not difficult: their clothing was "nothing much before and rather less than half of that behind." As for the children up to puberty, the only parts not visible were the soles of the feet. As they moved by, five or six a minute, the inspector called out to the clerk the code name of the type of the disease they had. The next inspector, a senior nurse, verified the diagnosis and marked the dosage of medicine necessary with chalk on the ebony blackboard of the patient's back.

The preparation for the injection was a little masterpiece in itself. One worker soaped the right buttock, a second rinsed it, and a third disinfected it. Meanwhile, another series of workers prepared for the injections: one opened vials, a second filled syringes sterilized by a third, and two injectors deftly pressed the needles home as the patients leaned over a horizontal bamboo pole. By 3:00 P.M., 2,900 persons had been treated.

In Indonesia, where there were more than ten million cases of the disease, Dr. Kodijat, one of the really great Indonesians, worked out a simpler method, which reached the people in their own villages. On the appointed day, case-finders (young men with high-school educations and three months of training in finding open yaws cases) came to the village. The headman then beat on his hollow log for the villagers to assemble. Everyone with yaws received a card. A few days later, the injector arrived, and the headman called in the card-holders by a special signal on the hollow log. Brown buttocks were bared, the needle flashed, and the job was done. One case-finder could examine more than one hundred persons a day this way, and an injector could treat many more than that.

By 1960, more than ten million persons had been cured. We did it within ten years. And there was no problem for the future because the clinics in those neighborhoods, including the "mantris" (male nurses) who were looking after the health of the neighborhoods, had stores of penicillin. People knew what to do if a case came up in their village. They simply went to the "mantri" and asked for a dose of penicillin that cured it. They literally wiped out the disease. It's almost nonexistent in Asia now, even in Indonesia.

The effect on the people of Indonesia was striking. They were extremely thankful and expressed it in many ways. One of the most unusual was in a remote area where the animistic religion was still strong, where they hold the banyan tree sacred. On this banyan tree they hung votive gifts in thanks to the gods for cures, just as you find in many Catholic regions of the world.

I remember visiting one of those banyan trees, which was completely hung with votive gifts of thanks because every family in that village apparently had had yaws. It was hung like a Christmas tree.

In terms of children's lives saved, the campaign against yaws was less important than that for malaria eradication. Mosquitoes bite adults as greedily as they do infants, but malaria kills a lot more babies than it does grown-ups. When I was in Asia, it killed one out of every five babies before its first birthday.

In 1946, DDT had only recently been discovered as a highly effective insecticide against the mosquitoes that carry malaria. The method of residual spraying of the insides of houses and cattle sheds was just being tested. Not until later, about 1957, did the eradication programs really get started. We were frightened into action by the fear that mosquitoes would become resistant to DDT; we believed we had to work fast.

The idea of stopping malaria by spraying the walls of living rooms once or twice a year sounds simple. In practice, it meant reaching perhaps seventy-five million houses in India alone. By "reaching" the homes we meant getting the spray teams inside the houses to do the spraying. In Muslim countries, especially, this was not always easy.

When the team, approaching a village, heard the clapping

Above: Sam Keeny, UNICEF's Asian adventurer and first regional director, holds a year-old child. He had a way with Asia's children.

Opposite: At Brebes, an Indonesian village, a male nurse is trained to detect yaws. His job: to identify all sufferers, then round them up for penicillin shots.

Elephants hauled penicillin, syringes, vans with loudspeakers, and health teams to remote parts of Thailand, helping to eradicate yaws.
TROPICAL MEDICINE FACULTY, MHIPOL UNIVERSITY, BANGKOK

of hands, they were not deceived into thinking that this was applause for their work. They knew that the men of the village were warning the women that strangers were near and that the women should hide. Once inside the house, the men had to be careful not to soil the housewives' treasures. In the poorest village houses there was next to nothing to protect, but in the cities there was bedding, maybe even a bit of lace. At first, people were wary. In time the teams were usually welcomed and householders were proud to point to the sign on their outer wall: DDT (with date). In 1966, when my work on family planning for the Population Council for East Asia took me to one of the remote villages behind the mountains in Iran, I found the DDT sign on every house. All this was new in Asia—and in most of the world. Many years ago, I remember sitting in an outpatient clinic, watching the doctor examining a girl of eight who had malaria. "Please save this one for me, doctor," pleaded the mother. "I've lost my four others from this fever and I can't bear to watch the last one go."

The goal of eradicating malaria was not achieved. There were all sorts of technical and logistic reasons. In some places mosquitoes did become immune to DDT, and other chemicals developed by WHO were more expensive. The battle took more and more money out of health budgets. Some governments ran out of funds or were slow in paying the spray teams. When that happened, sprayers simply quit and programs folded. However, in 1964, the World Health Organization reported some success: more than one-fifth of all the people on earth—some 680 million persons in previously malarious areas—were now living in areas completely or almost free of malaria, and some two million, most of them children, were being saved each year. Behind those figures lies a story of enormous effort, energy, and money, for the drive against malaria was the most expensive of all.

Take India, where deaths had been running as high as a million a year. While the disease wasn't eradicated, India pretty well cleared it out. Deaths dropped to under thirty thousand a year. Taiwan was the one country in all of Asia declared malaria-free.

After malaria, tuberculosis was the greatest child-killer in Asia. India was one of the worst situations. We had a very good head of the tuberculosis division of Indian services there, and a young WHO doctor named Halfdan Mahler (currently WHO director-general) doing his first field work. When the International Tuberculosis Campaign ended its work in mid-1951, UNICEF gave BCG vaccines and financed the training of lay vaccinators.

Campaigns were organized state by state. I remember being whisked off to see the marvels of the lightning vaccination campaign in the capital, Delhi. Eighty centers were being used. Bands in the city and drummers in the outlying villages assembled the children. The Delhi Flying Club dropped fifty thousand leaflets explaining the two injections each child needed: one to see whether it already harbored the deadly bacillus, and then a BCG vaccination for those who weren't already infected.

Loudspeakers on UNICEF jeeps told people that the test was useless unless they returned to be vaccinated if they needed it. Loudspeakers, gramophones, and comic films may not be traditional tools of scientific medicine, but the successful organizers of mass programs were strictly pragmatic.

As we rode from one center to another, we heard of achievements incredible by all previous standards. A field unit of about 25 persons is supposed to test about 32,000 individuals a month and vaccinate those who are not already infected. In Delhi, 11 persons in a single day had tested 16,500 children and would probably complete their vaccinations during a second day. One hero had tested 5,500 children in one day.

News of these achievements was broadcast every night on the radio in Delhi and heard all over India. Within weeks, several states that had been coy about promising money for statewide campaigns wired in that the money had been found. As our mission chief in India wrote, "We are now watching the BCG campaigns as closely as end-of-cricket scores."

We had another opportunity to protect children. This time it was their eyes. Millions of children in the region had trachoma, an eye disease that has been around for centuries. It thrives in hot, dusty places where hygiene is under par. Dirty handkerchiefs, towels, and flies spread it. Like yaws, it doesn't kill. But it blinds. In the past, trachoma was the world's leading cause of blindness. In the fifties, suddenly we had a cure: newly discovered antibiotic ointments—aureomycin and terramycin—and luckily, the price was one UNICEF could afford.

In Taiwan, in 1953, two million people were afflicted. That seemed a good place to begin. A start was made with seven thousand schoolchildren in a pilot project with the help of a WHO trachoma expert. Doctors taught teachers the routine. Pupils were their aides.

I dropped in a year later to see how these kids were doing. It was astonishing. A classroom eye-care drill was in progress. Children moved with clockwork precision. When the teacher gave the signal to begin, fifty children each put on a numbered armband. One read out the names of those to be treated, while another got a basin of soap and water, so that everyone could wash his hands. A third gave out tubes of ointment, each numbered to avoid cross-infection. They lined up. The teacher pulled down the lower lids of every infected youngster, squeezing ointment into the corners. The last step was to press small squares of tissue paper over the lids to help spread the ointment inside the eye. Tubes were collected. Children returned to their seats. Only five minutes had gone by.

By 1959, nearly 6.5 million Asian children were treated. You could say that many of these were saved from blindness. There is still, however, a long way to go.

The mass-disease campaigns reached into communities never previously served by health services. They showed the feasibility of the large-scale use of volunteers in health activities. They also made clear that, after an intensive attack

Above: In Anand, India, the first plant in the world to successfully dry buffalo milk opened in 1955. UNICEF contributed the equipment to this dairy and to two hundred milk plants all over the developing world.

Opposite: Rubbing it in: Taiwanese students practice applying antibiotic ointment to their classmates' eyes. It takes two doses daily for two months to cure trachoma. Before a campaign to eliminate it in 1954, over half of Taiwan's children suffered from trachoma. Two years later, the eyes of nearly two million schoolchildren in the nation had been examined, and over a million treated successfully.

phase, they should be integrated into permanent health and welfare structures.

Most of the babies, at least in Asia, were (and still are) delivered by a "traditional birth attendant," usually a self-employed village woman. She is generally very popular because, in addition to delivering the baby, she helps feed the father, the children, and the animals, if any. In the 1950s and 1960s, tens of thousands of birth attendants (seven thousand in the Philippines, more than that in Thailand, and perhaps five times that in Indonesia) were given simple training in delivery and referring potentially complicated cases to the health services. This training is probably one of the great achievements of those decades.

Untrained midwives previously had had no contact with organized medicine whatsoever. Now the idea of germs was inculcated into them. It took the form of "keep your hands really clean—out of the birth canal during delivery, avoid contaminating, and let nature do the job." We provided a very simple midwifery kit, which became standard for use by tens of thousands. It was given to a birth attendant after she had completed her apprenticeship under a trained midwife. These birth attendants were invited to come in for courses, and in some places, they came in for a course of several months. In other places, they'd come for weekends over a year, or in their spare time over several years. When they finally could do the job to the satisfaction of their supervisor, they were given the midwifery kit. This was an aluminum box about a foot by ten inches big, by eight inches deep, which contained all the essentials for aid in the delivery. Carefully designed by UNICEF and WHO, it was in great demand. You could even boil water for the delivery in it.

I remember that once in East Bengal (now Bangladesh), during the flood season, I wanted to go visit a couple of clinics. The whole countryside was flooded maybe four or five feet. So we went out in a rowboat. The clinic was just about a foot above water level. Everything around was water as far as you could see. Here in the room with us were two of these traditional birth attendants. I had with me a Bengalese doctor who spoke good English and was an excellent interpreter. A storm came up, and everyone was afraid to go back because there were waves several feet high. While waiting for the storm to abate, I asked these birth attendants if they had attended the training courses. "Yes," they said. "Did you like the courses?" I asked. "What do you think? We were doing it on our own time and at our own expense—if we didn't like it, we wouldn't have gone," they snapped back. They had already gained their midwife kits and were very proud of them. I had approved the issue of tens of thousands of these kits, but only then did I see fully what it meant to get them into use.

We were asked to build a penicillin plant in India. What I didn't know about penicillin would fill volumes. But with Minister of Finance Desai, we took a barren area in Bombay State close to the little city of Poona in the hills, and together

One of the great achievements of the past thirty-five years: Over
five hundred thousand nurses, midwives and traditional birth
attendants were trained on UNICEF stipends. A
professionally trained midwife near New Delhi (left) shows a
new mother how to bathe her infant. In a Philippine village
(right) a retrained traditional birth attendant helps a new mother.

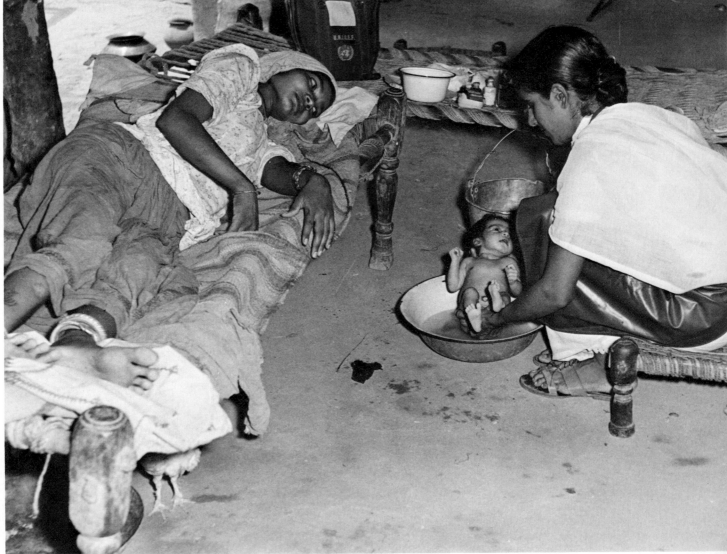

built a plant there that eventually became one of the largest single producers of penicillin in the world. A city of about fifteen thousand employees and their families sprang up around it.

Penicillin was in its infant days when we brought out to Asia the man who had developed the original plant at McGill University. With him as adviser, we agreed to provide all the production machinery if the Indian government would build the housing for it.

I remember the negotiations with Prime Minister Nehru. He wasn't a chemist, but he was a darn good lawyer, and he asked some searching questions. We argued for the government's taking over the plant instead of giving it to one of the big commercial companies of the pharmaceutical world. We specified that all the penicillin produced above a certain amount should be given to the hospitals and to doctors in government service for use with the poor. Nehru agreed.

Fortunately, there was a wonderful breakthrough while they were building the plant. The "brewers" learned how to grow the penicillin not only on the surface of liquid, but through the whole body of the liquid. This multiplied the amount that could be turned out, and production far exceeded expectations.

We did a similar job with two DDT plants and had an infinite number of technical problems to solve. One plant was in India, the other up in Peshawar, Pakistan, near the Khyber Pass. I remember learning quite a bit of chemistry; I had never taken it in school. But then, every day I spent in Asia I learned something new, surprising, and often hopeful. The most hopeful thing of all was to see with my own eyes that the disease and misery of children in the villages grew less and less with each day of UNICEF aid.

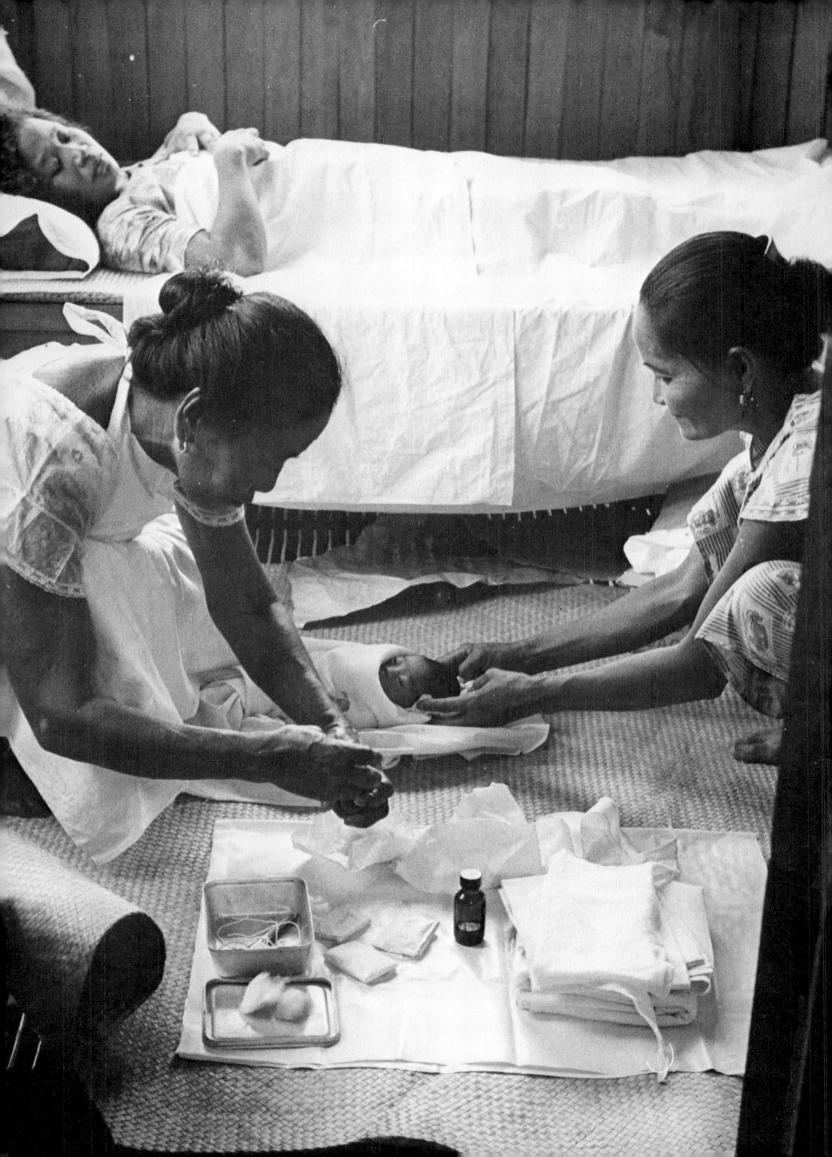

IV. The Nobel Prize, 1965

"Everyone has understood the language of UNICEF. . . . Even the most reluctant person is bound to admit that in action UNICEF has proved that compassion knows no national boundaries. Aid is given to all children without any distinction of race, creed, nationality, or political conviction. . . . UNICEF has become an international device capable of liberating hundreds of millions of children from ignorance, disease, malnutrition, and starvation. . . . The aim of UNICEF is to spread a table decked with all the good things that Nature provides for all the children of the world. . . . UNICEF offers young people an alternative worth living and working for, a world with freedom for all people, equality between all races, brotherhood among all men."

—from Nobel Citation awarding UNICEF the
Nobel Prize for Peace
December 10, 1965

A golden moment: the Nobel Prize for Peace was conferred on UNICEF at Oslo University, December 1965. Accepting the gold medal and scroll was Henry R. Labouisse, executive director. Delegation members include (left to right): Professor Robert Debré of France, dean of UNICEF's Executive Board; Mrs. Adelaide Sinclair of Canada, deputy executive director for programming, and Mrs. Zena Harman of Israel, chairman of UNICEF's Executive Board.

V. Goodwill Ambassadors

The real heroes

by Danny Kaye

Every life is an unwritten novel, but the story of how I got mixed up with UNICEF more than thirty years ago and all the crazy and wonderful things that happened to me since could easily make a Hollywood movie.

Just take the opening scene: After a personal appearance in London, I boarded a Stratocruiser flight for the United States. When we were six hundred miles out over the Atlantic and everyone was fast asleep, suddenly a crew member shook me awake: "You'd better get up, Mr. Kaye, because we may have to ditch!" So I got out of bed. It was very scary. Everybody was being given life rafts, food and flashlights. We had developed propeller trouble. The "prop" was free-wheeling; it was wild, there was no controlling it. I walked up and down the aisle, asking everybody to take off his shoes and to tie the life raft to his wrist in case we had to plunge into the water. The pilot, with some exceptionally good maneuvering, waited until he sensed the propeller was about to be torn loose, pulled the plane up into a near-stall, and the propeller dropped off and passed under, rather than into, the wings. Luck was very much on our side. We got back to Shannon Airport safely and caught another plane home.

Sitting next to me on that second plane was a man named Maurice Pate. Now, if you asked Central Casting to send up an actor to play the part of the director of an international humanitarian children's organization and they sent out Maurice Pate, you'd say they knew their business. Maurice was tall and stately, an imposing figure with silver hair and a quiet yet warm manner. He had spent half his life helping the world's unfortunate children, and he began explaining to me what UNICEF's work was.

Six months later Maurice Pate read in the newspapers that I was going on a trip around the world and he asked me to lunch with him at the big glass box, the United Nations building. He told me: "You know, people are having a lot of trouble identifying UNICEF." (The UN then, as now, was riddled with initials—WPPL and FPR and PPS.) "If you would stop at some of our installations and then come back and go on the radio or write a magazine article," said Maurice, "it would help us a great deal." "Well, I'll do a little better than that," I promised. "I'll try to make a documentary."

Returning to Hollywood, I went to see a man called Y. Frank Freeman, head of Paramount Pictures, about Maur-

Top: Danny Kaye, the original kid from Brooklyn, circa 1915.

Left: Danny Kaye drawn from life by Oscar Berger, early 1950s.

Opposite: Kaye comforts a near-dying Bangladeshi infant in a refugee camp in India, 1971

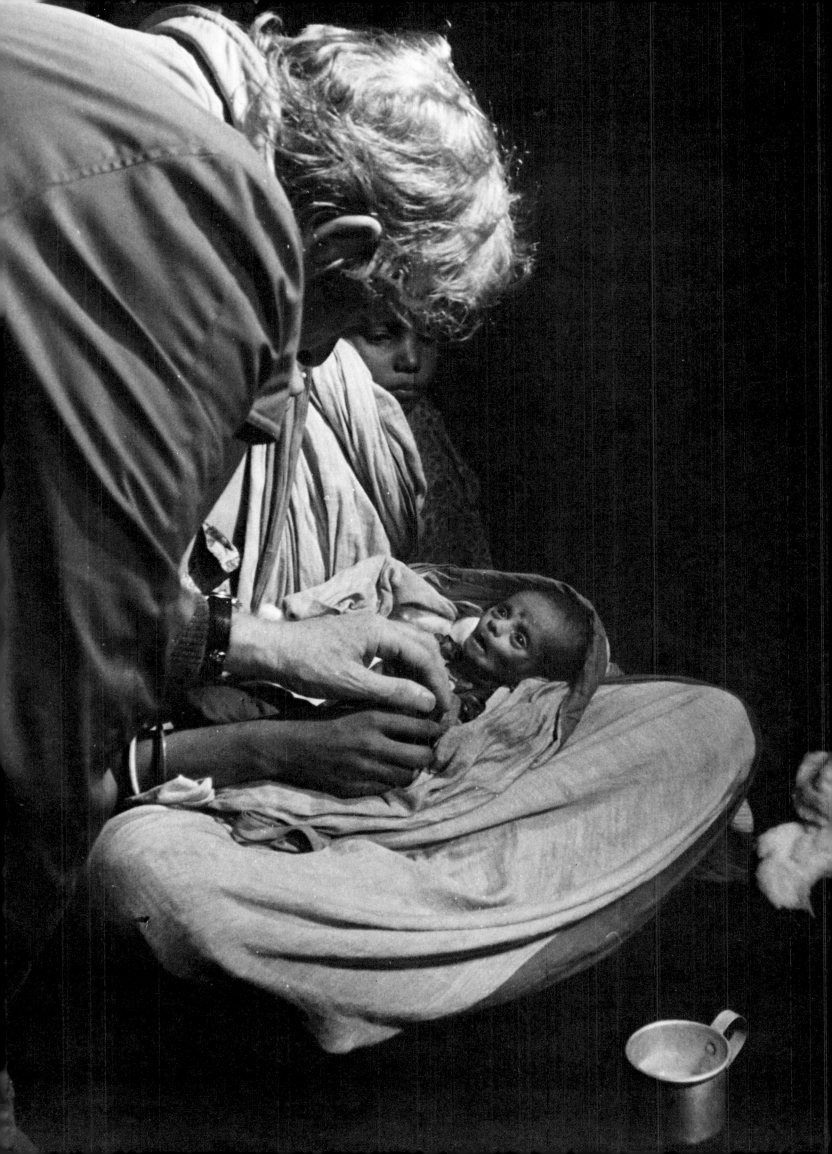

Top: Kaye amuses Boonting (left) and his friends during filming of *Assignment: Children* in the Thai village of Tungkaponghow. Once a victim of yaws, Boonting's spectacular cure with a shot of UNICEF penicillin is one of the film's highlights.

Above: During a home visit to the Trudeau family in Ottawa on Halloween, 1975, Kaye cottons up to Sasha the leopard and Justin the tiger, while mother Margaret enjoys the fun.

ice's proposal. Frank gave me two cameramen and I don't know how many hundreds of thousands of feet of film, and we took a trip to Asia to see what was being done to help the children and to make a film about it. Paramount decided to underwrite the expense of our trip, release the film to commercial theaters, and give the proceeds to UNICEF. All we had to do was make it.

Before we took off, in the spring of 1954, Maurice Pate and Dag Hammarskjöld, United Nations secretary-general at the time, appointed me ambassador-at-large, "charged with making known the needs of children throughout the world." I couldn't have been more delighted, more pleased, more honored.

Our first stop was the UN in Geneva, where we had a two-hour press conference. It was kind of shattering. The reporters seemed to be thinking: Danny Kaye, comedian, movie actor, vaudevillian—what's he going on this trip for, and what's he getting out of all this and how does it fit together?

I had no answer. I didn't know what I was going to do. I hadn't any idea of how I would shoot the film. We had no script, no props. The exciting thing was that we ended up shooting exactly what we saw—children in Burma, India, Indonesia, Korea, Thailand, and Japan. Today, people might call what we did something fancy like *cinéma vérité*. But that expression hadn't been invented yet, so we just went ahead and made the film.

To my surprise, everywhere I went I was accorded full diplomatic honors. In India, cheering crowds greeted us at the airport. Madame Pandit, Prime Minister Nehru's sister, gave us a diplomatic reception. It wasn't me they were honoring, of course, but UNICEF.

I found that UNICEF was the biggest factor in the struggle for the health of kids and mothers all over the world. In India, I beat a double-ended drum, and long lines of Indian youngsters followed me to a health post. It was amazing to see teams of health volunteers working for hours and hours, even though it was 109 degrees in the shade. They vaccinated as many as two thousand kids a day.

I witnessed the fight against malaria, too. In India, human muscle was creating DDT plants to start an eradication program. In Burma, I saw malaria workers, true to their unique cultural tradition, wash their feet before going into each village house to spray walls and ceilings. Doctors probed children's bellies for an enlarged spleen—the telltale sign of malaria—while I probed for concealed laughter.

Everywhere, the children were the real stars of our film. And that goes double for seven-year-old Sam, whom we met in a Thai village. Sam's real name was Boonting Choeykholai. I simply couldn't pronounce it, so I decided to call him Sam. We came to his village to film a small miracle happening at the local health center. Just like a million other Thai youngsters, little Sam had yaws. His body was covered with big, open red sores—the kind that make you feel a little bit ill when you first look at them. Six of his brothers and sisters also had the contagious, crippling disease.

Kaye's attempts to fast-dance earn him chuckles from leprosy victims in a Nigerian village.

I watched Sam being given a shot of penicillin provided by UNICEF, and he took it without a quiver. Fourteen days later—even before we finished shooting our film—his sores had completely dried up. A drug costing less than five cents had cured him, and his family and friends as well.

When our film *Assignment: Children* was released a year later, in 1955, people all over the world got to know about Sam as well as the other children UNICEF was helping. The film was translated into nineteen languages and viewed by I don't know how many millions of people. It is possible that more people saw that film than any other film I made.

I met Sam again years later at a reunion held by UNICEF in Tokyo, for children representing every Asian country UNICEF has worked in. By then Sam had become a tall, strong, healthy and handsome seventeen-year-old. He worked on his father's rice paddy. Once he recognized me, Sam never left my side. Because we didn't speak each other's language, it was rather difficult to communicate; so in trying to thank me and UNICEF, he merely put his hand on my shoulder. It was the most eloquent expression of love I have ever encountered.

Thanks to the ever-widening work of UNICEF, Sam's

"EVER SINCE DANNY KAYE'S VISIT THEY EXPECT ALL OF US TO PERFOEM!"

Top: Kaye's promotional flight for Trick-or-Treat for UNICEF in 1975 put him in a whole new category: the "World's Fastest-Flying Entertainer," according to the Guinness Book of Records. Kaye piloted the UNICEF One plane to sixty-five Canadian and U.S. cities in five days. This was one of five such flights he undertook from 1965 to 1975.

Bottom: Although he can't read a note of music, Kaye has guest-conducted some of the world's leading symphony orchestras, such as the London Symphony Orchestra. Here he is shown rehearsing with them for a 1975 benefit performance of *An Evening with Danny Kaye*. In this case, his show helped the musicians' pension fund, but Kaye also conducts often for UNICEF.

story—a child saved by one injection or one medical examination from a life of misery or early death—has been repeated millions of times around the world, spreading the word that children can be cured of malnutrition, of disease, of despair—if only we care enough to help UNICEF do it.

Most of my life I have dealt with children, and somehow I can communicate with them. I don't know how, but it hasn't been any work, it hasn't been any trial. For me, one of the great experiences of my life was finding out that you don't need words to communicate with a child anywhere in the world. Sometimes I'd wander through a village and just sit down on the ground, certain that curiosity would eventually lead the children to me. When they got close enough, I'd make a funny face and there'd be giggles. Someone would make a funny face back at me, and then we'd have a fine contest going. They were relaxed. They saw in me a reflection of themselves. Children don't know who I am. They don't care. I'm just an adult they can have fun with. When I can communicate with a child without speech but through a smile or a funny face, I become aware of love. Most children have built-in radar. You can't fool them. They know when someone feels love and concern for them, and they know when someone is just pretending.

My experience has shown me that children are the same, and they laugh at the same things, all over the world. It's not hard. You repeat a certain rhyme to the point of absurdity. You switch roles. You become a child and the child becomes the grown-up. You pretend. You roar like a lion and run as fast as you can; you flounder and fall down and can't catch up or can't escape. If you can get one child in a group to laugh—with you or at you—then the whole group will laugh. And if the grown-ups are standing around, they too will laugh with their children. I'd listen hard to get the rhythm and sound of each language, because one of the many things I learned in my UNICEF travels is that children and grown-ups alike flip if you so much as utter a single phrase in their tongue.

I'm told that there are people who say: "Oh, UNICEF—that's the Danny Kaye organization!" Who wouldn't be terribly flattered? But let's set the record straight: I'm one of many, many volunteers. And I don't think of myself as a hero for making countless trips around the world, giving speeches and performances, making films to help draw support for UNICEF. Nor am I a hero for flying the "UNICEF One" jet across the United States and Canada in 1975. That flight was the craziest and most wonderful experience of my life. We promoted Trick-or-Treat for UNICEF in over sixty-five cities in fewer than five days.

The real heroes are the people I've met in my travels who devote their lives, their energies, their emotions—without publicity, without fanfare, without great remuneration—to help children survive in this world. That's what really got me hooked on working for UNICEF all these years.

The great strength of UNICEF is that politics don't count

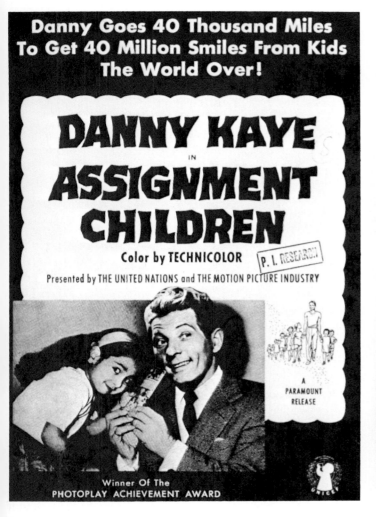

where children are concerned. That's what makes it so special. How can you love an Israeli child and not an Arab child; a North Korean child and not a South Korean child; an Indian child and not a Pakistani child? It's impossible. You can't tell the difference.

I help UNICEF because I want a happy, healthy, peaceful world. The sick, orphaned, hungry children UNICEF helps are a force for peace because they grow up remembering that people around the world have joined hands to help them. It's the most exciting thing in the world to say to a child, "I'm going to make you an ambassador for UNICEF. You're going to take this orange box [the Trick-or-Treat box] and go to somebody's house, and that money is going to save a child's life somewhere in the world." Kids are really very moved by the fact that they can do something to influence another child's life from so far away.

Deep inside, behind all the clowning and cutting up, I'm never more serious than when I talk about children. It's not funny that children continue to die from diarrhea, from preventable diseases.

I have a letter. It came soon after I returned from visiting refugee camps set up in India. That was in 1971, when millions of people had fled what was then East Pakistan, before Bangladesh became a nation. The Indian letter commended me for filming and making known the suffering of mothers and children in those camps. That letter means so much to me because at that time, there were people who questioned whether it wasn't "out of place" for a comedian like me to bring his funny face into such a tragic situation. Unfortunately, suffering doesn't go out of style, and the number of people who are aware of it and will do something about it must be made to grow.

In 1982, I was the lucky fellow who received the Humanitarian Oscar in Hollywood. At the time, I said that I felt a little guilty about all the praise because it was really no hardship at all. The truth is that, whatever I may have given, I have gotten back a thousandfold.

I believe deeply that children are more powerful than oil, more beautiful than rivers, more precious than any other natural resource a country can have. I feel that the most rewarding thing I have ever done in my life is to be associated with UNICEF. As long as I have the energy and the time, I will continue to devote myself to making a child healthier and happier somewhere in the world.

Opposite: The
foreigner:
Surrounded by
Indian youngsters
and adults, Ustinov
invokes a blessing
from above on all.

Barking for UNICEF

by Peter Ustinov

UNICEF came into my consciousness when I was asked
to host a huge benefit concert for the organization, at the
Paris Odéon in 1968. The invitation came from Leon Davico,
then chief of UNICEF Information in Europe. I can't remember the exact details, but there were at least four orchestras,
a Polish dance ensemble, a Russian dance ensemble, Mario
del Monaco, and a Romanian choir. The wings, even at the
Odéon, were so full you could hardly move!

The Poles started the evening with a mountaineer dance—
a long line of men swinging axes. One of them cut through my
microphone cable by mistake, so I had to shout for the rest of
the evening. I ended up a hoarser but happier man, asking
myself what sort of organization this was that could engender
such goodwill. After that I was as hooked on UNICEF as
others can be on a drug or on tobacco.

Of course, when my children were younger, I had a whole
lot of brochures which had been given away free by UNICEF.
My children had sold them and given the money to UNICEF.
I was very touched and impressed. But only after this concert
did I begin to take an active interest in the organization. I like
to think it's always been a part of my nature to pay something
back. My thought has always been that, if you happen to be
lucky enough to get on in this world, your responsibilities
increase; they don't diminish. Having been blessed with four
children who are more or less agreeable to talk to and more or
less good to look at, I thought the time to repay my debt was
while everything was going well.

In the past, as far as Europe is concerned, my function has
been to try and perform in galas and television specials as a
kind of anchorman. It's a side I don't like very much—the
money-raising side—but it's imperative in an organization
which is constituted in such a way that governments respond
according to private contributions. In countries like France
and Belgium, I should say that a quarter of the people who
come up and say they like something that I have done, or
disliked it or whatever, also say, "Thanks for all you're doing
for UNICEF." So, in that sense, I think that UNICEF is
above criticism.

I've done commercials for UNICEF in Australia and in
Canada that, on the whole, have gone very well. I've played
a lot of different characters in TV spots: a magician, a chef, a
football player, a hippie, a union leader, a big businessman,
Santa Claus, a cowboy and, if memory serves, a Canadian
forest ranger. The hippie and the businessman were the good
ideas of the Canadian publicity people, who were volunteering their creative services in the finest tradition of UNICEF.
It was a challenge to act out the different roles. In 1984, the
UNICEF greeting-card people came up with something new:
a commercial set inside a postal box. I was supposed to be
seated inside a replica of a London mailbox. A card was

Peter Ustinov,
caricatured (above);
sketched as a baby
(below) by his artist
mother, Nadezhda
Leontievna, at home
in London.

COURTESY PETER USTINOV

Bangkok, 1979: Barking like a dog can substitute for knowing a foreign language—it's a sound everyone recognizes.

dropped into it. I tore the card apart, sending half to your proverbial "Aunt Lucy" and the other half to a child in a country that needed help. Quite frankly, it wasn't easy for me to fit inside a postal box. But I'm not by temperament a Mother Teresa, who can merge into crowded slums and quietly do good things. I have to go on doing what I'm doing. I did that particular spot in French, Spanish, German, and, of course, English.

I found extraordinary welcomes in Thailand, Jordan, and Guatemala when I went out for UNICEF. I couldn't help noticing that the people who are most effective in *all* places are foreigners to those places. In other words, a Tanzanian working in Sri Lanka can be very effective just because he's different.

This was extremely apparent in Guatemala, where suddenly a nun appeared who was not at all Guatemalan by appearance. She was dressed in the uniform of Mother Teresa's order, and I said, "What are you doing here?" She said, "We came for the earthquake." I said, "What are you doing now? Are you waiting for the next earthquake?" And she looked at me cannily and said, "I know what you are asking. You are asking what are nuns from India doing here?" I said, "Exactly!" "Well, you know," she said, "we're different from these people, and they look up to us because they've never seen people like us before, and therefore we can do the things that Guatemalans can't." And I said, "Well, that's absolutely logical because Mother Teresa herself is not Indian, and therefore she has managed to do things in Calcutta

Happiness is . . . riding piggyback on Peter Ustinov.

There are occupational hazards to being a Goodwill Ambassador. Having children pull at your beard (at a school in Paris), for example.

Ustinov with son Igor and daughters Andrea and Pavla in the South of France, 1963. "I feel guilty, guilty of happiness. . . . What is working for UNICEF but a regard for a family larger than your own?"

that are impossible for the Indians."

When you do travel around a great deal, seeing many different people, you realize that babies are virtually indistinguishable. Listening to them, you don't know whether you're hearing a Japanese child or a black child from Africa—they make the same noise. They have not yet been formed by language and the rudiments of culture. Even older children—up to about ten or eleven years of age—are very similar. Their reactions are similar; their generosities and cruelties are similar. They instinctively make such good raw material; they're so well-inclined toward each other, on the whole, and their intentions are so laudable.

If you're suddenly presented to a whole lot of Thai children or Kenyan children or whatever children, and you don't know their language, your means of expression are very limited. You can't just grin and bow. Everybody does *that*. You have to find something out of common experience, and common experience is often the dog. Barking like a dog is a good substitute for language. I use the trick often because a dog makes a noise everybody recognizes.

I must say I hate the word *underdeveloped;* there are so many people in underdeveloped countries who are highly developed and so many people in developed countries who will never develop at all. In the so-called "developed world," which could just as well be called "the confused world," each

individual is permanently faced with a never-ending series of political, financial, and ethical choices. Often these are made without the time or the facts necessary for mature judgments. In the optimistically named "developing world," the choices are fewer but reach further—between starvation and survival, disease and health, literacy and illiteracy. UNICEF is the bridge between these two worlds. There may be those who quarrel occasionally about UNICEF's priorities, but nobody can possibly quarrel with its aims. For children, my friends, are, of all our possessions, infinitely the most valuable. They are our future; they are our purity; they are those who ask the vital questions we used to ask at their age, before we became intoxicated by the maelstrom of answers, the heady delights of personal opinion, the joys and sorrows of maturity.

UNICEF is no charity. To claim it is a charity would be a scandalous reflection on our sense of values. UNICEF is a solemn commitment to sanity. UNICEF is a steadying sail for the mind, a constant and necessary instrument of balance, of sanity, for those of all political or religious persuasions. I'm absolutely rabid in favor of UNICEF. I have always felt that its greatest strength, and greatest weakness, lies in its being what it should be—nonreligious, apolitical, and really as neutral as a chameleon taking the color of whatever it lands on. Herein lies the secret of its success.

Dolls are not mere playthings. These two are used for
teaching, and are shipped from the UNIPAC warehouse in
Copenhagen, shown here.

NORDISK PRESSEFOTO / ALLAN MOE

"Beautiful inside and out": Liv Ullmann

The future Goodwill Ambassador surveys Shinjuku Park, Tokyo. Liv Ullmann was born in Japan to Norwegian parents.

Opposite: "Liv Ullmann is beautiful inside and out," said James P. Grant, who named her UNICEF's first woman ambassador in 1980. Ullmann is shown here among Ethiopian refugees on her first visit to Africa. An eyewitness to the unfolding of Africa's tragic drought, her testimony moved the U.S. Congress and parliament members abroad to approve greater relief aid. For UNICEF, Ullmann managed to overcome her fear of flying and traveled around the world. She often went up in rusty helicopters, landing "in the middle of nowhere" to reach remote refugee camps.

Below: Running with children in Hadran village, Yemen Arab Republic, puts Ullmann back in touch with her own childhood.

Bottom: Of an Ethiopian refugee camp where hunger was an acute fact of life, Ullmann recalls: "We passed a very old lady holding a small heap of dried nuts in her lap. I sat down next to her and watched her give some to a little boy. Then she looked at me, and, without a word, peeled a nut and put it in my mouth." Ullmann often cites this incredible gift from a starving person as an example of the "sharing of those who have nothing."

UNICEF PHOTO / HORST CERNI

UNICEF PHOTO / ARILD VOLLAN

In this Bangladesh village, Ullmann helps to sink a new well by holding her hand down over a metal pipe being pushed into the soft, silty soil. When she lifts her hand up, sludge squirts out. It takes eight hours to drill such a well in Bangladesh, where UNICEF has provided pipes and pumps for about six hundred thousand villages. "It was the first time I saw what clean water really means," Ullmann says. "I will never forget the feeling."

My thirty soybeans

by Tetsuko Kuroyanagi

I first became familiar with the name "UNICEF" shortly after World War II, when Danny Kaye visited Japan several times. I also knew that the powdered milk in the lunches provided then at elementary schools was the gift of UNICEF. If it had not been for UNICEF's powdered milk, a fearful number of people who grew up to be the mainstay of Japan would have either starved to death or would still be suffering the effects of malnutrition. During the war, a great many elementary-school children my own age died because they did not have enough to eat. I can remember days when I had nothing to eat but thirty roasted soybeans, and that was more than many had. I would be given the beans in a paper bag in the morning, and I would carefully count them and decide how I was going to spread them out through the day. Five perhaps for breakfast, ten for lunch, and so on. Then I would drink lots of water to make those beans swell up inside my stomach. I always made a point of keeping about three beans for bedtime—otherwise I would be so hungry I could not get to sleep. Once on my TV talk show an actor told me he survived during the war on what he called "Pacific Ocean Soup"—sea water diluted with a little tap water and then heated!

There is a lavish abundance of food now in Japan, and bookstore shelves overflow with advice on dieting. Half the pages of Japan's women's magazines are taken up with advertisements of ways to lose weight—and yet, the year before last in Tanzania and last year in Niger, on a UNICEF mission, I saw children starving. What shocked me in particular was to learn that starvation not only causes malnutrition and death but also brain damage. In Niger I saw a child six years old who could not walk, talk, or even stand. "What can be done?" I asked, as I held its hand and stroked it. I was told that once brain damage occurs, nutrition can no longer help. It broke my heart to see a group of about twenty infants, without even the strength to cry, just stare blankly into space.

My African trips did have their brighter moments, however. I arrived at a village in Niger just as water spurted forth from a well being dug by UNICEF. All five hundred or so inhabitants of the village clustered around the well with their pots and buckets and clapped their hands in applause, while the children ran about excitedly. It was the first time they had ever seen such clear, clean water, I was told. The aged village headman thanked me profusely and pressed three live chickens into my arms. I knew what precious gifts they were, but the chickens started pecking me and I wondered what to do. I was sure I couldn't take them back to Japan, so I said I would like all the children to make a feast of them. But I had to accept them first on behalf of the children. It was the first time in my life I had ever handled full-grown live chickens and it was rather alarming!

Tetsuko Kuroyanagi, the Barbara Walters of Japan, musters a brave smile during her first field trip for UNICEF, in Matumbulu, Tanzania, 1984. All around her was starvation.

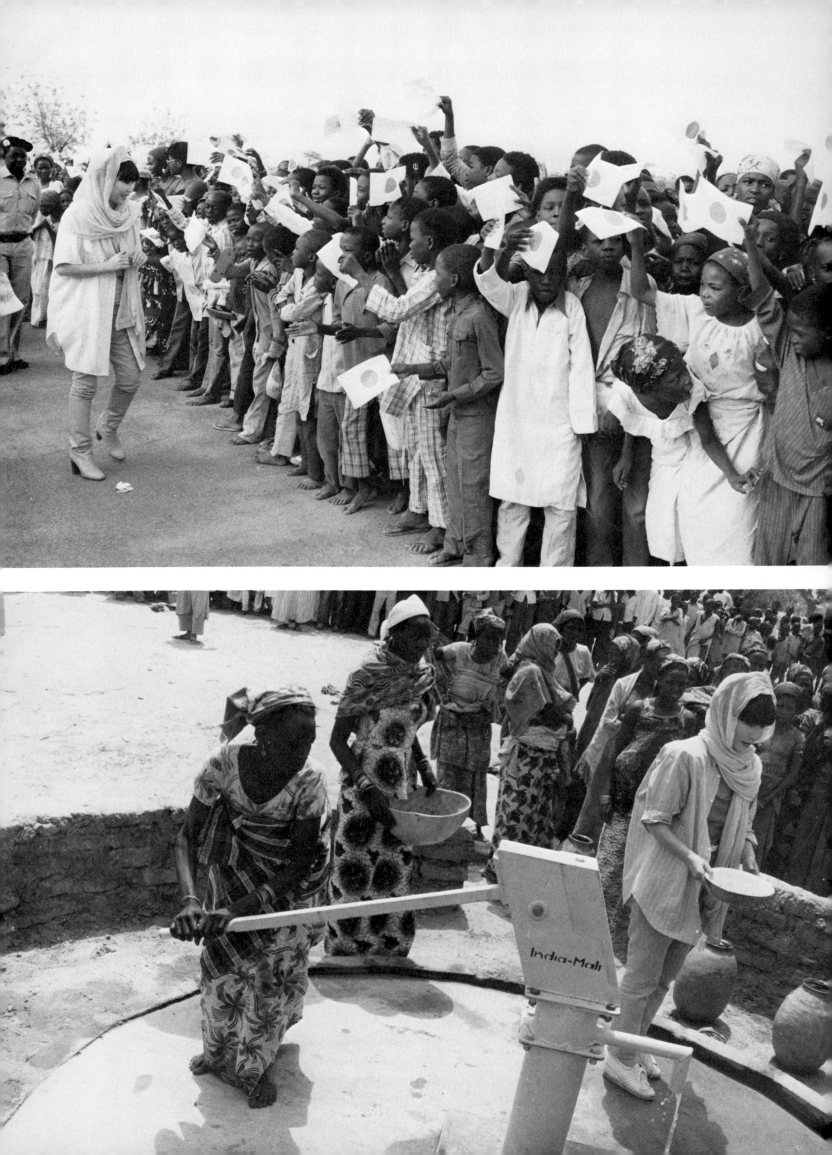

Left: Children throng the airport road in Dar es Salaam, singing and waving homemade Japanese flags, to greet Kuroyanagi upon her arrival.

Bottom left: A bright moment in the Niger village of Pilke I: Kuroyanagi celebrates the opening of a newly installed UNICEF pump. Women flock to fill dishes and jugs with the first clean water they have seen in years.

Below: Wherever she goes, she receives an enthusiastic response—even from the normally reserved Masai.

On both my trips to Africa, I was accompanied by crews from three Japanese television companies and two leading newspapers, as well as an independent news photographer. People in Japan were already aware of the problems in Africa and had been contributing money, but my trips stirred up fresh interest, and donations amounting to $750,000 were sent to my Goodwill Ambassador account. The contributions included a few dollars from kindergarten pupils, someone's very first old-age pension payment, and birthday money an elementary-school child had received.

When James P. Grant, UNICEF's executive director, visited Japan, he said that blankets were badly needed in refugee camps in countries such as Ethiopia where, while it may be as hot as forty degrees Centigrade in the daytime, the temperature can drop to zero at night. The response was wonderful. Some 1,800,000 blankets were collected, as well as enough money to cover the transportation cost of $2.50 per blanket. Japanese volunteers personally accompanied the blankets to the countries where they were needed, and, together with UNICEF workers, handed them over to the shivering recipients.

Japanese children have sent me countless letters filled with heartwarming messages, asking me to send them on to children in Africa. The plight of the Africans has taught Japanese children to feel compassion and concern for people less fortunate than themselves. The children have learned that there are people who are starving. They have learned that one can do something to help. They have learned about kindness. I believe it is good for children to learn these things when they are young. Also, I have had requests from all over Japan for me to come and lecture about Africa, showing, I think, the depth of the Japanese people's concern.

My book *Totto-chan: The Little Girl at the Window* has become the biggest best-seller in the history of Japanese

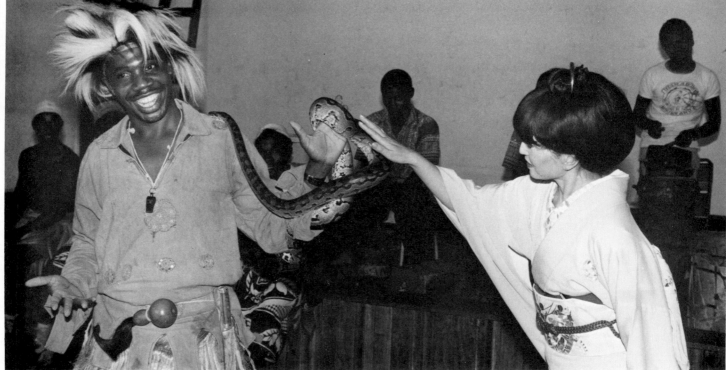

UNICEF PHOTO / HORST CERNI

publishing. Sales of the Japanese edition have now reached 6,500,000. The English translation was followed by translations into Thai, Malay, Indonesian, and Marathi, a language of central India, as well as European languages such as Finnish and Bulgarian, and also Polish, for which I was recently awarded the Janusz Korczak Prize. The book is my autobiography between the ages of six and nine. I wrote it as a memoir, but people read it as a treatise on education. Parts of it have been included in elementary and high-school textbooks not only in Japan but abroad, where the book is required reading at some universities. Children see it as a storybook. "The stories could be tales of any child growing up," wrote a reviewer for the *New York Times*, who continued, "Many of the chapters deal with universal themes: how children learn consideration for others, how they treat those who are different from them." Some people read it as poetry, others as literature. It seems to appeal to all ages.

When Mr. Grant was visiting Japan, Dorothy Britton's English translation of *Totto-chan* was handed to him by Sadako Ogata, former chairman of the UNICEF Executive Board, who urged him to read it. Mrs. Ogata is now a professor of international relations at Tokyo's Sophia University. Mr. Grant read *Totto-chan* in one night and the next morning went straight to the bookstore in his hotel, bought ten copies—all they had in stock—and took them back to New York, where he urged his colleagues to read it, too. As a result, I was appointed a UNICEF Goodwill Ambassador. It was all because of *Totto-chan* that I am now working to help the children of the world!

For the seventh year now I have been honored by being voted Japan's favorite television personality. I think it is mainly because of my talk show, "Tetsuko's Room," in which I interview a different guest for forty-five minutes each day. It was Japan's very first talk show and has been going on for eleven years. I also emcee the big Thursday night TV show called "The Best Ten," which features the week's ten most popular pop singers and is watched by thirty-five million people. The show is live, and happily I am able to talk about Africa, handicapped people, peace, and things like that. I wouldn't feel there was much point in having such a show if it were not for that.

I was trained to be a television actress by NHK, Japan's BBC-type broadcasting corporation. I liked acting on television, but nowadays I act only in legitimate theater and am just myself on television, interviewing people, emceeing shows and narrating documentaries. My original intention was to be an opera singer. Then I heard that NHK was looking for people to train as television actors, and I thought the experience would teach me how to be a good storyteller to my children when I got married, so I became NHK's first TV actress. Although I have as yet no children of my own to tell stories to, I have been privileged to bring stories to life for vast numbers of children through TV and radio. Having chosen what became my career with children in mind, I was overjoyed to be appointed UNICEF Goodwill Ambassador for Asia. I was happy to be able to contribute to the annual meeting of UNICEF national committees in London, in October 1985, by speaking at length on what I had observed in Africa. I look forward to doing what I can in the future to help make the lives of children in Asia a little happier.

A prince for all children

by H.R.H. Prince Talal Bin Abdul Aziz Al Saud

I began my humanitarian mission at the international level in 1980 as UNICEF's Special Envoy. I was inspired by a confluence of influences: the cultural values of Islam, which teach us to protect the weak and needy; Saudi Arabia's distinguished leadership tradition; and my country's unique geographical location.

Our father, His Majesty the late King Abdul-Aziz, implanted in our hearts and minds the deep-rooted Arab principles for human welfare. Our father—may God rest his soul—taught us the principles of justice and brotherly love. He taught us to help the troubled and to do good deeds for the poor and bereft. These concepts that stem from Islam characterize Arab communities. We base the education and upbringing of our young generations on them.

I feel that the Saudi citizen, in addition, has a special understanding of the hardships and agonies endured by his brothers in the developing world. We live in a desert. Water is precious, and many of the basic requisites for human life are lacking. It is not difficult for us to relate to similar conditions elsewhere.

All these things left an imprint on my mind and together provided an impetus to my working for mankind everywhere. The first question was how we could most effectively provide help. My experience in public endeavor helped me to realize that support should be directed at human development based on long-term scientific planning—rather than on meeting occasional pressing needs. Assistance should be directed to the development of future generations, who are the key to comprehensive advancement in any society. Working with UNICEF was ideal for carrying out these ideas, since its mandate is children's development.

My ties with UNICEF, and the fact that my international humanitarian work started with UNICEF, led to my helping found, in April 1981, the Arab Gulf Programme for United Nations Development Organisations (AGFUND). I felt that assistance should be collective, combining all Gulf Arab States, with voluntary contributions to one financial entity.

Kings, princes and presidents of the Gulf Arab States responded favorably. The idea was then developed and took form in the creation of AGFUND, which began making contributions to UNICEF and other United Nations organizations concerned with humanitarian and social development. At the initial stage of AGFUND's operation, these other organizations were the World Health Organization; the United Nations Development Programme; the United Nations Educational, Scientific, and Cultural Organization; the United Nations Environment Programme; and the Food and Agriculture Organization. The following bodies were added later: the United Nations Centre for Social Development and Humanitarian Affairs; the International Labour Organisa-

Giving children a fair shake: Prince Talal accepts an appointment in April 1980 as Special Envoy from James P. Grant, executive director. Thanks to the Prince's efforts since that date, UNICEF has received over eighty million dollars.

Opposite: The Prince holds his youngest daughter, sixteen-month-old Al Johara ("the jewel"), in 1982. "There is no difference among Muslim, Jewish, or Christian children. Politics makes such distinctions. Humanitarianism does not."

tion; the United Nations Relief and Works Agency for Palestine Refugees in the Near East; and the United Nations University.

Actual practice has proven that AGFUND is an important international body. It has fully performed its duties within its limited human and financial capabilities, in conformity with its unique nature, working with extraordinary flexibility to channel assistance through United Nations organizations and governments. Its assistance has had a direct impact on people. It is no exaggeration to say that its support has reached virtually the whole developing world—Africa, Asia, and Latin America. In the eyes of many, it has become an ideal means for providing governments and individuals with an opportunity for social development, particularly for maternal and child care.

During its first four years of operation, the total support AGFUND provided amounted to $145 million, out of which UNICEF received over $65 million from AGFUND's regular budget, and over $16 million from private donations. AGFUND's contributions included funds for emergencies and

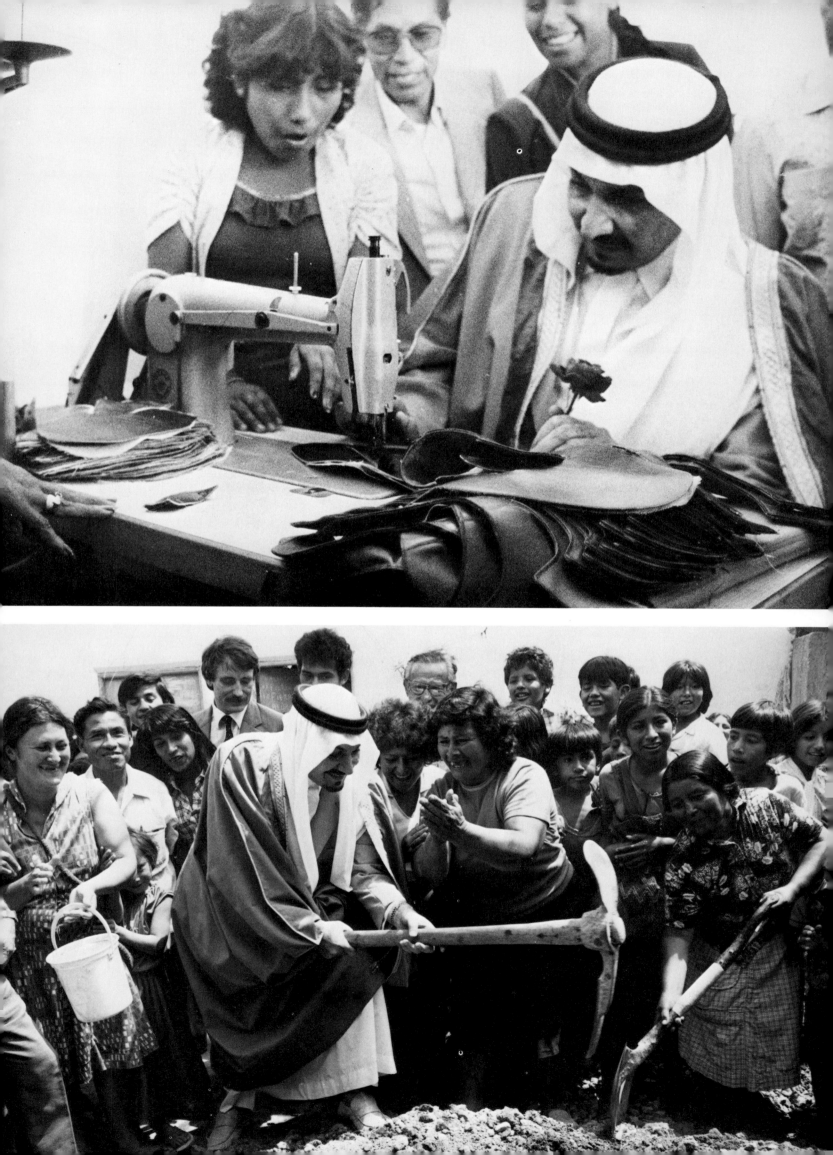

disasters in many countries, totaling $1 million for earthquake victims in the Yemen Arab Republic and $300,000 for those suffering from drought in Africa. These funds were channeled through UNICEF, the Saudi Red Crescent, the International Committee for the Red Cross, and the Office of the United Nations Disaster Relief Coordinator.

My experience with UNICEF has been unquestionably rich and exciting. I have become more familiar with the condition of children throughout the world, and with the many efforts by UNICEF to help the governments of the developing world in improving the condition of their children.

During field visits throughout the world, I witnessed the tragedies being lived through by children, tragedies on which whole volumes could be written. I became totally convinced that many problems could be avoided or handled with relatively little financial support and that, in many cases, effective social development *must* be based on maternal and child care. Dealing with these problems requires conscious will and rational management.

Thus arose in my mind an idea, for which I have appealed and continue to appeal. It is necessary to create, within the sovereign machinery of the state, supreme committees or councils charged with planning, executing and coordinating policies and projects for mothers and children. These would provide a sound, scientific beginning for social improvement in any developing country. Fortunately, many states have concurred with the idea and have established such bodies.

Though I have now relinquished my post as UNICEF's Special Envoy, I continue to view UNICEF as the pioneer organization in work for mothers and children, and I reaffirm my total commitment to cooperate with UNICEF and support it. The proof is that since I ended my formal assignment with UNICEF in December 1984, up to the beginning of November 1985 we have authorized and shall authorize for its projects, through AGFUND, nearly seven million dollars more.

Despite the changes in the economic conditions in the Gulf since AGFUND was founded, there is an overriding desire that it should continue to extend assistance to humanitarian programs of the United Nations organizations, including, of course, UNICEF. We firmly believe that the noble mission it undertakes deserves full support from governments and people alike.

UNICEF PHOTO / AKIL KIIAN

Above: With a Bangladeshi family in Dhaka.

VI. Volunteers Everywhere

Lifesavers

There is no better proof that UNICEF has become a household word all over the world, and that children help unite people everywhere, than in the incredible number and variety of volunteers who give their time, talent, energy, and money to UNICEF. Volunteers of all ages, from all walks of life, are UNICEF's lifeblood. Every day someone somewhere in the world does something inspiring or original, moving or funny, out of concern for children.

Take UNICEF's greeting-card campaign. There would have been no greeting-card operation at all if the world's artists hadn't voluntarily offered their creative work, or if private collectors and museum directors hadn't given UNICEF permission to reproduce leading works of art as cards, at no cost. Nor could UNICEF afford to pay the more than 250,000 volunteers around the world who sell millions of its cards in post offices, banks, building lobbies, beauty shops, supermarkets, or by going door to door. Some members of

UPI / BETTMANN NEWSPHOTOS

the Swedish Housewives Association think nothing of climbing into their Volvos and Saabs to travel long distances for UNICEF across the frozen north beyond the Arctic Circle, where temperatures hover at twenty below zero Fahrenheit. Their slogan: "Put on your woolies and sell UNICEF cards." You can't buy that kind of dedication. Without volunteers there would be no $14.8 million (from card profits in 1985) to buy vaccines, oral rehydration therapy packets, growth charts, high-dose vitamin A capsules—for children in developing countries.

"UNICEF appeals to people at every level. When I was in Hamburg in the Federal Republic," says Jack Mayer, greeting-card art and design officer for many years and a liaison with national committees for UNICEF in Europe, "this multimillionaire having his eighty-first birthday sent out a letter to all his friends saying, 'I have everything. Please send a gift to UNICEF instead.' On another occasion a workman came to the office of the Subcommittee in Hamburg, pulled a gold coin out of his overalls pocket, and gave it to the women. 'This is for the *Kinder*,' he said. The coin was worth about fifty dollars. In Norway, I saw little 'cub scouts' at the Sonja Henie Museum, ready to polish cars or shine shoes to raise money for UNICEF. Each wore a name tag. One said, 'My name is Knud. I polish shoes for UNICEF.'"

There are many other touching stories like these. The smallest contribution ever recorded by UNICEF came from a boy in Madison, Wisconsin, in 1953. It was three pennies wrapped in an old handkerchief addressed "To the World's Children from Jimmy." One year, members of the Transcona Pony League Baseball Club in Manitoba, Canada, decided to go without their team's traditional jackets, giving the money they would have spent on uniforms to UNICEF instead. In a surge of sympathy for hunger's youngest victims, American children have sent UNICEF their birthday money. Tupsy Molstad, who was head of the Norwegian Committee for UNICEF, told about a small girl named Trine, who literally used her head to raise money for UNICEF. Each time she did a headstand, Trine got ten cents, promptly sending it to the organization. Although confined to a wheelchair, thirteen-year-old John Haiko of Cedar Knolls, New Jersey, billed himself as a magician and entertainer and drew children to his home, where he starred in his own shows. The $1,009 he raised went to UNICEF. In a seaside Belgian resort, disabled youngsters on crutches or in wheelchairs sold greeting cards in the streets in order to help children in developing countries less fortunate than they.

Volunteers have made "Trick-or-Treat for UNICEF" grow like a magic seed across the United States and Canada. Similar campaigns have sprouted in Norway, Finland, and Ireland. The children do the collecting, and hundreds of thousands of adults—parents, teachers—help organize and sometimes escort the youngsters from door to door.

The idea that Halloween could be turned into "something good" first occurred to the Reverend Clyde and Mary Emma

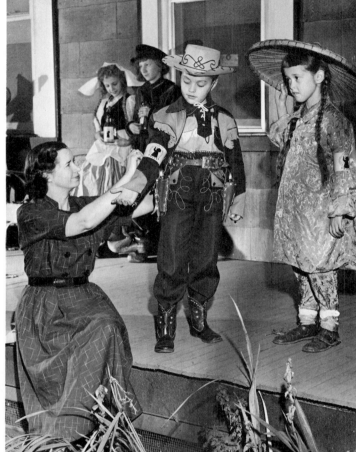

COURTESY OF REVEREND AND MRS. ALLISON

Opposite: New York, 1948. Borden Inc.'s mascot, Elsie the Cow, paraded across Forty-second Street to raise money for the United Nations Appeal for Children. Part of the funds went to UNICEF to send milk to Europe.

Above: Seeing Elsie in another UNICEF parade in Philadelphia sparked the idea in Mary Emma Allison's mind that children should Trick-or-Treat for UNICEF rather than just for themselves. On the porch of her Philadelphia home in October 1952, Mrs. Allison adjusts UNICEF armbands as daughter Mickey (in Chinese hat) and other parish children prepare to Trick-or-Treat for UNICEF.

Below: Mighty Mouse used his muscle in 1961 to promote Trick-or-Treat for UNICEF on posters, radio, and TV in the United States. Contributions hit two million dollars that year.

Bottom left: The trick is to treat the world's children well. At the height of their TV fame, Lassie and Timmy posed for a UNICEF promotional poster. Lassie was honorary ambassador during the 1959 Trick-or-Treat campaign.

Bottom right: Halloween chairfrog: Kermit the Frog, who headed up the 1980 and 1981 campaigns in the United States, is shown here with Muppet creator Jim Henson and UNICEF volunteers.

trick or treat for UNICEF

HELP THE CRUSADE AGAINST HUNGER AND DISEASE AMONG "ALL THE WORLD'S CHILDREN"

© TERRYTOONS

MIGHTY MOUSE™

THE UNITED NATIONS CHILDREN'S FUND HELPS MILLIONS OF NEEDY CHILDREN AND MOTHERS IN MORE THAN 100 COUNTRIES

Our Trick is to Treat "ALL THE WORLD's CHILDREN"

1981 Chairfrog

UNICEF

Allison in the early 1950s, in a Philadelphia suburb. Clyde Allison was then a young editor looking for ideas for a national Presbyterian publication aimed at junior-high-school groups. One day Mary Emma happened to be downtown when Elsie, the Borden Company cow, was parading along the main street. Mrs. Allison followed the cow to Wanamaker's department store, where a booth was set up to collect money for UNICEF's milk-feeding programs. Why not, she thought, have *children* collect money for other hungry children through UNICEF? The idea was promoted by Clyde Allison through his publication. Not long after, the three young Allison children and their friends set out door to door to Trick-or-Treat for UNICEF in Bridesburg, their new home. Their parents supervised, and so started a new custom. Under the auspices of the U.S. Committee for UNICEF, three million children across the United States—including the grandchildren of Clyde and Mary Emma Allison—take part in Trick-or-Treat for UNICEF. Altogether Trick-or-Treaters have brought eighty million dollars into UNICEF's coffers and have spread goodwill among millions of people.

Since 1956, Canadians have also taken the idea of Trick-or-Treat for UNICEF to their hearts. Despite declining numbers of children in school, some 1.4 million youngsters across Canada, in 1985, collected about 2.3 million Canadian dollars, as compared to 666,825 Canadian dollars in 1970. That leap forward reflects the fact that Canada's school administrators and teachers have used Trick-or-Treat to promote feelings of affinity among their young for those in developing countries.

Celebrating a UNICEF Halloween benefits the children collecting as much as those receiving. Lyndon B. Johnson recognized this when, in 1967, by U.S. presidential proclamation, he made October 31 National UNICEF Day. And so it has been ever since, with every U.S. president following suit.

Other countries, too, have seen a real human value to their boys and girls collecting for children's welfare. What Halloween is to North American children, *Julebukk* ("Christmas buck" or "goat") is to Norway's youngsters. On this ancient Norse holiday, which falls twelve nights after Christmas, youngsters dress up in costumes and go from door to door, singing hymns and folk songs, and asking for handouts. Since 1966, the Norwegian girl and boy scouts, some in masks or costumes, others in scout uniforms, have collected kröner door to door for UNICEF. At the same time, the youngsters distribute pamphlets telling what UNICEF does. Since 1966,

Below: A youthful delegation to the White House. Julie Nixon Eisenhower receives Trick-or-Treaters for UNICEF on October 27, 1971. Each year, a First Family member welcomes children in connection with National UNICEF Day, celebrated October 31 by presidential proclamation.

Bottom: Mila Mulroney, wife of Canadian Prime Minister Brian Mulroney, and three of their four children, Mark, Benedict, and Caroline, pose for a 1985 poster promoting Trick-or-Treat for UNICEF. Canadian enthusiasm for UNICEF fund-raising at Halloween broke through the two-million-dollar mark in 1985.

THE WHITE HOUSE

CANAPRESS / CANADIAN COMMITTEE FOR UNICEF

Los Angeles aviatrix Brooke Knapp departs from Washington, D.C.'s National Airport on her record-breaking February 1984 Flight for the World's Children. Setting a new around-the-world speed record for all classes of civilian aircraft of forty-four hours, thirty-two minutes, fifty-three seconds, Knapp also raised over $500,000 for UNICEF from sponsor companies and individuals.

these youthful ambassadors have collected $1,214,285 and kept their elders informed of UNICEF's work.

On the day her eleventh grandchild, Robert, was born, Mrs. Herbert A. Toops of Columbus, Ohio, happened to receive a UNICEF leaflet, which said: "Every second, three more children are born—the vast majority into poverty-stricken families in the underdeveloped countries." It occurred to Mrs. Toops to divide her gift of fifty dollars to her new grandchild into three parts, so that each of his contemporaries, or "fellow triplets" somewhere in the world, might have an equal share. With her check to UNICEF, Mrs. Toops wrote: "In a world which has shrunk so much during our lifetime, the welfare of our own grandchildren must be intimately bound up with the welfare of their contemporaries."

Concern for children can surface anywhere. One morning in June 1967, it surfaced in Great Bitter Lake, Suez, where fourteen ships were immobilized during Arab-Israeli hostilities. The captain of one ship decided to auction off his luxurious beard before returning home. Seamen from all the ships gathered aboard the quarterdeck of the captain's ship. His beard raised more than two hundred dollars. The seamen, representing eight different nationalities, unanimously voted to donate the money to UNICEF.

Spain's modern-day Infanta, Her Royal Highness Margarita de Borbón y Borbón, sister of King Juan Carlos, is a princess who empathizes with those less fortunate than she. In her own words: "We must be poor with the poor—otherwise our lives have no meaning. We must light the way

with lives that will serve as something to hope for, for those who live in the dark tunnel of suffering and despair." Although bereft of her eyesight, the princess has run the annual UNICEF greeting-card campaign, arranging for volunteers to staff tables inside and outside Madrid's leading shops and department stores. On more than one occasion, she has sold cards alongside other volunteers.

In 1966, when famine in India was at its most severe, a young Yale University junior named John Bers was so moved by the plight of starving children on the subcontinent that he sparked a Food for India fast. The Yale YMCA took up Bers's idea. The university agreed to pay fifty cents for every student who agreed to miss the evening cafeteria meal on April 28, 1966. At every table setting, a place card invited students to fast for India on that night, and some two thousand participated. After that, a wave of "fasts for India" swept across U.S. college campuses. The money raised was sent to the U.S. Committee for UNICEF, earmarked for UNICEF's Applied Nutrition Projects in India. These projects helped village families, including schoolchildren, to raise vegetables, fish, and small animals to become more food-sufficient.

"The food for India idea is probably the best idea I ever came up with in my life," Bers said in a recent interview. Married, with two children ages seven and fourteen, Bers works for a telecommunications business in Morton Grove, Illinois. "I have nothing but admiration for the people of India. The India fast wasn't a giveaway. UNICEF's pro-

Below: The ongoing success of UNICEF is dependent upon good citizens like trucker Christopher Groome of Ireland. Moved by the plight of African children, Groome organized a convoy of forty-three other Tesco Supermarket truckers who, on July 13, 1985, drove across the country from Dublin to Galway to raise funds. They collected close to thirteen thousand dollars from other good citizens along the way.

Bottom: Thousands of Belgian children carried and sold water door to door throughout the province of Namur in 1979–1982 to dramatize what the shortage of safe water meant to their counterparts throughout the developing world. The $33,333.33 they raised helped UNICEF well-drilling programs in water-scarce Bolivian villages.

FRANK PENNELL

BELGIAN COMMITTEE FOR UNICEF

COURTESY OF PEPSI-COLA INTERNATIONAL

grams were designed to teach people how to employ modern agricultural techniques. The Indian people pulled themselves out of their desperate situation."

On learning that their counterparts in many developing countries drink impure water—and in fact walk miles each day to carry that water home—the schoolchildren of Namur province in Belgium were shocked. With the help of a network of teachers and the blessings of both the Governor and Bishop of Namur, thousands of them, ages ten to thirteen, took part in a series of "Water Marches." From June 1979 to October 1982, they went from town to town, village to village, house to house throughout the province, selling glasses of water. At each door they would say: "May I inform you that at this moment a child is dying because it drank impure water? I've decided to save its life, to give it safe water. [This water was provided by local firms.] Will you buy a glass of water from me?" The children charged eleven cents a glass and together collected $33,333.33. They raised the consciousness and concern of everybody in the province. The money was sent to UNICEF to speed well-drilling and provide safe water for Bolivian children.

The same sense of responsibility has permeated Italy's three biggest trade unions. Their membership ranges from auto mechanics to doctors and lawyers. In November 1985, the heads of the unions—Franco Marini, Confederazione Italiana del Sindacati Lavoratori (CISL); Luciano Lama, Confederazione Generale Italiana del Lavoro (CGIL); and Giorgio Benvenuto, Unione Italiana del Lavoro (UIL)—took an extraordinary step. Putting aside their political differences, they made a joint appeal to their ten million members to donate one hour's pay to UNICEF. The object was to bring safe drinking water to men, women, and children in Mali's poorest, drought-stricken rural areas. First responses have been encouraging indeed. When the three union leaders were asked what made them do this, they answered, "We have children too."

In 1982, James P. Grant reported, "Far from being priceless, a child's life was worth less than one hundred dollars this year. Many millions of children's deaths could have been prevented at the cost of one hundred dollars per child." Fourth-graders at the Bedwell Elementary School in Bernardsville, New Jersey, lost no time in sending in one hundred dollars, their joint earnings from doing chores at home. Their letter said: "Dear UNICEF, We have enclosed one hundred dollars to save a child's life. We hope the child will be happy and live a long life."

Jawaharlal Nehru said: "Children are one the world over, and they could become a unifying factor in a world that is torn apart by strident and narrow nationalism." If the foregoing stories have not proved his words, the stories that follow will. They are written by five of UNICEF's outstanding volunteers.

The French butcher

by Claude Perret

As with so many things in life, I first heard of UNICEF quite by accident. In December 1967, I participated in a radio game program called "Sunday's Millionaire," and won $2,000. Before going down to the radio station, Europe 1, to collect the prize, I made out a smaller check, which I intended to give to a radio station charity. While we were celebrating with champagne, I listened to a news program. One of the persons interviewed was a UNICEF official, and he talked about the needs of children. I thought I'd do better to give my modest contribution to UNICEF.

Two months later, in February 1968, I received a telephone call from André Avril, who worked for the French National Committee for UNICEF. "Would you like to go on working for UNICEF, not giving money, but being a part of it?" he asked me. Since I owned a shop, he thought perhaps I could sell UNICEF greeting cards. Well, why not? A butcher could sell greeting cards just as well as a stationer.

In 1968, I was the only greeting-card outlet in the thirteenth *arrondissement*. It was obvious that with my small sales, I wasn't going to change much in children's lives. So I looked around in the neighborhood for other volunteers. Today I have a network of eight sellers. Among them, three are hairdressers, one runs a gas station, another owns a dress shop, and still another sells insurance. The best "retail points" are the local Prisunic grocery chain store and a stationery shop. Actually, it's less surprising that a butcher sells UNICEF cards than that a stationer does. When a stationer sells a box of UNICEF cards, he is competing with himself. Not only does he make no money whatsoever on the cards, but he doesn't sell commercial cards either, on which he would make quite a profit.

It's a curious thing, but my food customers are very different sorts of people from my UNICEF card customers. Of course, some people who come in to buy, say, a duck pâté or a bottle of Cahors wine (except for cheese you can find a whole meal in my shop) see the UNICEF poster with children and a display of the cards, and end up buying a box.

I've been selling UNICEF cards now for seventeen years, and I've learned something about human nature and the French people in the process. Initially, I thought the world was divided between those who were familiar with UNICEF cards and those who weren't. My first sales coincided pretty much with UNICEF's efforts to make itself known to the French public, and in the late 1960s, barely one out of ten thousand people seemed to have heard of UNICEF. Now that nearly everyone in France is familiar with the organization, I've come to believe that there are those who care about humanitarian causes and those who don't. Those who don't care are afraid of "getting involved." They see the cards, but make a point of not asking about them.

Some customers feel that by purchasing a box or two, they can easily accomplish a good deed. This thought soothes their conscience and motivates them to do something worthwhile. Others buy specifically with the children of developing countries in mind. Buying UNICEF material is at least a gesture and a practical act. Occasionally, people who buy cards listen to me talk about what is done with the money raised, and they, in turn, become UNICEF volunteers. For example, the insurance agent who sells a lot of cards now started by purchasing a box in my butcher shop.

Often, though, when I talk about UNICEF with people who enter my butcher shop, someone will say to me, "Oh, the money will never reach the people in the Third World. It will go into politicians' pockets." I explain how UNICEF works, that it offers material assistance in the form of vaccines, trucks, educational material, technical advice, and so on. I tell them that UNICEF gives help to countries that have plans. Or someone will see a box of ten cards and say, "Can I have eight? I only want to write to eight people." This doesn't make you believe in the generosity of the human race. People seem to think I make as much money on cards as I do on cutlets. Some can't grasp the idea that a person does something for nothing.

I don't limit my activities to selling ten thousand cards a year. I ride around the neighborhood on my moped, distributing UNICEF material to the eight sellers two or three times a week. I don't have much free time because I work from six or seven in the morning until eight at night six days a week, and I'm alone in my shop. When I can find a moment, I go from house to house and place UNICEF leaflets and booklets in mailboxes.

In France, it's a tradition to send postcards to family and friends when on vacation. Usually the picture is of a boat or a setting sun and a Mediterranean beach. Well, I prefer to send UNICEF cards all year round. In fact, we call them "correspondence cards" in France, and try to encourage people to use them for all purposes.

A couple of years ago, an article about me appeared in the United States, and a chap in Philadelphia dropped me a card with a picture on it. It was his butcher shop, and he sold UNICEF cards, too. I couldn't send him a picture of my five-by-five-meter butcher shop—it's just too modest.

As told to Paul Ress

Fifty-three-year-old Claude Perret, a Paris-born horse butcher, stacks UNICEF greeting cards in the midst of his pâtés, mustards, salamis, hams, pet foods, and wine, and sells them enthusiastically. The Left Bank card vendeur *is probably the best-known UNICEF volunteer in France.*

Thoughtfulness: As Christmas approaches, Parisian butcher Claude Perret helps customers like Anne Paternot select UNICEF cards with the same care he gives to their steaks and chops.

The German impresario

by Uli Heister

In the summer of 1983, I was obliged to give up my profession because I was seriously ill. Up until then, my profession had been my whole life. I'd been an actor and a producer, and in the four years before I'd fallen ill, I had been Peter Streibeck's personal adviser at the Thalia Theater in Hamburg. All of a sudden I was an early retiree who spent his time painting, reading, playing musical instruments and putting on plays with students. But I wasn't satisfied with all that. One evening I was watching a television talk show in which Liv Ullmann appeared. Until then, for me, Liv Ullmann had been a highly respected colleague whom I knew from films and for her commitment to UNICEF. She was describing her work and her experiences in the Third World. Then came the following sentence: "Do you know that in the Third World forty thousand children die every day?" She looked straight into the camera and added: "That means now . . . and now . . . and now . . . and now."

Since that evening that sentence has been echoing in my head. I couldn't sleep anymore at night for imagining that instead of quiet deaths around the globe, forty thousand times a day—in other words, every two seconds—a cannon is fired off near me. That would make me both deaf and insane in two minutes at the most. But those unknown children die so quietly that their death hardly bothers anybody. Before the end of the program, I'd decided to speak up, to speak up for those who can no longer speak up for themselves because they're weak. Since that day, this task has been my whole life. But what could I do? I could still use the telephone and I knew how to type. I had a certain amount of know-how. I'd learned how to be an organizer. So I began to organize a series of events under the slogan "Artists Aid UNICEF." I wanted to bring artists in all fields to Frankfurt, to appear, free of charge, for an evening or matinee performance to benefit UNICEF. The net proceeds would go to help a UNICEF water project in the Sudan. I figured that each artist who took part should provide one UNICEF water pump for the Sudan.

First, I tried the idea out on my closest friends, and everyone I asked was enthusiastic about it. In a fortnight, I had put together the program for the coming autumn: actor Peter Streibeck reading Tucholsky; a Thalia Theater performance of Franz Kafka's *Report to an Academy*; Richard

Thirty-nine-year-old Uli Heister has been confined to a wheelchair for the past year. Despite this, Frankfurt-born Uli has been organizing galas for UNICEF, and says: "I'm doing better than I ever have in my life."

Münch with *The Light Side of Goethe* (*Heiterer Goethe*), and singer Eva Maria Hagen doing an evening of *Chansons*. I had the artists but no hall. I soon gave up the idea of using any of the small halls for public functions on the outskirts of Frankfurt. I believed that only the best was good enough for the children of the world: a central location easy to reach, a place with special significance for the public. So I turned to the Frankfurt Old Opera. After a long talk, Ulrich Schwab, then general manager, let me have the Hindemith Hall at the opera house for "Artists Aid UNICEF." From September to December 1984, we made at least sixteen thousand dollars. In November 1984, I fell seriously ill again. My left leg had to be amputated at the top of the thigh, and at the same time I was given an artificial kidney. For a week I was a complete wreck. But a Catholic chaplain, in his down-to-earth Baltic way, raised my spirits. And there was Liv Ullmann. By chance, her talk show was repeated on television, and I vowed to pass on the kindness that I had benefited from, in that time of need, to suffering children around the world.

I recovered quickly. At the beginning of February 1985, I was sitting at my typewriter and making plans once again. Although I was now in a wheelchair and had to go for dialysis three times a week, every other day I spent almost twelve hours at my desk, continuing where I had left off in December. I soon reestablished the contacts I had made the previous year. In early May, we started the series "Artists Aid UNICEF" for the second time. We began with a jazz concert by Bill Ramsey. A week later Lilli Palmer read Hack's *Conversation at Frau von Stein's House about the Absent Herr von Goethe* (*Ein Gespräch im Hause Stein über den abwesenden Herrn von Goethe*).

Now it's autumn 1985. The coming season will be a good one. Many well-known artists have already promised to come, including actors Siegfried Lowitz and Peter Horton, film actress Senta Berger and author Günther Grass. Like me, they've realized that needy children in far-off countries are our children. They're showing solidarity and facing up to their responsibilities.

One of the great German director-producers, Fritz Kortner, once said: "Actors are people who put their childhood in their trouser pockets so that now and then they can take it out to play with again." I, too, have a childhood that I can "take out again." I have the privilege of being alive. Many children in the world don't have that privilege.

I'm now confined to a wheelchair, but I'm free, free to do something meaningful. I have just a small pension, but I'm rich because I have time for other people, and that makes me very happy.

As told to Claudia Oberascher, UNICEF National Committee—Federal Republic of Germany

Dedication: Confined to a German hospital because of severe diabetes, former actor and producer Uli Heister has been organizing galas at which singers, poets, and artists perform free for UNICEF.

The Belgian steelworker

by Jean Patti

I had been told that UNICEF was a "middle-class charity," so when I came across the word "profession" on a volunteer form, I wrote "worker" with pleasure. A few days later I received a telephone call from José Wuidar, a full-time Belgian UNICEF Committee campaigner whose task it is to "take UNICEF to the people." Like me, José had been a trade unionist, and he wanted to see what could be done to get factory support for UNICEF. Not many UNICEF volunteers, he told me, described themselves as workers.

When the Belgian Committee launched a national campaign to collect old X-rays, recover the silver nitrate in them, and spend the money for children in the Third World, I immediately thought of the X-rays of ten thousand Cockerill workers taken by the factory medical service. (I have worked at the Cockerill-Sambre steel plant in Liège for some fifteen years.) I was promised a huge number of these, but received very few. I put pressure on union leaders, who promised to raise the question with the factory doctors. I mimeographed five thousand leaflets, explaining what UNICEF planned to do with the old X-rays, and handed them out all over the vast

---

Jean Patti is a thirty-eight-year-old Belgian-born steel worker who volunteers more than half his free time to UNICEF. He forms local UNICEF committees and collects old X-rays for silver nitrate recuperation. Patti has made UNICEF a familiar word among factory workers.

MICHEL WALDMANN

rolling mill. But nothing worked. I only harvested two hundred or three hundred. Then I was told about an abandoned Cockerill factory hospital where I might find some X-rays.

There, in a pitch-dark basement, I located a tremendous cache—a silver mine. I reckon there were twenty-five thousand of them, every one in a dust-covered envelope. Altogether, they weighed well over a ton. What a job my wife, her father, and I had carrying the dust-laden X-rays up the equivalent of four flights of stairs! We found a broken-down operating room stretcher with only three wheels and transported them on it to a borrowed truck. I then took the loot to my own cellar, where an assembly line of volunteers removed the envelopes one by one and tried to tie the X-rays in small bales. You can't imagine how slippery X-rays are. It's like putting a cord around a pack of eels.

I called up two Liège newspapers to say I needed a truck to carry UNICEF's X-rays to a metal recovery unit in Louvain. They both published stories about that and I got more than one hundred offers of assistance. Ours was the largest single contribution made to the Belgian Committee's campaign, and it received widespread publicity. On the strength of that publicity, I launched a UNICEF greeting-card campaign at the steel plant. Today I think I can fairly say that UNICEF and its activities are one of the principal subjects of conversation in my plant.

I don't limit my work for UNICEF to the factory, although I think that's perhaps where I'm most effective. I have two children—Xavier, ten, and Nathalie, five—at the neighborhood public school, and I'm president of the Parent-Teachers Association. I give a lot of UNICEF educational material to the teachers and encourage them to use it in class. Of course, I also promote the sale of greeting cards.

I am asked occasionally what my own motivations are. To begin with, I think that my humanism—if I may use that word—derives from my family background. My father Luigi was an Italian coal-miner. One Sunday in 1946, he and six thousand other Italian immigrant laborers arrived on an overnight train in Liège. The next morning they were all 2,500 feet underground, digging coal. We lived in atrocious conditions, in a shack without any inside toilet facilities, and not even a septic tank in the yard. There was one cold-water tap for the whole house. We were terribly poor. I learned to identify a piece of coal in a pile of slag, and I was sent to the fields to pick daisies for salad.

Tuberculosis was widespread among children in working-class families, and polio and meningitis were common. I grew up among dozens of very sick children. Later, one of my own children got very ill and almost died before my eyes. A child's look—a child of any race—has something special about it.

One thing that really sticks in my memory is a mine explosion that took place when I was six. I can still see those twenty-six coffins, all in a line. I went to school with so many poor, fatherless children. The mine director asked for volun-

Opposite: Generosity: Belgian widow Josée Mignolet hands postman Jacques Warenghien her late husband's X-rays. The Belgian Committee for UNICEF has raised more than $300,000 from a five-year, nationwide used-X-ray collection.

Below: Commitment: Jean Patti, a Belgian factory worker, has become a used-X-ray detective, finding hidden caches and inspiring fellow workers to join in. Under Patti's leadership, workers at the Cockerill-Sambre steel plant in Liège have made the largest single contribution to the used-X-ray collection campaign in Belgium.

teers to go down in the pits, though it was still dangerous, to look for survivors. My father volunteered. I guess volunteering runs in the family. When they found out after three days that my father had seven children, they brought him to the surface, fast.

My childhood was marked by anguish, and it bore more than a little resemblance to the lives of millions of poor children in the world today.

After a skimpy technical education, I became a garage mechanic. At the age of seventeen, I joined the Belgian merchant marine. Over a period of about four years, I sailed on an oil tanker and a banana boat to the Gulf of Mexico, South America, and Africa. Once, when my ship was anchored in an Ecuadorean port, I was horrified to see children sleeping in the street fifty yards away. Their only cover was a banana leaf. They used to stick their hands through a porthole and try to grab chickens' heads and legs from the galley. I saw other families living permanently in railroad freight cars. I

began to reflect, although I was still very young. I returned to Belgium, went to work in the steel mill and, at the age of twenty-four, got married. Four years later my son was born and, partly because of him, I started to think of what I could do for other children. It was a few years later that I saw that UNICEF pamphlet at the Liège fair. "You, too, can do something for children," it said.

I have met remarkable human beings, many good people, since I began volunteer work for UNICEF five years ago. Of course, not everyone is decent or kindhearted. One day a selfish person told me, "There are two kinds of people in the world—those who receive kicks in the rear end and those who give them. As for me, I'm in the second group." I unrolled a UNICEF poster showing an emaciated African child bent over in a despairing position. I said to the man, "Is that the kind you want to kick?"

As told to Paul Ress

His hobbies—growing fruit and selling UNICEF cards—
keep him young. So says retired seventy-five-year-old
cemetery gardener Harry Bull-Nielsen.

HANS BOOLCHO

The Danish cyclist

by Harry Bull-Nielsen

My interest in UNICEF's work began back in my childhood—long before there was a UNICEF. My father aroused
my curiosity in international affairs and peace work. As a
member of what was then called "Fredsforeningen" (the
Peace Association), a forerunner of the United Nations
Association, he campaigned all his life for peace and justice.
I have tried to do the same.

At the age of twelve, I went from door to door, collecting
contributions for the relief of those left destitute by World
War I. That was in 1922. I joined the local United Nations
Association branch and, when the Danish UNICEF Committee was established in 1954, wanted to take an active share in
helping poor children around the world, so I became a
voluntary seller of UNICEF cards.

Just as I went from door to door as a child, I have—
throughout the major part of my adult life—biked from house
to house, selling UNICEF cards. On the whole, it is rarely
necessary for me to persuade people to buy UNICEF cards
today. In my first years as a card-seller, I naturally had to

*By biking door to door to sell UNICEF cards to friends and
neighbors in Odder, Central Jutland, Harry Bull-Nielsen has become the top card-seller in Denmark. Some neighbors tease the
seventy-five-year-old grandfather, saying, "We prefer to buy
UNICEF cards right away because if we don't, we know you won't
leave!"*

spend a lot of time convincing people. The cards were not as
nice then as they are now, and consequently I only sold them
to those who wanted to support a good cause. Today everyone knows what UNICEF is achieving, *and* the cards have
become much prettier. I have no problems selling—in fact, it
often happens that if I have not yet had time to come round to
their houses, my customers call *me* up. They simply expect
me to call on them! My visits seem to have become a tradition
in Odder in the months preceding Christmas.

Of course, my sales district is not limited to the town. I also
ride to all the farms on the outskirts and environs of Odder. I
sell UNICEF cards on Saturdays. But never on Sundays—
one would not like to offend anyone! In most places I am
invited in, but once in a while I do also sell some parcels right
at the doorstep.

I also sell UNICEF cards to the employees in the town
hall, in the banks, and in large industrial complexes. In the
local branch of the savings bank, *Sparekassen SDS*, Leo
Damgaard is my contact. He has a way of persuading his
colleagues to buy and use UNICEF cards and other articles,
and he works very systematically. It is always a question of
picking the right kind of people to help you with your work!

There are many ways in which to attract new customers for
UNICEF cards. My interest in fruit-growing has won me
many. Last winter, I went round pruning apple and pear trees
in ninety-six different gardens. This coming winter I will be
off to do the same job again. People tell other people I have
helped them, and then these people, too, call to ask for my
assistance. Obviously, I try to sell UNICEF cards to all those
people whose trees I prune.

My affiliation with the local branch of the UN Association
has also helped me establish good contacts to boost my sales
of UNICEF cards. Just before a meeting of the UN Association, I usually contact the local newspapers and the big
regional paper of Central Jutland, *Aarhus Stiftstidende*. I
throw in something about my sales of UNICEF cards, and
once one newspaper prints the story, the other papers want it
too. I have told about my UNICEF card activities on Danish
television. In recognition of my UNICEF work, I have
received an "Initiative Prize"—a fine silver cup—from the
Aarhus Stiftstidende.

Without my wife's support, I would never have been able
to sell so many cards. Time and again, she has waited with
dinner until I came home at around 9.30 P.M., after selling all
afternoon and most of the evening. After dinner, I would
spread all the cards out on the table and reshuffle them into a
new series that I thought might sell better than the original
combinations. I have spent hours and hours on this job. I
have often been away from my family all day Saturday, yet I
have never heard one word of reproach from them. We have
been blessed with children and grandchildren, and my wife
and I agree that everyone has to make his contribution to the
poor children of this world.

As told to Susanne Neertoft, Danish Committee for UNICEF

Persistence: For thirty years, neither rain nor snow has kept Bull-Nielsen off the roads. He has sold more greeting cards than anyone else in Denmark, raising nearly fifty thousand dollars.

The Swiss delegate

by Dr. Hans Conzett

People ask me why UNICEF is so well respected, so popular. First, the work of UNICEF is something that shows. People can understand the needs of children. They are able to see what is being done to meet those needs. Progress can be demonstrated, and the form of the help is usually specific, practical, and concrete. Second, attitudes toward UNICEF are shaped by the fact that people—especially Europeans—remember what UNICEF did for the children in countries devastated by World War II. This has inspired confidence in UNICEF's work elsewhere.

My life with UNICEF began at my home on Lake Zurich, in 1959, during a visit from Willie Meyer, an old school friend of mine. He was then working out of UNICEF's European office in Paris, helping to organize UNICEF national committees in Europe. He came to me because we were friends and because we shared the same personal ideals for justice and for the well-being of children. UNICEF hoped such committees would help to make people more aware of the tremendous needs of children in developing countries and what UNICEF was doing about them.

There were already nine committees in western Europe. Several influential child-care organizations in Switzerland were openly opposed to any newcomers in the field. But there was also strong support for the idea of a Swiss committee. The objectives of UNICEF were certainly in line with Switzerland's politically neutral, humanitarian traditions. Offered membership on UNICEF's Executive Board shortly after UNICEF was created, Switzerland, though not a member of the UN, is the only non-superpower to have achieved continuous board membership, having been reelected each time its term of office ended. It is also the only country to have had three board chairmen.

The more than thirty national committees for UNICEF have much in common—a high degree of autonomy, for example. While there are major differences, the committees collaborate closely with each other. Our committee made a decision at the outset to remain independent of the government. The Swedish committee, on the other hand, has had close government ties from the start. Others, like the commit-

tee in the Federal Republic of Germany, have a mixture of governmental and nongovernmental members. Those in eastern Europe work closely with their governments.

Committees sell greeting cards, calendars, and other products, and have special fund-raising campaigns to raise money for UNICEF's long-term development programs and emergency relief. More and more, their informational and educational campaigns have been able to win the public's confidence. And when citizens and organizations express strong support for UNICEF, governments feel justified, sometimes obliged, to make substantial contributions to UNICEF. The Swiss government, for example, has steadily increased its contribution. Any cuts in UNICEF funds would probably generate a public clamor, and the government knows it.

Our experience as a national committee began in 1959, when UNICEF's first executive director, Maurice Pate, requested formal approval for a Swiss committee from our foreign minister, Dr. Max Petitpierre. Petitpierre gave it with enthusiasm. Then he asked me to serve as the committee's first chairman, and I accepted with pleasure and pride. Later, when Dr. Petitpierre offered the committee a government subsidy, we turned it down. That way we felt we could remain independent of government control, be able to speak up freely when we felt the government was wrong or dragging its feet, and lobby for higher contributions.

The first year was rough. The greeting-card campaign was a more difficult undertaking than we had imagined, especially for a group of eight people who were supposed to handle all of the new committee's business. Andrée Lappé (now the committee's external relations officer) was the committee's first staff member—and for a time the only one. She had managed a minor miracle by selling most of the thirteen thousand boxes of cards sent by the UNICEF Paris office. But it wasn't enough. Despite the motivation and hard work of people like her, we ended our first year with a deficit.

A turning point came in 1960, with our first visit by a UNICEF staff member from the field. It was the UNICEF representative in Brazil, a countrywoman of mine—Gertrud Lutz. She had offered to spend part of her home leave speaking to volunteers and other groups in various Swiss cities about the urgent needs of children in developing countries, the work of UNICEF and her own efforts in Brazil. Wherever she went, her deep-rooted commitment inspired all who heard her. She had a great impact on the volunteers, whose importance I cannot stress strongly enough. They help keep operating costs down, enable us to reach greater numbers of people on a personal basis, and provide a reliable measure of our growth and popularity. Most important, they keep UNICEF a "people-to-people" organization.

Our fund-raising—on a serious basis—really began in 1961. We were eager to increase the amount of milk powder being sent to developing countries for children suffering from kwashiorkor and other nutritional deficiencies. With the help of Swiss milk producers, shops selling milk products, and the

Switzerland's Hans Conzett epitomizes the team spirit that binds together governments, UNICEF national committees, and its Executive Board and Secretariat with public-spirited citizens in a global partnership of concern and action for the well-being of children.

A lawyer, publisher, and former Parliamentarian, Dr. Conzett has devoted almost three decades to the building of UNICEF. He helped to found the Swiss National Committee for UNICEF in 1959 and has been its chairman ever since. He has headed the Swiss delegation to the UNICEF Executive Board since 1964, serving as chairman of the board's programme committee (1970–1974) and chairman of the board (1975–1976). He was president of the Swiss Parliament in 1967–1968.

UNICEF DHAKA PHOTO

media, we carried out a nationwide campaign to sell special one-franc coupons to raise funds for the milk. We collected about $450,000.

For a milk-producing country like Switzerland, the campaign had a special appeal. Later, it was a logical development for the Swiss to concentrate on UNICEF-assisted programs in milk conservation, child nutrition, nutrition education, and clean water and environmental sanitation.

Over the years, we brought into the Swiss delegation experts from various professions, as did other governments. These experts have had considerable impact on their governments' development-aid policies. They add another dimension to the long-time good relationship that unites the board, executive director, and Secretariat. Consultations, correspondence, and all kinds of pre-board and post-board meetings help to keep our partnership alive and productive all year long. One of UNICEF's strengths is that candid, realistic opinions have been welcomed, indeed sought, by the UNICEF Secretariat.

My first trip as chairman of the UNICEF Board was to Bangladesh and Japan in 1975. As chairman, I had access to high-level government leaders, and as a former Parliamentarian and member of the Inter-Parliamentary Union, I had numerous valuable contacts throughout Japan. In the years that followed, Japan raised its contribution fivefold. I believe that similar visits of other board chairmen and key board members, as well as UNICEF Goodwill Ambassadors, have done much to generate wider support for UNICEF.

The International Year of the Child (1979) was an enormous success in Switzerland—and throughout the world. One lasting result of IYC was our deep involvement in "development education." This meant introducing Swiss children to the concept of world interdependence. We have invested a great deal of time, money, and energy in making the aims of development education an integral part of the educational system throughout Switzerland. Our Forum School for One World was created in 1982 specifically for the purpose of evaluating development-education teaching materials. In ten or twenty years, we hope Swiss students will know better how to contribute to international understanding and justice and build a better world. We may have a long way to go, but school authorities and teachers' organizations alike have recognized the need, and that is a strong starting point.

VII.
Musicians for UNICEF

Rocking with reason

Rock music was a political and social force long before the brilliant successes of Band-Aid, Live-Aid, and U.S.A. for Africa. On August 1, 1971, George Harrison and his friend Ravi Shankar set an example for the rest of the world when they put together the Concert for Bangladesh. At that time, no one knew that civil war had broken out in East Pakistan, or that ten million people, mostly women and children, were fleeing for their lives to India.

The idea for the concert came from Shankar, who is himself Bengali and a noted classical sitar player. Nobody really knew until the day of the concert who would perform. Nearly forty-five thousand people jammed Madison Square Garden in New York to overflowing for two star-studded performances, in what was more a super jam session than an organized concert.

The biggest drawing cards at the Concert for Bangladesh were the two former Beatles—Harrison and drummer Ringo Starr. They were joined on stage by Bob Dylan, Eric Clapton, Leon Russell, and Ravi Shankar. George Harrison ended the evening concert with his brand-new song, "Bangla Desh." Its last line went: "Now I'm asking all of you to help and save some lives."

"The awareness is more important than the money," George Harrison said at the time. "Even if we make eight million dollars, it's still small compared to the size of the problem. We're trying to relieve the agony. It just happens to be East Pakistan now. Last year it was Biafra. It happens all the time. Any war is bad." Ravi Shankar put it this way: "It's like trying to ignite—to pass on the responsibility to everyone else. I think this aim has been achieved."

"This act of private individuals moved the whole Bangladesh tragedy into the public consciousness before even the governments were willing to face up to it," said UNICEF Director of Information Paul B. Edwards. "The world was looking on in stunned horror, when Ravi and George drove it into their minds, particularly the minds of young people." And hundreds of young people began calling the office of the U.S. Committee for UNICEF, not only to offer money, but to ask how else they could help.

The Bangladesh concert, album, and videotape was the

Bottom: Noted sitarist Ravi Shankar raised more than he'd ever hoped at the Concert for Bangladesh: more than ten million dollars instead of the estimated fifty thousand dollars. That stands as the largest sum ever raised from one single event for UNICEF.

George Harrison (below) and Ravi Shankar proved, with the Concert for Bangladesh, what a social and political force rock music could be.

WE ARE THE CHILDREN   131

In 1979, the UN General Assembly served as backdrop for a galaxy of stars—including ABBA, the Bee Gees, Rita Coolidge, Andy Gibb, John Denver, Earth Wind and Fire, Donna Summer, Kris Kristofferson, Olivia Newton-John, and Rod Stewart. The "Music for UNICEF" concert kicked off the International Year of the Child.

UNICEF PHOTO / RUBY MERA

single largest benefit ever held in terms of both money raised—over ten million dollars—and audience reached—millions of people—until 1985, when the British Band-Aid and U.S.A. for Africa organizations broke all previous records for fundraising.

If ever there was an impressive and original idea, it was the event "Music for UNICEF: A Gift of Song," created in 1979 by the Bee Gees with Australian producer Robert Stigwood and British TV personality David Frost. The plan was to hold a musical salute to the world's children in the United Nations General Assembly Hall in January, to kick off the International Year of the Child. Each performing star would sing his own original composition, at the same time donating all its future royalties to UNICEF.

"We made a lot of money in the past two years," Barry Gibb, Bee Gee songwriter and performer, explained at the time, "and we'd like to give some of it back. My conscience tells me I'm making too much money not to give some to underprivileged children. They're the defenseless ones."

As his brother Robin Gibb put it, "We knew there were enormous problems with starvation and with medicine and education for children. And the more money these people could get in a hurry, the better."

On January 9, 1979, the "Music for UNICEF" concert assembled performers who had never appeared in concert together before: ABBA, the Bee Gees, Rod Stewart, Rita Coolidge, John Denver, Earth Wind and Fire, Andy Gibb, Kris Kristofferson, Donna Summer, and Olivia Newton-John. The United Nations General Assembly Hall was put to use for the first time as a platform for popular music, to be televised around the world. The occasion also marked the first time so many composer-performers had ever made outright gifts of the copyrights and royalties of their songs to an organization.

"A lot of artists really want to give something back," executive coproducer Robert Stigwood said at the time, "so it's really from the heart. Also, I think UNICEF is the most worthwhile charity for kids around the world. Its overhead is incredibly low, so the money does get out there and do its job."

The Bee Gees—brothers Barry, Maurice, and Robin Gibb—kicked off the entire project by donating royalties from "Too Much Heaven." In 1979, that song hit the top of the charts, bringing UNICEF's programs a heavenly half a million dollars.

Running a close second was Rod Stewart's gift song. At

Below: The Bee Gees—from left: Maurice, Barry, and Robin Gibb— donated the rights to "Too Much Heaven" in perpetuity, to the U.S. Committee for UNICEF.

Below center: "Do Ya Think I'm Sexy?" Rod Stewart's voice echoed in a General Assembly hall accustomed to more solemn deliberations.

Bottom: The "Music for UNICEF" concert marked the first appearance in the United States of the Swedish group ABBA.

UNICEF PHOTO / RUBY MERA

UNICEF PHOTO / RUBY MERA

the last minute, Stewart, who had planned to perform an "oldie," "Maggie Mae," switched over to "Do Ya Think I'm Sexy?" Dressed in outrageous crimson tights, tan socks, and boots at rehearsal, he wiggled and strutted his stuff, giving his latest hit his all, and then some. UNICEF officials raised their eyebrows. Charged with safeguarding the image of the United Nations during that night's concert, they feared Stewart's performance, heightened by the song's suggestive lyrics, would affront the UN's dignity and offend the 250 million viewers in seventy countries where the concert was being telecast.

Some hours before show time, Jack Ling, UNICEF's director of information, confronted Stewart over the good taste of his body movements. They compromised on the "Elvis Presley" solution. Inside the General Assembly Hall the audience caught every twist and turn of Stewart's pelvis. The worldwide television audience saw him only from the waist up. They heard none of his lyrics; the background noise was used to drown them out. Not only was the concert a big success, but no one complained. "Do Ya Think I'm Sexy?" went on to become one of the all-time hit songs. As Ling said recently: "I think I was a pretty good judge of what was potentially offensive, but a pretty bad judge of hit songs."

UNICEF PHOTO / RUBY MERA

WE ARE THE CHILDREN   133

Some five million dollars has been raised from album sales, television license fees, and the publishing rights to all twelve "Music for UNICEF" songs. A list of them and their composer-performers follows:

"Too Much Heaven"   The Bee Gees
"Do Ya Think I'm Sexy?"   Rod Stewart
"Chiquitita"   ABBA
"Rhymes and Reasons"   John Denver
"That's The Way of The World"   Earth Wind & Fire
"I Go For You"   Andy Gibb
"Beautiful Child"   Fleetwood Mac
"Mimi's Song"   Donna Summer
"Fallen Angels"   Kris Kristofferson/Rita Coolidge
"The Key"   Olivia Newton-John
"Daytime"   Cat Stevens
"Malheur A Celui Qui Blesse Un Enfant"   Enrico Macias

"In London, in 1979, some fellow who was supposed to represent Kurt Waldheim [UN secretary-general] wrote on Mayfair Hotel stationery that Waldheim wanted to know if we would do something for charity," Paul McCartney remembers. "Then a letter came from Waldheim himself, saying, 'I have never authorized anyone to ask, on my behalf, if you would do anything. It is a hoax. But, seeing as you're now involved, *would* you do something?' We sent back a telegram saying, yes, we'd do a show."

That's how McCartney began putting together the greatest superstar jam London had ever seen for a humanitarian cause. The benefit lasted four nights—from December 26 to 29, 1979—during which McCartney, Queen, the Clash, Rockestra, the Who, and other top British rock talent gave marathon performances for starving children in Kampuchea (Cambodia).

On the last night, McCartney, sweat glistening down his face and neck, gave a masterful rendition of his song, "Let It Be." That song ended the Concerts for the People of Kampuchea, and the decade, on a high note of concern for the suffering of Kampuchea's children. By raising more than $530,000, McCartney and his friends helped UNICEF feed and heal sick and hungry children caught in the tragedy.

Using their personal magnetism and the power of rock music, Paul McCartney, George Harrison, and the Bee Gees raised the consciousness of other rock performers and millions of their young fans. The message they sent out helped pave the way for the phenomenal success of the Live-Aid concert and the U.S.A. for Africa recording of 1985. And the Band-Aid/Live-Aid organizations have given three million dollars from the proceeds to UNICEF so that small children in five drought-stricken African countries, including Ethiopia and the Sudan, could be immunized against the main child-killing diseases.

Paul McCartney (below) helped assemble the greatest superstar jam for a humanitarian cause London had ever seen, during Christmas week 1979. Four days of "Concerts for the People of Kampuchea" featured such British rock elite as The Who, Pretenders, Queen, and Rockpile.

VIII. Greeting Cards

How it all began

The creative spark set off nearly forty years ago by a seven-year-old girl named Jitka started UNICEF down the greeting-card road. Other, more famous artists followed in her footsteps. Like Jitka, they made gifts of their original designs to UNICEF. Together, the child-artist and a handful of grand old masters helped put UNICEF's new venture on the artistic map of the world.

In 1947, Jitka Samkova, from the Czech village of Rudolfov, composed a drawing on the theme: "happiness in a country at peace." Her painting showed five little girls dancing around a maypole. It expressed so much joy that her teacher, Josef Bartouska, sent it along with eight other drawings to UNICEF's office in Prague. There, Mission Chief Helena Glassey chose Jitka's drawing to reproduce on a poster publicizing UNICEF. The poster hung in feeding centers all over the country.

News of a "wonderful drawing by a child" reached UNICEF's offices in New York in 1949, and when officials saw the Czech poster, they decided to publish it as a year-end greeting card. Only a few thousand copies were printed. It was offered for sale, not to the public, but to UNICEF and UN staff only, at a nominal price—enough to cover printing costs but not to make profits. Not only did it quickly sell out, but it drew so much favorable comment that people began urging Maurice Pate to issue cards like it every year.

Pate, however, was concerned that charges of commercialization might be leveled against the organization if cards were sold for profit. His rationale for finally proceeding with the venture in 1950–1951 was not for profit but for public awareness—"so UNICEF's name would become known." In 1951, the UNICEF Executive Board approved the small sum of four thousand dollars to finance production and sale of half a million cards to the public. Pate advanced five thousand dollars from his private bank account to guarantee the new card campaign. Luckily, sixteen thousand dollars in income was realized, so Pate's personal check was never cashed.

The next year—1952—inspiration struck Nora Edmunds, first director of the greeting-card campaign. Why not ask Raoul Dufy, who was living in a Paris suburb, to create and donate an original design to UNICEF?

A determined young woman sent from UNICEF's Paris office made many visits over a period of months to the artist's country studio. On her first visit, Dufy said to her, "I have just the thing for you—a watercolor of the Brooklyn Bridge."

"Very nice," she replied, "but what does that have to do with the United Nations?" "Nothing," the artist agreed. He promised to produce an appropriate design in two weeks.

On the young woman's fourth visit, she insisted on staying while the famous artist (then seventy-five years old and suffering from arthritis) re-created his impressions of the United Nations building. Flanking the building were three of New York's most elegant bridges, including the bridge Dufy loved most of all: the Brooklyn Bridge. The artist had had the last word. But UNICEF was the winner. Dufy's charming watercolor design sold out before Christmas 1952. Its freshness attracted just the attention UNICEF needed.

Not long after this, Dufy died. But other masters followed him. The very next year, Henri Matisse, from his wheelchair at age eighty-four, created a collage, *Torch of Hope,* to symbolize the work and spirit of the United Nations. To Matisse, the black handle symbolized man's materialism; the blue flame above, the world rising toward more spiritual values; and the yellow flare at the top, human hope.

Among those whose special talents made a big splash was satirical artist Saul Steinberg. Chosen as United Nations artist of the year in 1956, Steinberg also agreed to create a design expressing the spirit of the United Nations. His first offering was a large sketch of a group of penguins. "What's the connection?" asked Nora Edmunds, puzzled by his choice of subject matter. "Why, those are the delegates chatting to each other," the artist quickly replied. "In this country," Mrs. Edmunds pointed out, "being called a bird-brain is an insult." Mr. Steinberg readily agreed to do another sketch: an exquisite and highly successful watercolor drawn with pen and ink, entitled *United Nations—Bridge to Peace.*

Marc Chagall, Pablo Picasso, Salvador Dali, Georgia O'Keeffe, Andrew Wyeth, Joan Miró, Paul Klee, Wassily Kandinsky, and Jean Dubuffet were among other renowned painters who lent their genius and prestige to help the greeting-card campaign. Not only did some of these artists create designs for and give the reproduction rights to UNICEF; in the beginning, they handed over their originals as well. These art gifts made it possible for UNICEF to reproduce cards that were highly faithful to the colors of the original art.

In 1968, the main sales agents of the cards, the UNICEF national committees, became active participants in selecting the art. To add variety to the annual process and to reach a wider card-buying public, former art and design officer Jack P. Mayer, along with greeting-card director Margaret Sharkey, chose pieces from the world's major museum collections.

Until 1972, original art was shipped to color-separation experts in Brussels by airplane like clockwork and without incident. In June of that year, nineteen paintings, including a priceless Indian miniature from a private collector in the United States, were carefully packed and marked for air shipment, as usual, to Brussels, via Sabena Airlines. But the art never arrived. Tracers produced no leads. Card production for the 1973 and 1974 collections had to go forward using

UNICEF

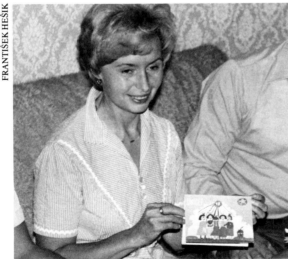

FRANTĪŠEK HEŠIK

Far left: Artist Jitka Samkova as a young girl.

Left: Jitka today, holding her original design.

Above: After the war, seven-year-old Jitka Samkova painted a "thank-you" on glass because paper was scarce. Her design became the first official UNICEF greeting card in 1949. It was reissued in the United States in 1986 for UNICEF's fortieth anniversary.

the only available means: color transparencies taken in New York. Of far greater concern was whether to break the news to the artists and private collectors immediately or wait and hope that the art would surface. Insurance money alone couldn't compensate for irreplaceable originals. Six months later, in November, a Sabena official called to say that the missing shipment had been found in the very heart of Africa, in the airport at Kinshasa, capital of Zaire (formerly the

Belgian Congo). Rather than risk a repeat of such a caper, director Margaret Sharkey changed the *modus operandi*. The greeting-card operation never shipped original art again.

In their early years, UNICEF cards were sent mainly for Christmas and New Year in largely Western, Christian countries: the United States, Canada, the United Kingdom, the Federal Republic of Germany, and France. Today, UNICEF cards help people celebrating Hanukkah, Dewali (India's

festival of lights), the birth of Buddha (Wesak), Jewish New Year, and Id al-Fitr (the Islamic feast day), and the possibilities for offending different groups are innumerable. How does UNICEF navigate safely through unknown cross-cultural, interreligious and racial shoals in selecting and offering its cards? It is assisted by an International Art Committee, a body that includes representatives of UNICEF national committees around the world and art specialists. Both groups rotate every year, bringing fresh vision to the critical selection process. Each year the committee considers over a thousand possible designs and selects one out of six—the best from an artistic, sales, and cross-cultural viewpoint.

Over the years, the art committee has helped UNICEF develop its own set of taboos or guidelines for card selection. For example: No snow scenes showing hunters carrying guns are permitted; no nudes (except for a nursing mother and child); there must be no sexual overtones; no racial or cultural stereotypes—no Africans wearing grass skirts, Europeans with blond pigtails and blue eyes, Chinese figures in coolie hats, or Americans with Indian headdresses.

Respecting different religious beliefs is, of course, vital. According to Roy C. Moyer, former chief of art and design, Muslims would be offended if quotations from the Koran appeared on Islamic cards. In orthodox Muslim tradition, respect for the Koran dictates that the holy book may not be placed on a shelf below waist level. For a quotation from the Koran to appear on a greeting card would clearly be offensive. The card might fall on the floor or be stepped on.

In the Orthodox Jewish faith, concern centers around God's holy name in Hebrew letters. Its use on a Jewish New Year or Hanukkah card would be unacceptable, since greeting cards might be thrown out or torn up—an affront to God.

Not to be overlooked are negative connotations that certain colors have in some parts of the world. Europeans associate a black background with death. Blackbirds are considered omens of death to them. Cards evoking such strong feelings are eliminated from the selections geared to European audiences.

The biggest challenge the art committee faces every year is choosing which design best expresses the themes of peace and brotherhood. The abstract message is a challenge for artists to express in new and striking ways. There are only so many symbols: the perennial dove with an olive branch in its mouth; the lion and the lamb; intertwining arms for brotherhood—and only so many different variations on those themes.

It may surprise no one that the cards with the most universal appeal of all depict children, flowers, or animals.

The secret of UNICEF's greeting-card success may not have changed at all since the early fifties, when Nora Edmunds offered her philosophy: "I have always tried to have the cards as colorful and gay as possible. We all know the story of UNICEF's children is sad. So I think we ought to show the children happy—*after* UNICEF has helped them."

Left: *Joie de vivre:* Chagall in his studio, at age ninety.

LOOMIS DEAN, LIFE
© TIME, INC.

Marc Chagall: "My colors must sing!"

"At ninety-three, Marc Chagall would come dancing in," reported Jack Mayer, one of UNICEF's two art and design officers. "His wife, Vava, had to pull him away from his work for our meetings. His *joie de vivre* was extraordinary, and he was just as young as he could be in his attitude."

In 1980–1981, Mayer visited the artist four times at his home in St. Paul de Vence, France, to win Chagall's approval for an art poster that shows a young child being kissed by an angel—symbolic of peace and love. The poster was a blowup of the four central panels in Chagall's gift to the United Nations—his magnificent stained-glass memorial window to Dag Hammarskjöld.

UNICEF made four different color proofs to try to meet Chagall's standards, over which Mayer and the artist conferred. "Of course, he was being a perfectionist," Mayer recalled. "He told me, 'My colors must sing. You have to capture them on this poster!' Chagall insisted on matching the poster reds to those in his stained-glass window. He felt they weren't intense enough on the first proofs and that this weakened the force of the poster. He knew and I knew that you couldn't get stained-glass colors on a printed poster," Mayer explained. "What he wanted was the very best reproduction possible."

Up to the last minute, on Mayer's fourth trip, it was still touch-and-go as to whether Chagall would say yes—or opt for yet a fifth proof. Finally Vava, his wife, said, "Enough is enough!" And Chagall, who was extremely eager to contribute to UNICEF, gave his approval.

"It's a privilege," the artist told Mayer, "to have my work in some way alleviate the misery of little children in want." In 1982–1983, Chagall's poster—the first art poster UNICEF ever produced—did just that. It sold out in the United States and was a huge success in Europe.

The Card-makers of Nepal

by Kathleen Peterson

Normally, greeting cards don't mean a lot to people who cannot read. But in Nepal, where less than one-third of all men and 10 percent of all women are literate, greeting cards have become the centerpiece of a community-development project. That project is changing the lives of thousands of families. Begun in 1981, it is revitalizing two dying crafts in Nepal—papermaking and wood-block printing—by combining them in an industry that produces finished greeting cards for UNICEF to market all over the world.

The income generated from the industry is making possible clean drinking water, primary schools, nutrition programs and day-care centers for children living in rural villages and an urban community.

Papermaking is an extremely old and important cottage industry in many parts of Nepal's terraced middle-hill region. There, in the shadow of the exquisitely beautiful Nepalese Himalayas, subsistence-farm families manufacture paper during agriculturally slack periods as a means to earn additional income for precious food and basic commodities.

Papermaking was first introduced to Nepal in the eleventh century, and the craft has changed little over time. Rural Nepalese papermakers still use wooden mallets to beat pulp by hand and wooden frames stretched in cloth to mold paper.

Long prized for its durability and inherent resistance to insect and fungal deterioration, Nepalese paper was used for printing Buddhist scriptures in monastery libraries across Tibet. It was also the official paper of the government of Nepal, and today, even with the ready availability of cheaper machine-produced paper, it is used for all legal and financial documents that must survive the passage of time. Nepalese paper was also used for medicinal purposes, to make kites and window coverings, for religious block-prints and amulets, and as wrapping paper. It served as a major commodity in Tibetan and Nepalese trade for centuries.

All this changed, however, with the introduction of machine-made paper from India and the destruction of most of Tibet's monasteries during the cultural revolution. Facing a drastically reduced outlet for the purchase of their paper, and suffering from the exploitative practices of middlemen and moneylenders, many papermakers over the past decade were forced to abandon their craft.

Similarly, wood-block printing, originally introduced by India, once played an important role in Nepal. Hand-carved wooden blocks were used to print patterns on locally woven cloth that was once the mainstay of Nepal's indigenous textile industry. The artisans who practice this craft have been sorely affected by the increasing popularity of imported machine-made cloth, and many of them, too, have been forced to give it up.

The UNICEF program coordinator for education and so-

Entire families involve themselves in papermaking, from the women who carry bundles of lokta *down the Himalayas, to the seven-year-olds who help clean, cook, and pound bark fiber into paper pulp.*

cial services in Nepal, Maria Diamanti, became aware of this situation and realized that there was an excellent opportunity for community development among these craft communities.

The government of Nepal concurred that selected communities of papermakers and wood-block printers could be linked together to produce greeting cards that could, in the initial stages, be sold through UNICEF's greeting-card program. Through the creative collaboration of the UNICEF office in Nepal, the UNICEF greeting-card operation, and the government, it was decided to capitalize on the unique skills of Nepal's craftsmen as a basis for a community-development project and for the benefit of UNICEF's greeting-card program.

Nepal was not new to me when I arrived in Katmandu in late 1981 for my first assignment with UNICEF as project officer for community development. I was fortunate in having already spent several years doing graduate research work in Nepal and was familiar with its people, rugged Himalayan terrain, and main working language, Nepali. I had worked with traditional Nepalese and Tibetan artisans, painters, and wood-carvers.

Prior to my arrival I frankly wondered if I wouldn't be torn by conflicting loyalties in my transition from academic researcher to development worker. I worried that my responsibilities to UNICEF as a communicator of new ideas and facilitator of social change might occasionally be at odds with the deep respect I had developed for traditional Nepalese culture and its people.

My concerns soon evaporated. Like so many UNICEF-assisted activities around the world, this project was founded on principles of strong community participation, and the two thousand families who were part of it were involved at each step of the way in identifying what their families' greatest needs were, as well as the most appropriate means to satisfy them. I found that although I was a source of information and ideas for the communities I worked with, it was they who used newly found organizational skills associated with their crafts to plan and implement projects that changed the face of their village life.

Like other income-generation projects, this one was designed to help families earn additional income. The handmade cards from Nepal are the first UNICEF cards produced by communities of people who are part of UNICEF's programs for children, and they are the best example I know of people helping people through the purchase of UNICEF cards. The sale of these cards helps support UNICEF and its programs for children around the world, as well as enabling the craftsmen who made them to run their own production units, provide jobs, pay for salaries, and support important services in health, child care, water, education, and sanitation that affect the entire community.

The Nepal project centered around three separate community groups living in different parts of the country. The overall strategy was to strengthen each of the elements in the produc-

Women pour liquid *lokta* onto frames to dry under the Himalayan sun. Each sheet needs at least ten hours of sunshine to dry, and yields eight cards. The high-quality paper produced lasts more than two hundred years.

tion chain—raw-material collection, papermaking, and production of greeting cards—and link them together for the benefit of the whole.

Nepalese paper is made from the bark of the Daphne shrub. Daphne is found in many countries of the world and proliferates in many parts of Nepal on shady northern slopes at altitudes of six to ten thousand feet. When cut correctly and harvested on a four-year rotation cycle, the Daphne plant is not damaged during the cutting process and regenerates new growth that will support papermaking over several years. The bark, or *lokta* as it is called, is cut by extremely poor, often landless, rural families living at higher altitudes than where Daphne forests are found. From the felling of the slender branches to the stripping of bark and its two-day transport of the bark to the papermaking site, this enterprise involves all family members. It also represents a significant source of income to families who must purchase most of their food.

The UNICEF project introduced improved forestry skills and management training that helped teach the *lokta*-collection families to better conserve and control their precious forest resource, thus allowing for the sustained development of the paper industry. The government, with help from UNICEF, also worked with these same families to build clean-drinking-water systems and improved primary schools, which were the two areas of greatest importance to local cutters of the Hatiya Forest Range.

The papermakers of Naglibang and Pang Panchayats are high-caste Hindu farmers who grow rice and maize on steep terraced slopes during summer and winter and make paper in the spring pre-monsoon months. Nearly 80 percent of the labor required in the twelve-hour process of cleaning, stripping, and cooking of the fiber, hand-pulping of the cooked bark, and molding and drying of individual paper sheets is done by women and children. Families comprise the basic paper-production unit, and families reap the direct profit from the sale of their paper. As in the *lokta*-cutting areas, families of poor paper producers were organized in this project into small groups. These groups were able to take advantage of low-cost credit, training, and marketing programs made available through the Small Farmer Development Project of the Agricultural Development Bank of Nepal.

The papermakers were the first to realize the human and material potential their loose federation of small-farmer groups represented. Within the first eighteen months of their involvement in the project, the papermakers had already begun the construction of a very ambitious clean-drinking-water system and were working on the second of five primary schools. In the next few years, the papermakers continued to start rural child-care centers, organize a community health system, establish fast-growing fuel-wood plantations, and form women's training and income-generation groups. Organized papermaking was the stimulus for community cooperation. I had the pleasure of watching this cooperation grow and flower many times over as the papermakers realized, with growing confidence, what they could achieve in all areas of community life.

The final link in the production chain involves the seventy-person printing workshop in urban Bhaktapur. The craftsmen in the largely female workshop smooth, cut, print, fold, and glue the handmade paper into finished greeting cards and envelopes. They use their new skills and improved economic resources to provide crèche and child-care facilities for their preschool children, health training, construction of latrines, and support for community health and child care in the area neighboring the workshop.

Between 1982 and 1986, approximately four million greeting cards were produced by these craftsmen and sold to UNICEF for distribution through its global network of national committees and volunteers in Europe and North America. Like all UNICEF cards, they carry the message of UNICEF and its work for children throughout the world. The greeting cards from Nepal, however, also carry another message—a message of community mobilization and empowerment through cooperation.

A UNICEF greeting card is a simple thing, after all, a bit of paper with a brief message. The cards made in Nepal carry an unwritten message of families helping themselves to find solutions to their needs. The families of Hatiya, Naglibang, Pang, and Bhaktapur are using UNICEF greeting cards as a means to counter the profound poverty and disease that surround their lives and devastate the health and development of their children. The cards are a symbol of hope for the children of Nepal and a way we can show our support for these families.

MARK FELSENTHAL

Top: At a day-care center for children in Bhaktapur in the Katmandu valley, mothers print, cut, fold, and assemble UNICEF cards in a printing workshop. Part of the cardmakers' profits go to support the center, so that while they work, their children can be involved in preschool learning under the guidance of locally trained teachers.

Above: The skills of a thousand years ago have not been forgotten. Craftsmen hand-carve traditional Nepali symbols, like crossed thunderbolts, on a wood block for UNICEF cards.

IX. Caught in Cross Fire

Lebanon to El Salvador

*Nation shall not lift up sword
against nation, neither shall
they learn war any more.*

—Isaiah 2:4

The image of the child caught in the cross fire, under the gun, the bomb, behind barbed wire, made homeless or parentless or disabled by war, touches everyone deeply. The longing for peace is as old as man. From time immemorial children have paid dearly for the deadly war games their parents play.

If anything, the forty years since the end of World War II have been even more turbulent and dangerous for children than those before. Millions have been caught in the backlash of recent major political struggles, in cataclysms writ large upon the canvas of recent political history: civil wars in China, Greece, Lebanon, Vietnam, and Cambodia; the partition of Palestine and of India; and battles—in Israel, Bangladesh, Nigeria, Zimbabwe, and other countries.

From the start, UNICEF's mandate has been to help children without regard to the political conflicts of their parents. When the Indian subcontinent was partitioned in 1947 into two independent nations—India and Pakistan—an extraordinary and unforeseen phenomenon took place. As many as twelve to fourteen million Hindu, Muslim, and Sikh refugees fled past each other across the new borders. Mothers and children made the harrowing journey. During that time, many children were orphaned.

When the refugees had reached their destination, they found the best efforts of both the new Indian and Pakistani governments inadequate for their needs. On both sides of the new borders, they faced the same sad litany of problems—including malnutrition, diarrhea, anemia among pregnant refugee women, and an acute shortage of warm children's clothing, especially in northern India and western Pakistan. In those early days of independence, UNICEF helped both governments with their refugee problem by providing milk, clothing, penicillin, and vaccine against tuberculosis, and by training health workers.

Following the partition of Palestine in 1948 and the outbreak of hostilities between the new Jewish state and its Arab neighbors, the UN Commission for Palestine and Count Folke Bernadotte (the UN mediator for Palestine) appealed to UNICEF to help ease "the desperate plight of both Arab and Jewish refugees." UNICEF answered the call, sending rations of milk, cod-liver oil, medical supplies, and blankets for mothers and children on both sides. UNICEF's supplies as well as its representatives were allowed to enter through Jerusalem's Mandelbaum Gate—the only crosspoint between Jordan and the new Israeli state. In the critical years that followed, some two hundred thousand orphaned survivors of the Nazi persecution as well as Jewish child refugees from North African and Middle Eastern countries—all new immigrants to a new state—benefited from that aid. At the same time, UNICEF set up emergency feeding programs and distributed food supplies to Palestinians. In 1949, the United Nations Relief and Works Agency for Palestine Refugees in the Near East (UNRWA) was created. For a number of years after, UNICEF aided some fifty thousand Palestinian refugee mothers and children in border villages outside UNRWA's mandate.

Across the Mediterranean, civil war in Greece threatened to tear the nation apart. From 1947 to 1949, thousands of refugee children streamed down from guerrilla-held mountainous areas in the north to get out of the cross fire. More than two hundred thousand became refugees in their own country. In refugee camps, children of guerrillas, no less than children whose families were loyal to the government, received milk, blankets, and vaccines sent by UNICEF.

During the Korean conflict (1953–1955), the Hungarian uprising (1956), and the Congo crisis (1960), shipments of UNICEF milk, blankets, and clothing helped children survive those emergencies.

The man who led UNICEF from 1965 to 1979, when UNICEF became an important developmental as well as humanitarian agency, was Henry R. Labouisse. Before becoming UNICEF's second executive director, he had already accomplished great things in foreign aid and international missions. He had played a key role in setting up the Marshall Plan operations in Europe following World War II; had been director of the U.S. nonmilitary foreign-aid program; had headed the United Nations Relief and Works Agency for Palestine Refugees in the Near East for four years; had been a special adviser to UN Secretary-General Dag Hammarskjöld in mobilizing experts for the Congo; and had acted as a consultant to the World Bank. His quiet, open-minded ability to get things done stood UNICEF in good stead during the crisis-filled years after 1965, and under his direction UNICEF broadened its scope to become a major partner in international-development activities.

The first major crisis of Labouisse's term, the Nigerian civil war, opened up a terrible chapter in that country's history. Between 1967 and 1970, the war brought untold suffering to millions of young children and mothers caught inside the blockade of the breakaway southeastern provinces, and in territory recaptured by the Nigerian army.

In the summer of 1968, the heartrending faces of starving children inside the Biafran enclave and areas affected by the

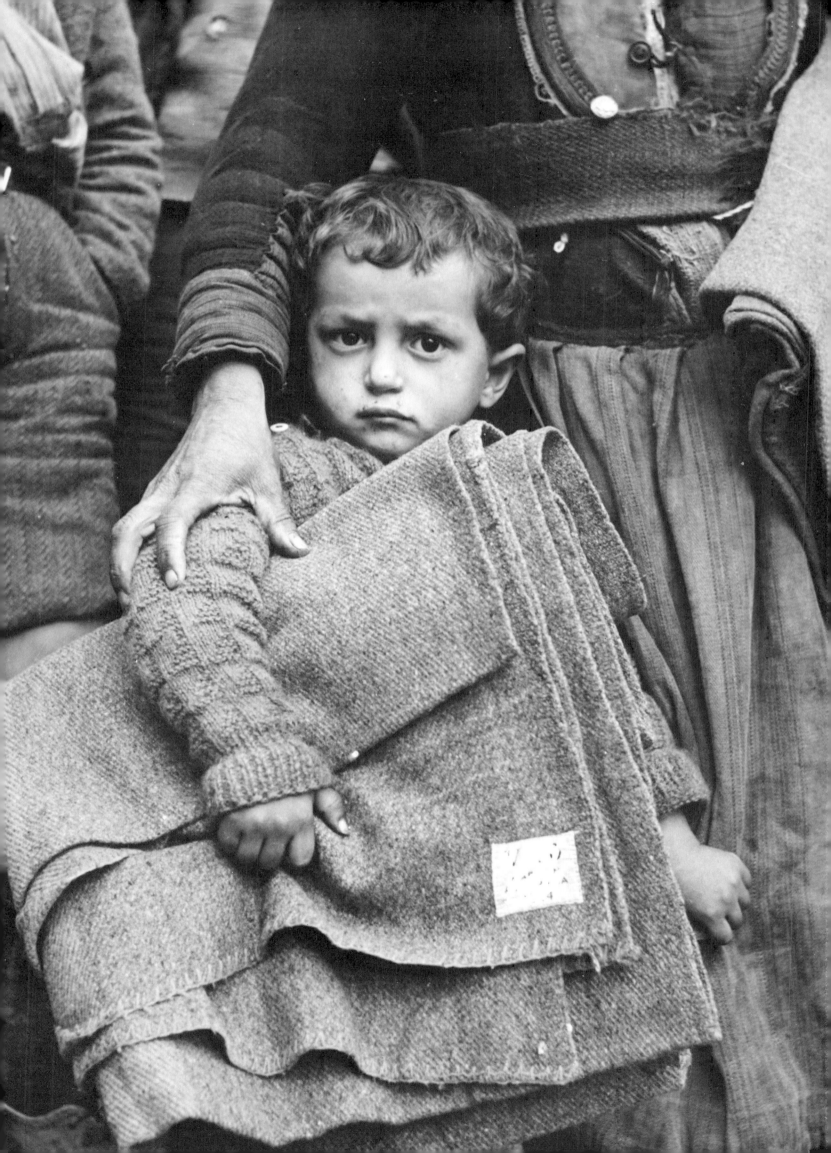

A train packed with Hindu refugees arrives in Amritsar en route to India in 1947, about the time modern India and Pakistan were created. Partition of the land into two countries was accompanied by violence and riots, causing one of the greatest mass movements of people in history. In its wake, more than eleven million Hindus, Muslims, and Sikhs were left homeless.

fighting made their way onto the front pages of newspapers around the world. Working closely with the International Committee of the Red Cross and with equally concerned world church groups, UNICEF airlifted urgently needed food and medicine to infants and children on both sides of the fighting lines.

After his visit to Nigeria in midsummer 1968, Labouisse wrote: "We went from village to village, inspecting various refugee camps, where groups of up to five thousand mothers and children huddled together, emaciated, listless, beyond the point of caring—just waiting for death. I witnessed the frightful suffering of the many thousands of refugees who have poured into that area (Uyo and Ikot Ekpene), which is now under federal control." Labouisse was unable to visit the Biafran-held area, where the worst-off babies and children were known to be.

In Lagos, he convinced General Yakubu Gowon, Nigeria's leader, that UNICEF wanted to help all of Nigeria's children, and that it was not partial to the Biafran cause. During their meeting, Labouisse proposed night relief flights, and General Gowon promised he would not shoot the planes down. With this tacit understanding, it was possible for the International Committee of the Red Cross to start night relief flights carrying children's therapeutic food and medicine.

In September 1968, two UNICEF helicopters based at Calabar began operating from dawn to dusk. To areas overrun by the fighting, even in those close to the front lines, they delivered between twelve and fifteen tons of children's food daily in double plastic bags. Relief workers waited below at designated delivery points to receive it. Pilots engaged by UNICEF broke records for a turnaround operation by reloading and refueling at Calabar in four minutes flat. Then they soared off again, over the swamps and creeks, for yet another food drop.

In addition, UNICEF shipped food and medical supplies to the then-Portuguese islands of São Tomé and Príncipe, as

Refugee children in
Camp Lahore,
Pakistan, receive
UNICEF milk in
1947.

UNITED NATIONS PHOTO

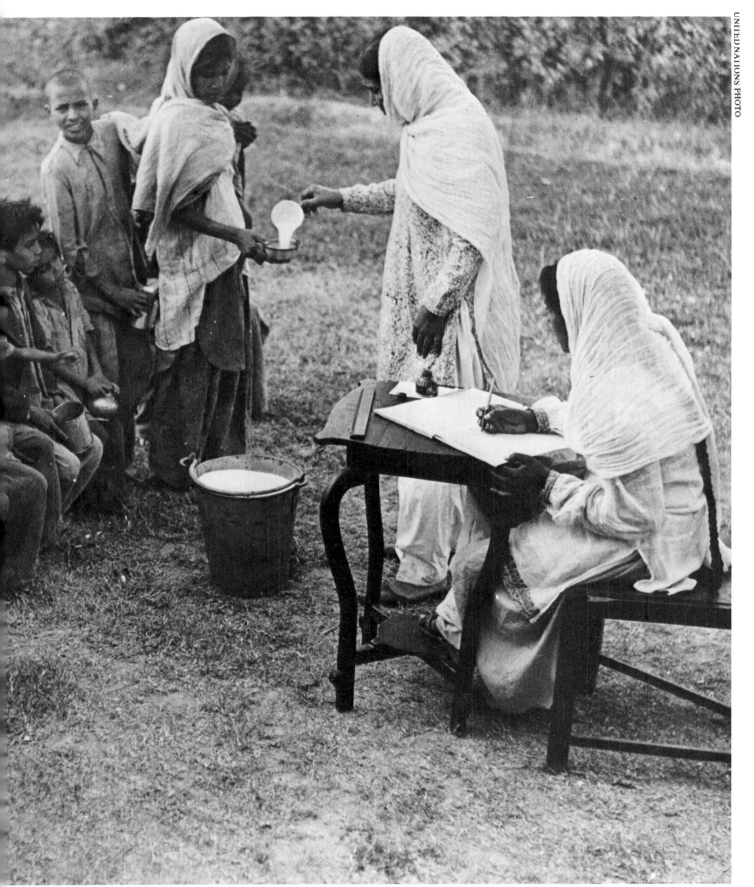

Above: In Nigeria's southeast province, where battle lines were constantly shifting during the 1967–1970 civil war, helicopters and ships brought food directly to starving refugee children.

Opposite: Severely malnourished child victims of the Nigeria-Biafra war, 1967–1970, were saved from starvation when special foods like CSM (corn-soy-milk mixture) and K-Mix-2 (high-energy food) were airdropped into their villages. Most recovered in six weeks.

well as the island of Fernando Poo, to be airlifted, whenever aircraft space was available, to seven hundred sick bays inside the beleaguered Biafran-held enclave.

There were many infants and children with advanced malnutrition. At the time, a special formula for children in such a weakened condition was not available. In mid-1969, at the request of Dr. Aaron Ifekwunigwe, head of Biafran pediatrics, UNICEF developed just such a therapeutic food: K-Mix-2. It was made of casein (a milk derivative), skim milk, and sucrose, to which palm or peanut oil and water were added. Although most children accepted the preparation eagerly from cup or spoon, those in an extremely weakened condition were fed via nasal tube. Even severely malnourished youngsters, with this special care and feeding, recovered within six weeks.

By January 1970, the war had ended. A period of intense rehabilitation began, in which children continued to need special feeding to restore their health. UNICEF continued to supply high-protein foods, drugs, and vaccines to immunize vulnerable child survivors against smallpox, measles, and tuberculosis. In addition, for a period of months, UNICEF found itself in the position of being the sole channel for the distribution of food to the general population in the territory. It provided large-scale warehousing and trucking and used hundreds of workers, who were paid in food, to distribute the supplies. In addition to a massive seven-million-dollar aid program, UNICEF provided new roofs and reequipped health centers and schools damaged during the civil war.

In early 1971, an upheaval of cosmic proportions began in East Pakistan, Asia's poorest country. As rebel forces tried to secede from Pakistan, a war of independence broke out, which lasted nine months. Most of the fighting took place in the densely populated countryside. It was so bitter and pervasive that to get out of the cross fire, some ten million people fled across the border into India to find food and safety.

The burden of rescuing this flood of sick, hungry humanity thus fell on India. Refugee camps were set up, and an appeal for help was made to the international community. Support on a vast scale flowed from UN agencies, including UNICEF, and from other international and voluntary organizations. By shipping quantities of K-Mix-2, the legacy of the Nigerian civil war, the vast majority of malnourished young children were restored to near-normal health. The onset of malnutrition among others was prevented through daily supplementary "feeds" of two kinds of precooked, sweetened, high-protein food supplied by the United States—CSM (corn-soy-milk mixture) and WSB (wheat-soy blend).

Incredibly, most of the refugees survived the ordeal. When Bangladesh finally won its independence in December 1971, the refugees went home by truck and rail. They carried with them plastic tarpaulins for shelter, and the blankets and cups they'd received from UNICEF during the Indian sojourn. There were, in addition to returning refugees, some twenty

Above: Child's play: Detonated rockets fascinate Vietnam war survivors near a Buddhist orphanage in 1972.

Opposite: Massive quantities of therapeutic foods, blankets, medicines, and clothing from UNICEF assisted ten million fleeing their homeland into India during the Bangladesh war of liberation in 1971.

million people who had been displaced inside the country. A network of feeding stations—more than 2,220—was set up at public and private schools throughout the country to sustain them. Over and above continuing food shipments during the emergency, UNICEF distributed drugs and medical equipment to stave off the threat of epidemics.

Meanwhile, in neighboring Vietnam, the war had escalated ominously. A unique situation developed for UNICEF concerning the suffering and trauma of tens of thousands of children in the north. In 1969 and 1970, they came under heavy bombing. There was deep concern on the part of some of UNICEF's main supporters, Sweden, France, Italy, and Poland, along with Mr. Labouisse, that the organization should fulfill its humanitarian mandate vis-à-vis children in the north. During the three-decade-long war, the north's leaders had not permitted any international aid into the country. Meanwhile, children in South Vietnam had been receiving UNICEF's aid since 1954.

A shipment of dark-blue cotton cloth from eastern Europe was the gift that helped UNICEF open a dialogue with Hanoi's leaders and win their trust. (The cloth was used to make school uniforms.) With the signing of the Vietnam peace pacts in 1973, UNICEF became the first United Nations organization to help alleviate the vast suffering of children in war-ruined villages in North Vietnam. According to Jacques Beaumont, one of the first UNICEF representatives to visit the north, the extreme poverty was striking. There was hardly a school or hospital that didn't need repair or rebuilding. And that is what UNICEF, with the approval of its Executive Board, set out to do: reequip schools and hospitals, and rehabilitate services for children in all parts of Vietnam. Urgently needed drugs, particularly antibiotics, and basic pediatric and other medical equipment were also supplied by UNICEF.

Across the border in Cambodia, in 1979, the Pol Pot regime fell, and the People's Republic of Kampuchea was formed. A guerrilla war continued in the countryside. Some six hundred thousand refugees began crossing the Thai border. Children and old people arrived exhausted after walking hundreds of kilometers through the jungle. Many of them were dying. They were fleeing both hunger and the guerrilla war. Their farms were in ruins, their schools and health services destroyed.

The peril of famine hung over the survivors, putting the remaining Kampuchean people at risk. In 1979, the United Nations named UNICEF "lead agency" for a massive, unprecedented relief and rehabilitation plan for Kampuchea. Never before had UNICEF handled a relief program on such a scale. An estimated five million people inside the country and in refugee camps along the Thai border were involved. The "lead agency" role was a vote of confidence in UNICEF's ability to see that aid would be distributed without political discrimination. It required close coordination with the International Committee of the Red Cross, other UN

No signs of war's trauma—these Vietnamese children's faces show only a zest for life.
UNICEF PHOTO / JACQUES DANOIS

Afghan mother Bibi Gul, age forty (second from the right),
stands in a bleak Pakistani government refugee camp with
her four children (left to right): Ahmed Shah, age nine; his
sister, Speen Gul, age five; Shah Zarina, age thirteen; and
Masud Zaman, age eight. They may be thinking about
Ghulam, their father, who stayed behind in their village.
Not all refugees in the camp are as lucky as this family,
who live in their own tent, provided by UNICEF.

agencies, and nongovernmental organizations. Henry Labouisse visited the new leaders in Phnom Penh and surveyed the relief operations along the Thai border. "When I visited Phnom Penh in November 1979, my talks with President Heng Samrin and his ministers, and what I saw with my own eyes, made me realize the extent of the tragedy. Millions of lives had been lost; the intelligentsia, the experienced cadres, had been decimated; agriculture was in shambles. Reconstruction had to start at zero. . . . I am firmly convinced that, over the months, our emergency assistance saved untold numbers of lives, greatly reduced suffering and opened the way to far-reaching rehabilitation programs."

When the Lebanese civil war erupted in April 1975, emergency relief again became the focus of UNICEF's work. By mid-1978, over a third of the country's population was displaced—nearly 1.3 million people, half of them children. Water supply and health care were two areas of greatest need. In the south, schools, hospitals, and dispensaries were rebuilt and reequipped. Wells were drilled, pipelines laid to bring safe water to communal water taps and health centers.

According to Charles Egger, for many years deputy executive director of UNICEF programs, "In Lebanon, UNICEF did not leave out any of the religious or political communities that had suffered a great deal and were in dire need . . . neither the Christian groups in the mountains of North Lebanon . . . nor the southern Muslims."

During the siege of Beirut in the summer of 1982, the UNICEF office in Beirut was kept open by longtime staff member Rachid Koleilat, the only senior UN official to remain in the threatened city. Powdered milk, canned food, and other goods were distributed from UNICEF's available stocks or purchased on the local market. Early in June, the first of five cargo planes brought in UNICEF relief supplies for mothers and children among the newly displaced persons.

The regular water supply was severely disrupted. In response to a request for help from the Ministry of Electricity and Hydraulic Resources, UNICEF water engineer Raymond Naimy, amid bullets, bombings, and strafings, scurried from one water emergency to another. Working around the clock, Naimy, with a crew of fourteen, drilled more than twelve wells at strategic locations. Large-capacity water tanks were installed at eighty-five locations in the city. Taking water from existing artesian wells, two UNICEF tankers made rounds twenty-four hours a day to replenish the tanks. Women and children queued up with their colorful plastic containers, buckets, cans, or anything else that would hold water. The code name of this emergency alternative-water system was "Operation Water Jug." It made Naimy—and UNICEF—heroes to the Lebanese.

Who would have thought it possible to stop the bitter civil war in El Salvador for the sake of children? James P. Grant, who became executive director of UNICEF in 1980, and José Napoleon Duarte, president of El Salvador, thought it was worth trying.

On Siesta Beach in Beirut, Lebanese children uprooted by the outbreak of civil war in 1975 take refuge in shacks where once wealthy people had weekend cabanas.

UNICEF PHOTO / TONY HEWETT

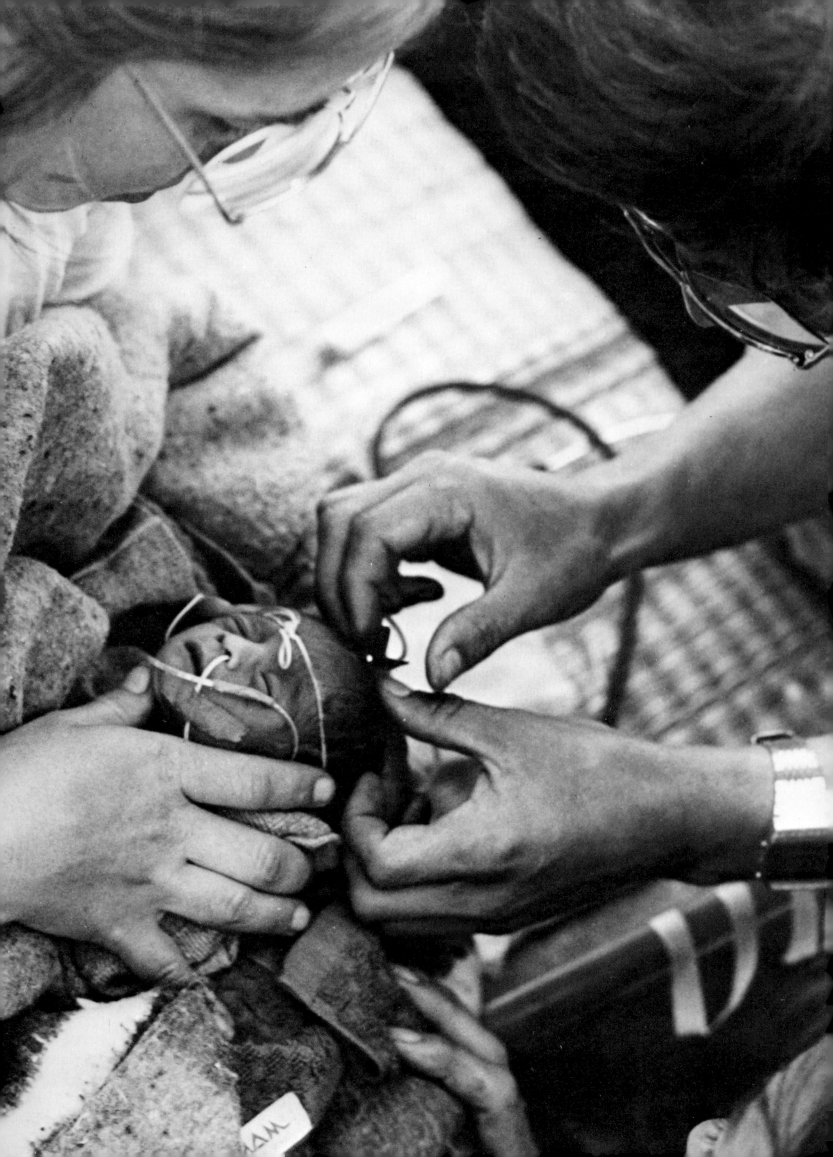

In a refugee camp along the Thai-Kampuchean border, doctors work to save the life of a newborn baby through nasal feeding. The swings of the political pendulum—revolution, famine, upheaval—in Kampuchea since 1974 have brought terrible hardships to both children and mothers inside the country and to some six hundred thousand refugees who fled into northern Thailand.

In December 1984, the two leaders agreed to suggest a "mini-truce" to guerrilla leaders so that a nationwide crash campaign could immunize all children under six. Archbishop Gregorio Rosa y Chavez mediated between the guerrillas and the government. Three separate "days of tranquillity"—February 3, March 3, and April 21—all Sundays—were declared in 1985. Advisers from the Honduran Red Cross helped oversee the campaign for which UNICEF provided—in addition to the impetus and optimism which sparked the campaign—$500,000 worth of vaccines. The vaccinations were mainly carried out by twenty thousand Health Ministry workers and volunteers. Also, teams of volunteers from the International Committee for the Red Cross vaccinated children in twenty villages in war-torn and conflict areas.

One compelling reason both sides agreed to the truce was the fact that there were more young children in El Salvador who died from preventable diseases (measles, tetanus, diphtheria, whooping cough, and polio) in 1984 than people who were killed by the fighting.

"We have had a day of peace," said President Duarte, "a day of life, and a day of hope." Said James P. Grant: "Great things are possible—even in a country at war, like El Salvador. For the first time in history, a major conflict has stopped to immunize children."

That miracle occurred again in 1986, on April 6 and May 25. On these two additional days of complete tranquillity, nearly 237,000 children and 57,000 women were immunized.

The breakthrough achieved in El Salvador has given impetus to the idea of declaring children "a neutral conflict-free zone in human relations." UNICEF is placing a new emphasis on practical ways to contribute to the protection of children during times of armed conflict, and to link immediate relief with long-term measures. It will also take active part in international efforts promoting compliance with international humanitarian laws and establishing norms for the protection and development of children everywhere in wars, including a Convention on the Rights of the Child.

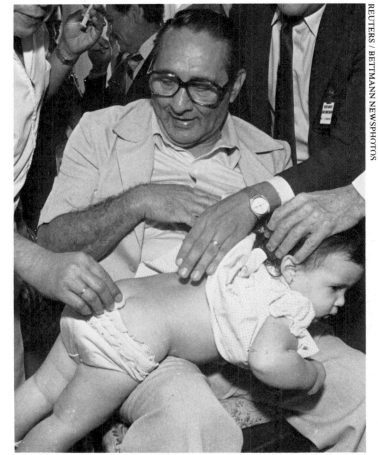

REUTERS / BETTMANN NEWSPHOTOS

"We have had a day of peace, a day of life, a day of hope," said El Salvador's President Duarte on February 3, 1985, the first of three days of tranquillity in the war-torn country. By agreement with guerrilla forces, all combat stopped so that 260,000 children could be immunized.

X. Child Survival

The miracle mix

By any stretch of the imagination, they are four of the most unlikely items with which to make any kind of revolution. There's nothing new, unproven, or radical about any of them. Three are "low-tech," low-cost, and have been around for years. The fourth is free, but goes back to Mother Eve. They are: a shiny aluminum foil packet containing an oral rehydration recipe; a syringe; a ten-cent sheet of graph paper; and mother's milk.

But in late 1982, when UNICEF's executive director, James P. Grant, began putting his mind, drive, optimism, and enthusiasm behind four techniques guaranteed to boost child survival rates, in partnership with WHO, he helped to spark a real change in the world's thinking.

In moving speeches, Grant has imbued the silent deaths of infants and small children from preventable causes—dehydration caused by diarrhea; immunizable diseases such as measles, whooping cough, or tetanus—with the same high drama as the deaths of children caught in cross fires of war or in the wake of drought or earthquake. Since 1982, his straight talk, combined with moral indignation, has made the Child Survival Revolution and methods to promote it something for the front pages of newspapers in New York, London, and Paris. "It is unconscionable," he insists, "to allow one child, let alone fifteen million children a year, to die from a preventable disease when we have the technology and the means of communication to prevent it."

The four techniques Grant recommends are simple, low-cost, and well-known: mass immunization of children against six fatal and disabling diseases; promotion of breast-feeding actively through every channel; monthly growth-monitoring by mothers; and the treatment of diarrhea with a homemade oral rehydration solution. They may not cure poverty, but Grant firmly believes they do provide a remarkable degree of protection for children against poverty's worst effects. And they are a spearhead for UNICEF's overall strategy to help countries accelerate efforts for the survival, health, and development of their children.

Fighting against poverty has been the focus of James Grant's career since the end of World War II. Before taking over at UNICEF in early 1980, he had been president of the Overseas Development Council from its start in 1969. Grant was director of the U.S. Agency for International Development's program in Turkey (1964–1967), after which he was named an assistant administrator of the worldwide A.I.D.

program. Under the Kennedy administration, he served as Deputy Assistant Secretary of State for Near East and South Asian Affairs. Born in China, UNICEF's current director is the son of an American doctor who founded the first schools of public health in China and India.

Grant has made the subject of children's diarrhea a matter for public discussion, introducing it at meetings, in talks at the highest government levels, at parties, and just about everywhere else. The reason is simple. Acute diarrhea is a problem of gigantic proportions, affecting nearly five hundred million children annually. A dehydrated baby losing its vital fluids is a sad sight indeed: lethargic, eyes dulled, skin wrinkled up like an old man's. When it cries, there are no longer any tears. It stops urinating. Within hours it can die. Nearly three million children do die in the stupor of dehydration each year, and a further two million from the combined effects of diarrhea and malnutrition. Most vulnerable are infants between the ages of six and eighteen months.

Grant's determined fight to stop such deaths starts with the tiny oral rehydration packets. These contain a powder that, when mixed in a liter of water, can restore the health of a dehydrated baby within twenty-four hours. Some have called this possibility "astonishing." A child's life can be saved by its mother at home for the ten-cent cost of the tiny aluminum packet of "miracle mix." Just a few years ago, it was believed that only intravenous feeding in a hospital—out of the reach of most Third World children—could do that. The *Lancet,* one of Britain's leading medical journals, has called oral rehydration therapy (ORT) "potentially the most important medical advance of this century."

In his pockets, Grant always carries samples with him. In the world's leading capitals, at meetings with prime ministers and foreign ministers, he mixes up a batch of the solution, offering up a toast to children's health. Since the formula combines sugar, salt, and a couple of other essential ingredients, the taste—"as salty as tears"—and the toast are sure to make an indelible impression on Grant's influential hosts.

The worldwide promotion of oral rehydration therapy has become the cornerstone of the Child Survival Revolution. Among the agencies that have joined forces in promoting its widespread use among mothers are the World Health Organization, the U.S. Agency for International Development, and the League of Red Cross Societies.

In 1985, UNICEF supplied about eighty developing countries with seventy million packets, making it the world's largest single supplier. It has also helped forty-one countries begin their own production of the lifesaving packets. In ninety countries, national campaigns promoting ORT's use have already been launched.

But *having* millions of the tiny aluminum packets is only the first step. Social marketing methods are being used in the Third World to get the oral rehydration message out to mothers. That message has two parts. One is that parents can make a homemade solution using eight parts sugar or molas-

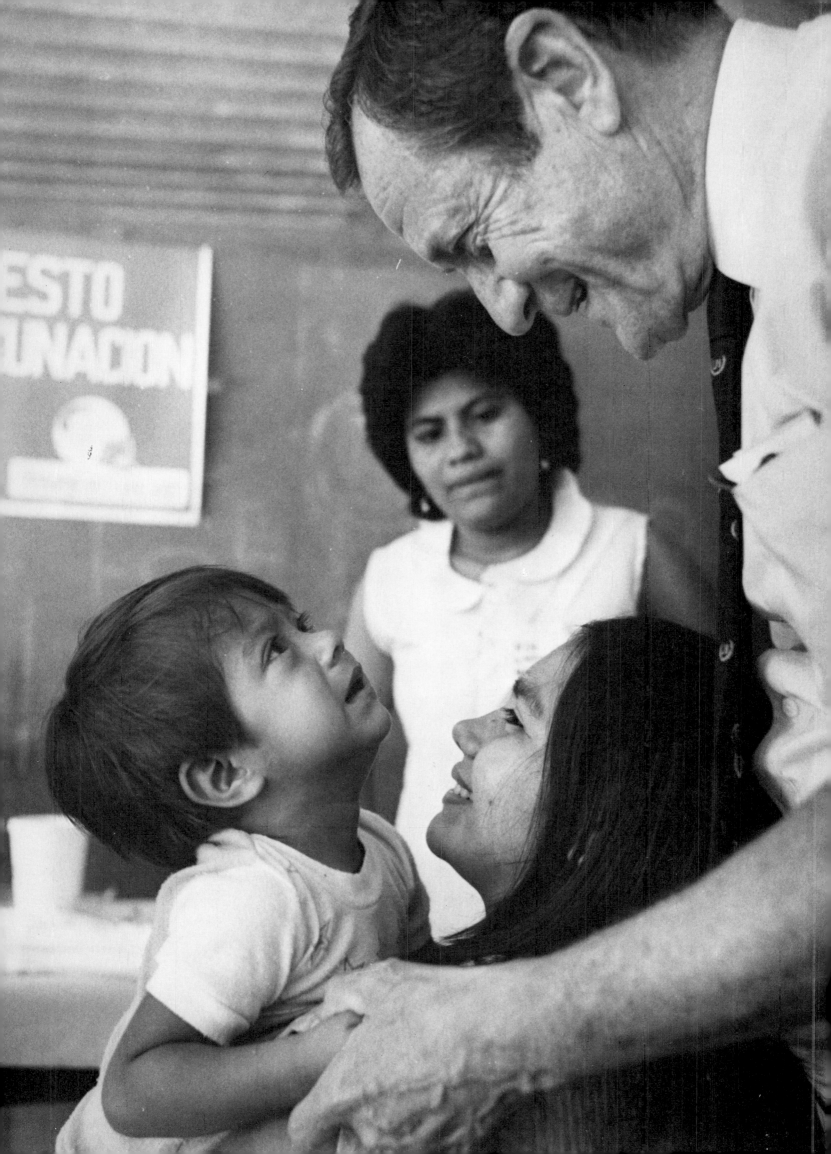

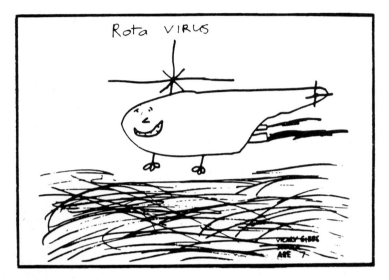

Rota VIRUS

Above: The rotavirus, thought to be responsible for a significant number of cases of diarrhea, is imaginatively depicted by Vicary Gibbs, age seven, who lives in Quetta, Pakistan. Vicary's father, Ken, is resident program officer there for UNICEF.

Opposite: Concern is written all over this Pakistani mother's face as her child receives intravenous rehydration at Rawalpindi General Hospital. Dehydration due to diarrhea and gastroenteritis kills nearly five million children yearly.

ses to one part salt in a liter of water. It is just as effective as the tiny packets in preventing dehydration in nine out of ten babies who get diarrhea. Alternative recipes use rice gruel or slightly salted vegetable soups. The other part of the message is that if the baby doesn't get better quickly, mothers should go to the local health worker for the little packet of oral rehydration salts to mix and give to their children. (A dehydrated child may need the extra ingredient in the packet—potassium—to retain more fluid and recover.) At the clinic, the health worker can also give mothers sound advice on continuing feeding and on preventing diarrhea in the first place.

The drama of a child's recovery has a powerful effect in convincing mothers of the necessity of ORT. When they see babies revive so quickly—even the sunken fontanel (the soft spot on top of the head) of a dehydrated baby can return to normal within as little as a half hour—mothers become educators themselves, teaching other mothers how to mix and administer the fluid. "Saving the life of one baby with acute dehydration can become a turning point for a whole village," Dr. David Werner, head of the Hesperian Foundation in Latin America, concludes.

In the midst of drought and famine in the Sudan, oral rehydration packets are combating diarrheal disease in overcrowded refugee camps and emergency feeding centers. "All who have used the salts—including the previously skeptical," UNICEF's office in Khartoum reports, "say that their effects are remarkable." The death rate from diarrheal diseases among vulnerable children in refugee camps has been remarkably low due to the use of ORT—usually under 5 percent, against the 30 percent or more that was once all-too common.

In Gambia, Africa's smallest country, mixing contests and "Happy Baby" lotteries have helped to spread the ORT word. These offer plastic measuring jugs and bars of soap or bags of rice as prizes for village mothers who can answer basic questions about ORT. Within eight months, two-thirds of all Gambian mothers learned how to mix the solution, and almost forty percent had started to use homemade ORT when their children had diarrhea.

Egypt, where some eighty thousand children die each year from diarrheal dehydration, leads the world in successfully promoting the use of oral rehydration salts. The substance was advertised on television in Alexandria in 1984 every night for a month at peak viewing times. This proved so successful that the commercial is now being broadcast nationally. In fact, it is reported to be the most widely recognized in Egypt. The message advocates not only early use of oral rehydration packets, but also continuing breast-feeding. Large numbers of Egyptian doctors and nurses have gone to special lectures and workshops to learn more about ORT. The program is already beginning to have an impact on the infant death rate nationwide.

Lifesaving packets cost less than a dime apiece. Modern-day "rediscovery" of oral rehydration therapy makes it possible for even illiterate parents to learn to treat their children at home, rather than depend on a hospital for intravenous feeding. Here, factory workers in Dhaka, Bangladesh, prepare the packets.

As a Bangladeshi mother demonstrates, a homemade ORT mixture can be fully effective in preventing dehydration from diarrhea. As parents become involved in treating their own children, death rates from dehydration drop dramatically.

**The solution for mothers at a
health center in Burkina Faso
(formerly Upper Volta). Sugar,
water, and salt—homemade
therapy.**

In Honduras, deaths from diarrheal dehydration are reported to be falling after a one-year campaign to market ORT via television and radio. With mass-media messages backed up by 1,200 health workers making home visits, over 90 percent of Honduran women now know about the new remedy, and almost half have begun using Litrosol—the local brand name for oral rehydration salts.

In Haiti, eight out of ten parents in the slums of Port-au-Prince and three out of ten in the rural areas have begun to use ORT. Almost 60 percent of all cases of childhood diarrhea in Nicaragua are being treated with it.

As a result of ORT education, in 1984 a half million children worldwide did not die from diarrheal diseases who otherwise would have. Given mobilization of all possible resources to teach parents the techniques, UNICEF believes that ORT can become available to half the world's families within the next five years. At that point, it will save the lives of some two million young children a year.

The "miracle mix" is also helping to transform the mind-set of parents from passive acceptance and fatalism to active participation in the good health of their children. That transformation is the inner core of the Child Survival Revolution.

The stories that follow describe how children's lives are being saved by three other key child survival techniques: mass immunizations, promotion of breast-feeding, and growth monitoring by mothers.

UNICEF PHOTO / MAGGIE MURRAY-LEE

WE ARE THE CHILDREN   173

The magic needle

Some are stoic, even heroic, never flinching as they bare arms or buttocks to the needle's jab. Others shriek and howl, striking terror in the hearts of children waiting behind them. No matter. It's all over in a second—pinpricks of pain yield years of protection for millions of youngsters against the six child-killing and disabling diseases: measles, polio, diphtheria, whooping cough, tetanus, and tuberculosis. That scene is being repeated all over the developing world in national campaigns aimed at achieving "universal child immunization" by 1990.

The major impetus for this UNICEF- and WHO-supported drive comes from technological breakthroughs. Vaccines are more heat-resistant and less expensive than ever before. Enormous progress has been made in improving cold chains of refrigeration. These use kerosene, bottled gas, electricity, solar energy or ice boxes to keep vaccines cool enough to remain potent from the time they leave the factory until they are injected into the child. As a result, immunization efforts are moving forward dramatically. In 1985, UNICEF provided some 445 million doses of vaccine to developing countries, triple the amount given two years earlier. It has assisted more than sixty-five countries in improving cold-chain and logistical systems.

But better technology alone is not enough. Behind the scenes, James P. Grant has been flying from capital to capital, tirelessly cajoling, convincing, sounding the clarion call to presidents and prime ministers to take up the challenge set by WHO in 1977 of mobilizing whole nations for immunization. In his view, "Immunization campaigns are good politics, good religion, good diplomacy for everyone."

In two of the largest countries in the world, leaders have committed themselves to pushing toward the 1990 goal. Prime Minister Rajiv Gandhi of India, a country where more than a million children die each year from vaccine-preventable diseases, has launched a plan to immunize all children as a "living memorial" to his mother, the late Indira Gandhi. In China, President Li Xian-nian announced a goal to extend immunization to at least 85 percent of the country by the end of 1988.

The lives of millions of children are being saved by these immunization campaigns. But there is great urgency. Although the numbers of children immunized have doubled and tripled in some countries, in others, vaccine-preventable diseases continue to kill almost four million children each year, leaving millions of others disabled.

"The biggest immunization problem," according to Grant, "is how to convince a mother and father to bring in their child each of the three times necessary for full immunization." An old adage sums up the most probable solution: "If the mountain won't come to Mohammed, then Mohammed will go to the mountain."

In Brazil, for example, in 1984 over ninety thousand vaccination posts were set up within walking distance of almost every family—in schools and community centers as well as clinics. No fewer than four hundred thousand volunteers from all strata of society manned them. And a saturation campaign brought the message to parents not only via advertisements, prime-time TV, and radio, but also through announcements at football stadiums, supermarkets, and shopping centers, informing them of where, when, and why their children should be immunized. The result: 2 million children under age two have been vaccinated against measles and 1.5 million protected against diphtheria, whooping cough, measles, and tetanus. The number of polio cases has been reduced from two thousand to forty a year.

In Colombia, ten thousand immunization posts were erected across the nation—in health clinics, schools, civic centers, marketplaces, and parks. Over 120,000 volunteers, along with the police and armed forces, helped with the campaign's logistics. Through the Colombian Red Cross, some 13,000 volunteers were trained to assist with the actual vaccination of 750,000 children in a campaign that has been called the "showpiece of the international immunization crusade." President Belisario Betancur used the power of the presidency and his considerable powers of persuasion to get Colombia's press, including opposition newspapers, to cooperate. He recruited the Church, the Red Cross, Rotarians, Lions, boy scouts, businessmen, and teachers. People received a veritable bombardment of reminder messages with lottery tickets, light bills, and bank statements. On each Sunday before national vaccination days, priests lectured about the importance of having children immunized and gave out flyers and posters advertising the three national vaccination dates.

In Nigeria, Africa's biggest country, to ensure that parents understood the need to inoculate their children, community leaders, traditional chiefs, religious leaders, and schoolteachers added their authority and backing. Posters, flyers, radio messages, songs, house-to-house visits, and loudspeaker vans—all publicized the vaccination sessions. The payoff is that eight to ten times as many children in the capital cities of all nineteen states were vaccinated each month in 1985 as compared with 1984. The cost for the complete five-booster package (which protected against the main childhood diseases) ran between four and five dollars for each child. In the area of Owo alone, experts from the Centers for Disease Control in Atlanta estimate that the immunization drive has forestalled 10,000 cases of measles, prevented over 300 deaths, and saved at least 150 children from blindness, deafness, or other disabilities.

After committing himself to a nationwide campaign, Prime Minister Ozal of Turkey came up with a novel way of delivering vaccines to forty-five thousand vaccination stations across the country. He used the refrigerated warehouses of the national meat and fish industries. The army

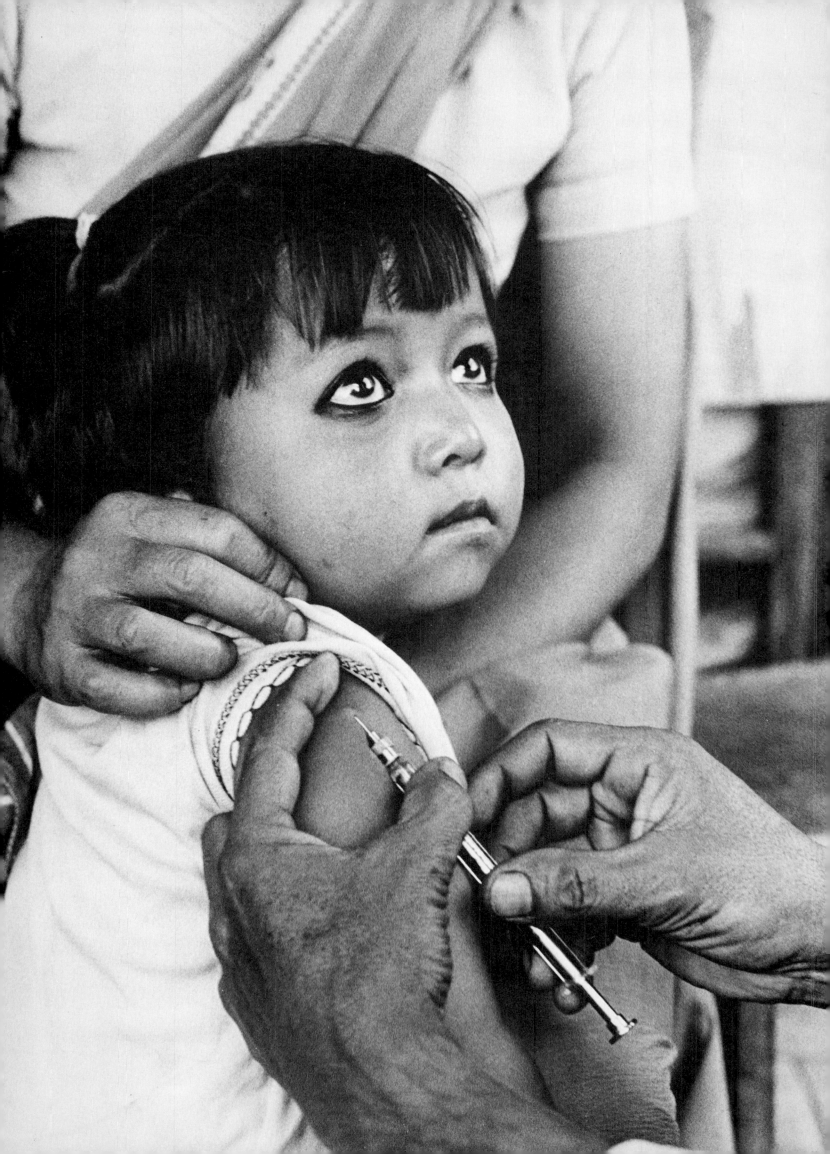

Susheel Varma, an auxiliary nurse/midwife, vaccinates a village child in Dhandlan, India. As a memorial to his mother, the late Indira Gandhi, Prime Minister Rajiv Gandhi has called for the immunization of all Indian children.

provided transport. Mothers and children who needed rides to vaccination points were driven by Turkish members of the Rotary International, which also contributed $2.1 million in vaccines. Teachers began work three weeks early to help prepare the campaign. Housewives in the capital, Ankara, made thirty thousand sandwiches so that health workers could stay at their posts for an entire twenty-four-hour-long Vaccination Day. Across the country, over four million children were vaccinated—two-thirds of the nation's children under five.

At a ceremony commemorating the fortieth anniversary of the United Nations in October 1985, ordinary citizens joined national leaders and ambassadors in declaring their commitment to immunization for all the world's children by 1990. Among those signing was Secretary-General Javier Pérez de Cuellar, who said: "The death of one child, when the death could have been avoided, is a rebuke to all humanity."

Political leaders of all persuasions must lead the way, bringing educational, agricultural, and other government ministries into partnership with the health sector. Strategic alliances must be forged with religious, professional, and community service groups, as well as the media. Widespread training of health auxiliaries (including thousands of vaccination teams); growth in the number of women's groups; increases in literacy; and the phenomenal spread of transistor radios and other communication media provide countries with new possibilities for social mobilization.

There is greater hope than ever before for the health of the world's children now that universal child immunization is within reach, a "possible dream." Entire nations, from the community up, are learning to mobilize, plan, and get technical support, giving new impetus to a host of other improvements in children's lives. In the story that follows, two health promoters describe their adventures in the jungles of Colombia's Pacific coast province, traveling by canoe, motorboat, and foot through mountainous jungle to vaccinate children in remote towns and villages.

Below: Scenes like this one in an Upper Volta village must be repeated daily around the world if the United Nations Children's Fund and WHO are to reach their goal of universal child immunization by 1990.

Bottom: A field day for mass immunization: This reminder decorated the 1985 Test Cricket Match between India and Sri Lanka in Colombo. It reached millions of TV viewers in Sri Lanka and all across the Indian subcontinent.

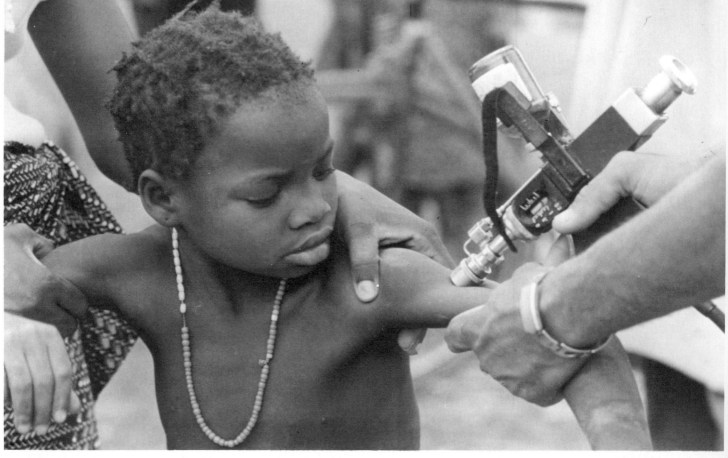

Bottoms up: A policeman immunizes a child during the third Colombian National Vaccination Day, summer 1984. Pulling out all the stops, the country mobilized every available resource, including police and army medics; thirteen thousand Red Cross vaccinators; over two hundred thousand teachers, and two thousand parish priests who preached immunization from their pulpits.

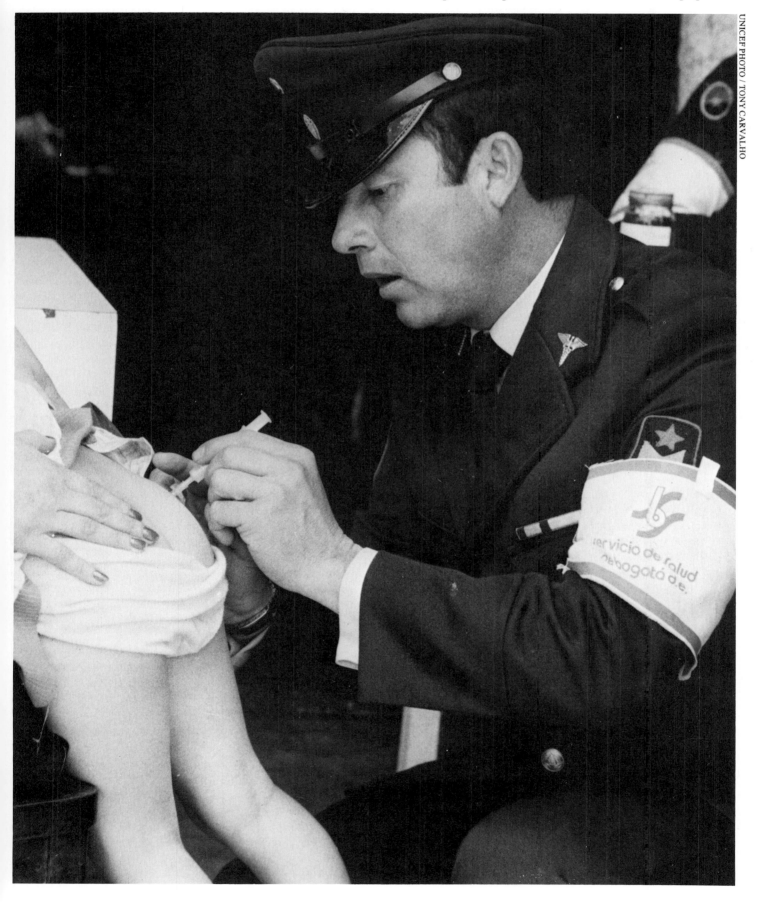

UNICEF PHOTO / TONY CARVALHO

A jungle story

by Patricia Lara

At 8:00 A.M. on October 19, 1985, the President of Colombia, Belisario Betancur, is vaccinating a child at the presidential palace in Bogotá. At the same moment, Amparo Martan and Rocio Hernandez are initiating a similar activity at their small health post in Partidero, deep in the jungles of Cauca Province. The town is in an impoverished area located twenty minutes by motorboat from the town of Guapi and thirty-five minutes from the Pacific Ocean. Only a few children have ever been vaccinated there. The two men are explaining to the mothers present that vaccinations are necessary to prevent disease and that possible reactions to the vaccine are no cause for alarm. It is 1985 and they are participating in the Second National Vaccination Crusade.

Dozens of mothers wait their turn. Some of the children run around the schoolhouse while others linger on their mothers' laps, casting terrified glances at the syringes and needles. The first woman steps forward. Her name is Maira Anchica. She is the mother of eight, and she has come to be vaccinated with two of her children.

"How old are you?" asks Amparo.

"I don't know," replies the woman.

Making a quick estimate, Amparo writes "38" on the registration form and then asks the age of the child. Again, the answer is vague. "He was born the year the river was flooded," says the mother.

Slowly, Amparo records similar unspecific information for most of the mothers and children while Rocio vaccinates amid cries of protest from the little ones.

Maira's husband works in the lumber mill at Partidero and earns approximately sixty-five dollars a month. This is all she, her husband, and eight children, ten chickens, two pigs, and an old dog have to live on. Her eldest son, who is eighteen, works as a fisherman and helps provide food for the entire family.

Yesica Chinchilla is another woman, like many of the region, who has no exact knowledge of her age nor the ages of her children. She too waits to be vaccinated. Yesica's husband, Juancho, is a fisherman who sells his catch to a nearby cold-storage plant. He earns the equivalent of forty dollars a month, the family's only income.

Maira and Yesica indicate that most families in the area have six or seven children. They do not practice birth control because they fear introducing foreign substances into their bodies and because their husbands simply will not allow it. The women explain that most males adhere to the popular saying that "each child is born with a loaf of bread under his arm." Both Maira and Yesica say they go to a physician only when the local herb doctor is unable to provide a cure. Their houses are made of wood built on stilts, with a family area, kitchen, and a room where five or six people sleep; their diet consists mostly of fish and bananas; and the most common diseases among them are malaria, tuberculosis, tetanus, gastroenteritis, and those caused by parasites.

Amparo Martan believes that the National Vaccination Crusade has been a success. More than fifty thousand volunteers have taken part in this effort, including senior-year high-school students, who volunteered to record information. The next National Vaccination Day will be held in November, and indications are that coverage could reach the 80-percent mark. Amparo proudly states that other countries, like El Salvador and Turkey, hope to duplicate the Colombian experience by mounting similar campaigns of their own. By the close of the first National Vaccination Day, Colombian health authorities estimate that approximately eighteen children were vaccinated per hour.

Amparo Martan, a short, plump woman, is the rural health promoter for Partidero. Here, in a ramshackle wooden schoolhouse, Amparo receives mothers and their children who have come by canoe along the nearly dry Guapi River, some traveling for almost an hour, others less. They have made the journey at the request of Amparo, who personally visited the five hundred homes in the area to tell people about the Vaccination Crusade. The community of Partidero chose her to be their health promoter. Later, she was officially appointed by the Ministry of Health and is now paid a salary equivalent to eighty-five dollars a month. Amparo is accepted by the community and exercises a considerable degree of influence among the people of the region. This is the key to her success.

Amparo explains that since this is a region where people can tune into foreign radio stations more easily than local ones, media support for the crusade was lacking. That is why she made house-to-house visits. "I distributed promotional material to all of the homes," she says. "Usually, at least one of the children knows how to read and will explain the information to the mother. If no one in the family can do this, then I read it to them."

Colombia now has forty-five hundred promoters like Amparo Martan working throughout the country. Most of them are between the ages of eighteen and thirty, and have at least five years of primary education plus additional training as health promoters. Their job is to visit homes, observe living conditions, make recommendations on personal hygiene and the disposal of waste, provide first-aid treatment, stitch wounds, and give talks on nutrition, gastrointestinal diseases, oral hygiene and family planning. Their role has been fundamental to the workings of the national health systems as well as to the success of the National Vaccination Crusade.

Rocio Hernandez, a staff member at the Guapi Hospital, is working with Amparo on this particular campaign. Guapi is a crowded town whose only source of electricity is an old generating plant that lights up the town at six in the evening and abandons it to darkness at midnight. One can reach Guapi by boat or by air via a small Twin Otter. It is a town typical of Colombia's Pacific coast, where the mortality rate for children is more than three times the average for the rest of the country. Three-fourths of the families in Guapi have a monthly salary of less than eighty-seven dollars. People earn their living mostly by gold mining, logging, and fishing. There are no roads and, in many places, no refrigeration facilities to allow for storage or marketing of fresh foods. But Guapi is a quiet, peaceful place.

Rocio Hernandez is a young woman with fine features and large, clear eyes. She formerly worked with the local hospital in Bahia Solano, another town situated on the shores of the Pacific and backed by the endless jungle of the Chocó region. It is one of the poorest areas of Colombia, where there are only thirty-four doctors to every forty-nine thousand square kilometers of territory.

One of the objectives of the Vaccination Crusade has been to ensure that mothers and children will not have to travel more than one hour in order to be vaccinated. Consequently, long and arduous travel is required of the health team.

"In April we visited an Indian tribe at Uva," says Rocio. "Their village is located two days away from Bahia Solano. We traveled thirteen hours by river and sea in canoe and motorboat, then walked another fifteen hours through mountainous jungle and across swamplands, accompanied by torrential rains, snakes, the cry of birds, the sound of running streams, and the wind in the trees. When we arrived," she adds, "the Indian health promoter called the tribe together and we were able to vaccinate all the children in addition to providing medical and dental care, plus lectures on hygiene."

The Indians, who represent 10 percent of the population in the Chocó region (the rest are mostly blacks), fashion bags and other craft items, which they offer for sale up and down the river. This activity, together with the sale of bananas, generates their entire income. They live in *tambas*, a type of dwelling built on stilts at a level approximately a meter above ground. In contrast to the homes of other Colombians, these have no interior divisions and are comprised of a single open space where twelve to fourteen families sleep.

The Indians normally attend to their bodily needs outside the *tambas*, on the ground or at the river, which is also the source of their drinking water. Rocio indicates that some are now beginning to boil the water used for human consumption, but that the change is slow in coming as most do not like the taste of boiled water. Cooking is done on the ground.

The humid and dark atmosphere is conducive to tuberculosis and malaria. One of the Indians reported having eighteen attacks of malaria in a single year. Neonatal tetanus is also common, as a machete or rusty knife is frequently used to cut

In Guapi, a village deep in the Cauca jungle, during Colombia's National Vaccination Crusade, an infant receives a shot from a nurse's aide (left) to protect it against diphtheria, whooping cough, and tetanus. Rural-health promoter Amparo Martan (right) observes the aide's technique.

UNICEF PHOTO / JAIME A. NINO

the umbilical cord. Gynecological examinations are difficult, as men refuse to allow their women to be examined.

Rocio Hernandez talks about some of the special customs and rites of this tribe. When a girl reaches puberty, the entire community embarks on a celebration that can last eight to fifteen days. The bodies of the young girls are painted with designs done in *jagua*, a black juice taken from the seeds of a special plant. This shows they are ready for marriage.

"They painted me with *jagua* designs when I went to vaccinate," says Rocio. "I had many admirers, even ones who wanted me to stay."

Because of the tremendous distances between villages, Rocio explains, rural areas were covered by the crusade at a later date. Urban areas, much easier for vaccination teams to get to, were covered on the day of the campaigns. "There were a lot of problems with transportation," she says. "We had to depend on the police and other institutions to supply us with boats and motors. Those belonging to the public health authorities were not enough. There were other problems as well. In some areas, it was impossible to refrigerate the vaccine because there was no electricity. Occasionally, the vaccine did not arrive in time. Some children still have not received the entire series because the mothers tire of bringing them in for vaccinating. However, thanks to assistance from UNICEF, in cooperation with 'PLADEICOP,' Colombia's Regional Plan for Integrated Development of the Pacific Coast, we will now be able to complete the job. There are still no figures as to how many people have been vaccinated in the Chocó region, but we hope to eventually cover 60 percent of the population."

Back to the breast

It is ironic that, while well-educated mothers in Europe and the United States today are returning to breast-feeding in droves, many poor mothers in developing countries are doing the opposite. They are choosing so-called "modern" artificial substitutes, which they cannot afford, often do not need, and are not able to use safely. Even if born under the poorest roof in the developing world, a baby who is exclusively breast-fed for the first four to six months of its life has a more solid basis for staying healthy and growing well.

"Fifteen years ago, in most industrialized countries, infant formula was thought to be equal to or better than mother's milk," James Grant observed. "Today we know the reverse is true. Scientists have rediscovered the merits of mother's milk." Not the least of those merits is that mother's milk contains at least six anti-infective agents, which work against many common illnesses of infancy.

On the other hand, infant formula has been called one of the industrialized world's "most dangerous exports to developing countries." Without clean water or sterilizing equipment, fuel and time for boiling water, or enough money to buy enough formula, mothers are unwittingly risking the health and lives of their infants.

The risk of death in infancy is about five times greater for babies who are bottle-fed than for babies who are breast-fed. That's the conclusion of the London School of Hygiene and Tropical Medicine, which drew together thirty-three comparative studies from around the world.

How to get that message out to health and hospital officials, pediatricians, nurses, midwives, mothers, fathers, and schoolchildren—soon to be parents themselves—remains the challenge. A worldwide effort to promote breast-feeding in all countries is currently under way on the part of UNICEF, WHO, and other concerned organizations. It is considered a key child survival technique.

A ten-year campaign on the part of health professionals, concerned private groups, and others to regulate the use of infant formula among Third World mothers achieved an important outcome. In 1981, the International Code of Marketing of Breast-milk Substitutes was put forward by the World Health Organization in collaboration with UNICEF and passed at the World Health Assembly.

Since the code's acceptance, over one hundred countries have begun campaigns to promote breast-feeding and to control the marketing of artificial substitutes. Some thirty-three governments have completely banned the advertising of infant formula to the public. At the same time, the media is actively cooperating in promoting breast-feeding in seventeen countries.

To convince mothers of the merits of breast-feeding, celebrities in Brazil and Haiti have nursed their babies on television. In Nigeria, actresses pose for posters while breast-feeding. It's the subject of puppet shows, popular songs, soap

Above: Poster provided by the Society of Pediatricians in Brazil, where the world's first national program to promote breast-feeding began in 1982.

Opposite: A young mother breast-feeds her child at a health center in Guayaquil, Ecuador. Breast-feeding for the first four to six months of life, with appropriate supplementations of breast milk during the latter half of the first year, is strongly recommended by UNICEF and the World Health Organization. Its decline in the developing world poses a significant threat to child health and survival.

Breast is best, but do most
mothers know which way of
feeding is better? In the waiting
room of a Togo health center, one
can observe contrasting styles.

operas, and national mass-media campaigns in the Philippines. Imams in Indonesia have become directly involved, and so has Mother Teresa. In Calcutta, the Nobel Laureate joined James Grant in an appeal to the media to help publicize the benefits of breast-feeding during the first critical months of life.

Dr. Natividad Relucio-Clavano, the head of pediatrics in a Filipino city hospital, went on a voyage of discovery abroad and came back with a new understanding of what was happening to newborn babies in the developing world, including her own town, Baguio City. A firsthand story follows, in which she tells how she won her struggle to promote breast-feeding. She changed the lives of babies not only in Baguio City, but all over the Philippines.

Dr. Clavano's story

For many years I was no different from countless doctors in the developing countries. I was a typical pediatrician, whose vision and work were limited to the four walls of a hospital. Instead of helping babies thrive, I was, without realizing it, encouraging practices which caused their sickness, and sometimes their death. I prescribed bottle-feeding routinely for babies, gave them formula milk, and went along with the infant-formula companies. I was, in fact, their friend, just like everyone else. The Baguio nursery had its share of colorful posters and calendars showing beautiful, healthy babies—advertisements for infant formula. We followed what we believed were the most up-to-date practices. Babies were separated from their mothers at birth and placed in the nursery. Mothers were not encouraged to breast-feed. Instead, we practiced delayed feeding or starvation periods on newborns, followed by feeding with water or glucose and then infant formula, and gave mothers free samples to take home and feed their babies.

We did all the things we did, not because we did not care, but simply because we did not know the truth about the benefits of breast-feeding and the perils of bottle-feeding. Our medical and nursing schools had simply ignored the subject. That sounds shocking—and it was!

I had to travel halfway around the world to finally discover the truth about something that would become the central issue of my life.

In 1974, I took leave from my job as head of the pediatrics department at Baguio General Hospital and Medical Center (now known as the Dr. Efraim C. Montemayor Memorial Medical Center) to study pediatric allergies in the United Kingdom. Halfway through my course, I was exposed to the work of Dr. David Morley and his colleagues at the University of London's Institute of Child Health. It was a turning point of my life. It gave new meaning to my concept of child care. For the first time, I understood the link between social conditions and infant mortality.

I was so shocked at learning the numbers of infant deaths

Below: A Nepali mother and child.

Opposite: Breast-feeding on the littered streets of Cairo.

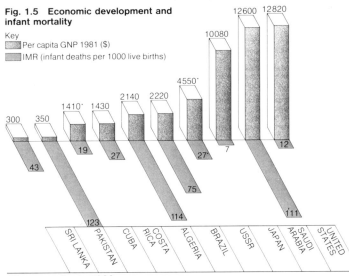

Fig. 1.5 Economic development and infant mortality

Key
Per capita GNP 1981 ($)
IMR (infant deaths per 1000 live births)

12600 12820
10080
4550
2140 2220
1410 1430
300 350

43
123 SRI LANKA
19 PAKISTAN
27 114 CUBA
COSTA RICA
27 ALGERIA
75 BRAZIL
7 USSR
JAPAN
111 SAUDI ARABIA
12 UNITED STATES

Figures refer to 1980.

Dr. Natividad Relucio-Clavano, a Filipino pioneer in promoting "rooming-in," holds a newborn baby.

due to preventable diseases that I decided to study tropical child health instead. In the new course, my eyes were opened to the crucial problem of the decline in breast-feeding. A lecture by Dr. Mavis Gunther, a breast-feeding advocate, enlightened me about the anti-infective properties of breast milk, which protect the baby from bacterial and viral diseases. So, breast milk is not only ideal nutritionally, it also protects the baby from infections.

Later, my travels to various Asian and African countries brought me face-to-face with the misery of malnutrition and the widespread deaths of bottle-fed babies. In one African cemetery, I saw countless baby graves decorated with empty infant-formula tins and feeding bottles. They were startling symbols of the terrible mistakes still being made in child care in many parts of the world.

I decided to start my own breast-feeding campaign. My primary goal: the elimination of milk formula and bottle-feeding at Baguio Hospital. On my return to the Philippines, my first problem was winning the support of my colleagues. How does one break the strong hold that commercial infant formula has on doctors, nurses, and other hospital staff? How does one change firmly rooted attitudes and practices?

First, I distributed materials on the virtues of breast-feeding and the dangers of infant formula. And I talked with hospital administrators, doctors, nurses, government officials, midwives, civic leaders, mothers—anyone concerned with child care—to persuade them that the changes were practical and economical. Wherever I could, I cornered people—in corridors, at parties, and at various seminars and conferences.

At first, many of my colleagues were astounded by my revelations about breast-feeding. Some were skeptical. Others were actively opposed to any change. My proposal came as a shock to doctors and nurses who had been taught to keep babies in the nurseries and on the bottle. But there were many who were impressed and gradually became convinced supporters. The infant-formula firms, however, did not know what to do with me.

Then, in 1975, I closed the doors of the Baguio Hospital nursery to the infant-formula salespeople and banned bottle-feeding. We stopped giving our babies the "starter" dose of formula. Everything conducive to bottle-feeding was removed, including gifts and free samples from the infant-food companies. We tore down the posters and calendars. In their place we put up the famous "baby-killer" posters, showing an emaciated baby inside a dirty feeding bottle.

We brought the babies to their mothers immediately after birth so that they could begin breast-feeding at once. This was usually thirty minutes or so after a natural delivery (and from two to four hours after a cesarean). Our new "rooming-in" policy encouraged mothers to keep their babies with them in the maternity wards and rooms to practice "on-demand" feeding. A special bond between mother and child was quickly established at the start. The mother learned the rudiments of infant care and felt more at ease with her baby and more confident when it was time to go home. The important thing was to give the babies back to their mothers, where they rightfully belonged. It was really nothing new.

Our program yielded immediate economic benefits. With mothers caring for their babies, we were able to release a number of nurses and midwives from nursery work for other duties. We required less electricity (for sterilization, heating bottles, and boiling water for formula). And we had fewer sick babies.

Some of the health workers released became the first personnel for our new Under-Six Clinic program (USC). Based on Dr. Morley's successful child-care program in Africa, it is basically a package of preventive and curative services for infants, children, and mothers. It includes the four child survival techniques—breast-feeding, growth monitoring, promotion of oral rehydration therapy for diarrhea, immunization—plus nutrition, detection and control of anemia, family planning, and treatment of acute and chronic illnesses. These programs—at rural health units or in slum areas—help to reach the neglected masses beyond the hospital. This is important in my country, since nine out of every ten births there take place at home.

In the ten years or more since I banned bottle-feeding from Baguio Hospital and started "rooming-in," much has happened. With UNICEF as sponsor and Dr. Wah Wong (its Philippine representative) as my mentor, I conducted a four-year study of ten thousand babies born in our hospital between 1973 and 1977. The study showed a dramatic reduction in infant deaths and infection among breast-fed babies. I believe it helped convince the Philippine Ministry of Health to adopt our breast-feeding and "rooming-in" practices in all government hospitals and clinics. The ministry also adopted our Under-Six Clinic program nationwide, with UNICEF providing equipment and training. These public Under-Six Clinics are expanding rapidly throughout the country.

More good news: Breast-feeding is finally being taught today as part of the curriculum in Philippine medical and nursing schools, and health workers are now being trained to promote it as well. One day soon we hope breast-feeding will be taught in all our primary and secondary schools, too.

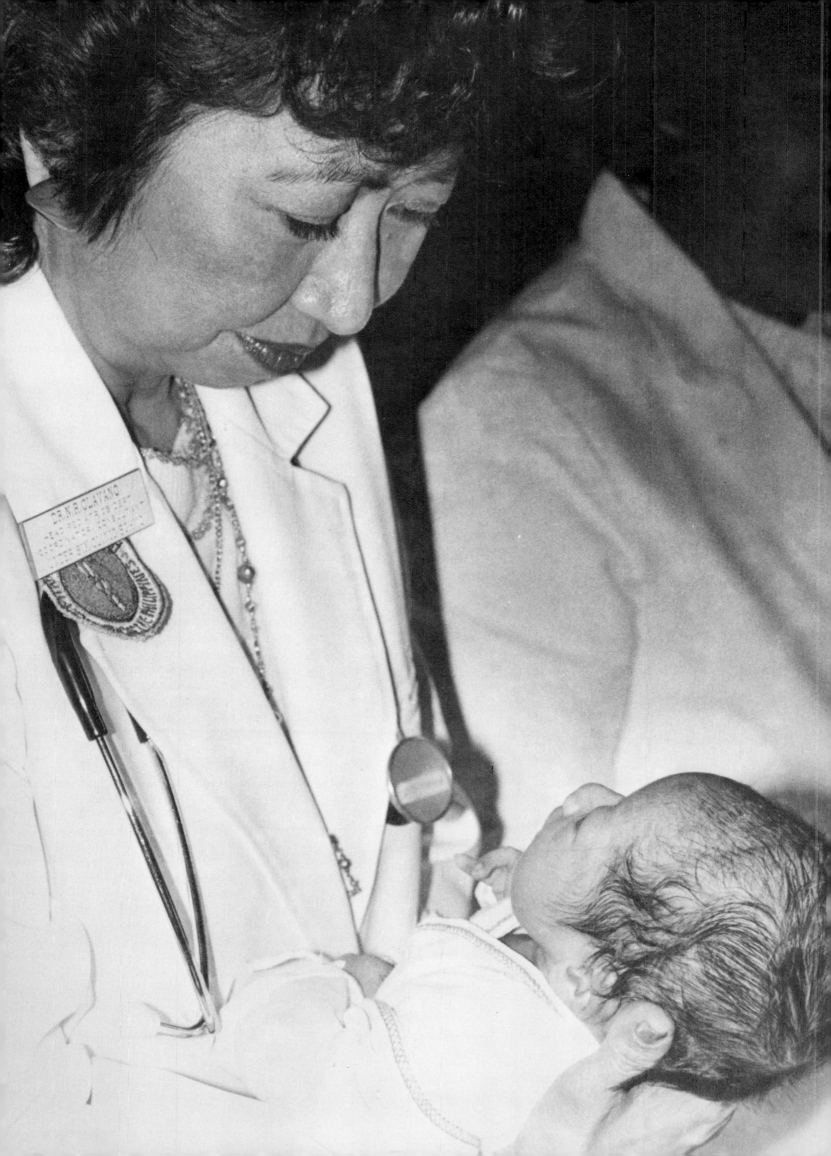

Telltale charts

Any mother in a typical village of a Third World country knows that her child should grow bigger and taller over time. What she doesn't easily and quickly recognize without a visual aid is slowed growth due to malnutrition—a condition afflicting millions of infants and toddlers throughout the developing world. A slowdown or drop in the normal, progressively rising weight curve of a child will usually show up months before there are obvious signs of malnutrition. A moderately chronically malnourished infant or toddler will look entirely normal, but be too small for its age, and will have lowered resistance to infection.

But a simple cardboard or ten-cent sheet of graph paper—that's as low-tech as you can get—can change that. Regular child-weighing and entering the results on a growth chart can make malnutrition visible to parents early, while it is still relatively inexpensive and simple to treat. The chart warns them that the child needs supplementary foods, more frequent feeding, or medical help.

The participation of village health workers is key to the success of child-weighing. They not only help mothers with the weighing and plotting of the child's growth curve, but also advise them of what foods to give a child who stops gaining or who loses weight. They also immunize the child against infectious diseases that can further hamper growth.

Given adequate information and support, even illiterate mothers can easily understand what the charts tell them about their children. A study in Ghana showed that although a little over half the mothers had no more than two years' schooling, after six months in the child-health program, 66 percent of them were able to interpret the charts correctly.

The experience of Project Poshak in India also confirms that mothers can interpret the charts. By the time of the project evaluation, all mothers interviewed knew that a plateau or downward slope showed the child was not sufficiently well nourished, and that this meant the child was not healthy and had a higher risk of catching disease. Seventy-six percent were able to mark their own child's position and to identify his or her health status correctly.

In Indonesia, where UNICEF has supplied fifteen million growth charts and 58,700 weighing scales, studies show that 95 percent of the trained village volunteers can use the growth charts. A survey of 2,500 mothers indicated six out of ten understood about child health and growth and the need to weigh children monthly. Trained village volunteers also teach mothers at what age to begin weaning a child and what diet it needs to continue growing normally.

Up to 2.5 million children are now being weighed regularly each month in Indonesia, and the results are being regularly posted on village notice boards, which show what percentage of the children have gained weight in the last month. From there the information is fed into a computer in Jakarta. It keeps track of the overall nutritional status of children. The goal is to cut the country's malnutrition rate in half.

Growth charts are now coming into use in over eighty countries. In the words of Dr. David Morley, professor of tropical child health at the University of London and one of the pioneers of low-cost ways to protect children's growth: "The potential impact of growth charts is nothing less than revolutionary. . . . It is this informed involvement of the mother in the struggle to make sure that the child puts on weight each and every month that is perhaps the greatest contribution the growth charts can make to child development and child health."

One mother in Madurai, southern India, put it in terms that other mothers instantly understand: "The growth chart is like an astrologer's prediction for your child; buy one for him."

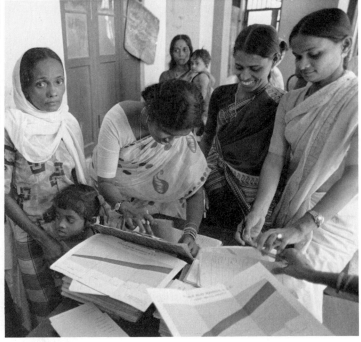

UNICEF PHOTO / SEAN SPRAGUE

Above: At a nutrition center in Kerala, India, mothers learn to plot a baby's weight on growth charts.

Opposite: A midwife weighs a newborn baby in a net scale, which comes as part of a UNICEF kit. Under Ghana's law, a midwife is completely responsible for mother and child until seven days after birth.

Below: Anxious mothers, like this one in Chad, by studying their children's growth charts regularly, can navigate away from malnutrition themselves— and prevent up to half of all cases among their children.

In Thailand (bottom) and Pakistan (opposite), mothers learn the importance of plotting a child's growth.

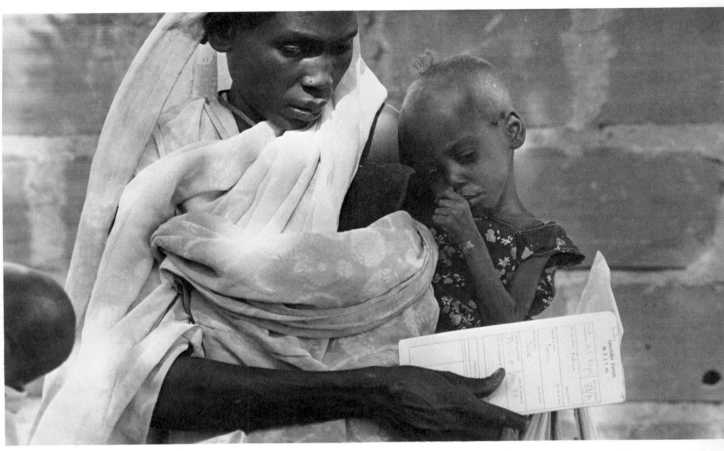

XI. Africa's Crisis

A smile in darkness
by John Richardson

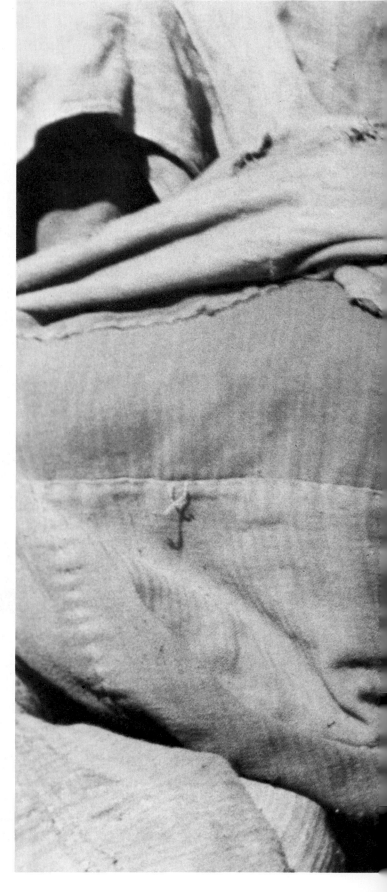

Terrible anxieties haunted me at the end of 1984. I was working for UNICEF in New York at the time, editing *UNICEF News*. The sad tidings had just hit the world like a sledgehammer: Africa was in deep trouble, and people were dying of starvation in staggering numbers. Something had to be done to save them, and it had to be done fast. I had lived in Africa, where I experienced some of my most cherished and difficult moments. I knew I had to go back to help.

World concern at the time was extraordinary. I remember a couple of affluent New York women traveling into Manhattan on a commuter bus. It was a few weeks after the famous BBC film from Ethiopia had triggered avalanches of tearful telephone calls to relief agencies from people who wanted to help save lives. The two of them sat behind me for the forty-minute ride, dressed in fur coats and an abundance of jewelry. They started their morning conversing about a fashion show at one of the New York hotels. I kept thinking about Ethiopia, secretly condemning these women for being so self-absorbed and oblivious.

But they surprised me, because the next topic of conversation was Ethiopia. "I can't take it," one of the women told her friend. "I can't watch children die on television. I'm not eating lunch this week. I'm going to send the money to UNICEF or CARE instead."

It was like that then. People had been touched at the bottom of their hearts, and they responded not with the calculated moves of political ideologues who signed on to causes because they fit their political views or served their interests, but because of what they had seen on television, read about in newspapers, and imagined in their minds: it had made them cry. This was powerful, because it was the purest of human reactions for most people. It was an emotional response.

Several weeks later, I was in Ethiopia as information officer and press liaison for UNICEF and the United Nations secretary-general's representative in charge of emergency relief. The media flooded to Ethiopia, and later the Sudan. Servicing them—providing information, arranging trips, scheduling interviews with diplomats and aid workers, keeping them company—was a full-time, often exhausting job. It was the media that generated such enormous response; they were perhaps the most indispensable element in the whole drama. Without them, most of us would never have gone to help, and

At the Herbo Shelter in the Wollo region of northern
Ethiopia, newly admitted mothers and children are
screened to determine their nutritional and health status.
When necessary, they are treated with UNICEF-supplied
medicines and vaccines.

thousands would have died in total anonymity.

UNICEF understood this well, and was one of the agencies that made a special effort to use the media to alert donors to the need for help. When I later worked for UNICEF in the Sudan, I was one of the key people in the emergency effort, and often spent twelve- or fifteen-hour days handling the endless stream of journalists, celebrities, and donor representatives.

The Sudan is an enormous territory, the largest country in Africa. Scattered over thousands of miles of semidesert were several million people who were close to the end of their resources. Five years had passed with no rain. They lived on the fringes of a desert that was rapidly eating its way south. UNICEF was able to fill some critical gaps in the emergency effort by providing a variety of supplies—Land-Rovers, feeding kits, blankets, medicines, supplementary food—to smaller, nongovernmental agencies that were responding in large numbers to the famine.

By the middle of 1985, the world was perhaps as aware as it was going to be of Africa's problems. Ethiopia and the Sudan were at the head of a long list of countries the United Nations said were suffering from critical food shortages. There were the Sahelian countries in the northern part of Africa—among them Chad, Mali, Niger, Burkina Faso, and Mauritania—and a group of countries in southern Africa, the worst of which were Angola and Mozambique, where drought and civil conflict had ruined crops and cut off food supplies.

The famine had been going on for some time. Like others who had lived and worked in Africa, I had known about it. I had raised money and worked for OXFAM-America during the Sahelian famine of the early 1970s; I had written about the effects of prolonged drought in southern Zimbabwe in 1982; I had traveled in the northern regions of Kenya, where serious problems were developing in the early 1980s, and I had read isolated reports of the seven million people suffering terrible famine in northern Ethiopia. I knew enough about Africa to realize that famine was not always the result of drought and nature's stinginess. I had gone as a journalist to Uganda, where hunger was a result of war, drought, *and* large-scale social and economic breakdown. And I knew the jungles of central Africa, so lush and green, where many have trouble feeding themselves and children regularly die in high numbers from malnutrition.

For those who wanted to see them, the signs of approaching disaster were all around. I remember with great clarity a trip I made in early 1984 to the town of Afmadu, in southern Somalia, a livestock center in a region inhabited by nomads. The Somalis who accompanied me knew that drought was beginning to take its toll. The last forty kilometers of road to the town was littered with dead cattle. Some had dropped in the road that morning, still alive, and were waiting to die. One of them, a large white ox, had had its innards ripped from its body. There was a large hole in its stomach, and we could see its heart beating in the pile of intestines and organs lying in the dust at its side. The animal was alive, and tears were streaming down its face. By the time we returned along the road a few hours later, the vultures had arrived and were picking over the animal's carcass. Death had struck hard. After the animals died, nomads told us, people would start dying too.

But even the most hardened relief workers and journalists were not prepared for much of what was happening by 1984. What the world saw on television was the worst of it—the horrible outcome of years of steady, unyielding deterioration of land, economy, and spirit. For those of us who were there, it was a difficult confrontation.

There was the shock of Mekele Hospital in northern Ethiopia—of having a tall, twelve-year-old skeletal boy dangled in front of my eyes, of seeing an old man jerking around in a bed with a tube up his nose, his body reduced by famine to a bony profile. There was the sense of shame at being led by a doctor into a room of slowly dying elders, of having him pull the covers off an emaciated, defeated old woman, her ruined body no longer anything but a spectacle for the eyes of visitors. There were the small children, crying frantically, so obviously confused and frightened in such a heartless, hopeless world. And there was the awful sight, one that got worse over a period of a few minutes, of a little baby trying to get milk from his mother's empty breast, hitting her in growing frustration, turning his little head aside in exasperation, and finally giving up. He leaned against his mother and looked off into the distance, defeated. All of it was there, including the horrible, wasted, yellowed faces of death.

Death could be hidden for a while behind the smiles of the living, behind the shrieks and laughter of the little children who followed me around and tugged at my sleeve, behind the sterility of facts and figures and charts that were conjured up to present the spectacle in palatable form to initiates who passed through. But it couldn't be hidden for too long, because even the little encounters built up and wore down resistance, and eventually established their own incontrovertible reality.

Some people I saw in the famine camps of Ethiopia were simply beyond it, and what was frightening and disturbing was that one could no longer communicate with them, no longer fashion even the most ill-fitting bridge to overcome that horrible feeling of isolation and impotence. But there were many others, particularly some of the children, who still maintained their hopeful innocence. There were those like the shriveled little boy I saw in one of the intensive-care wards run by an Italian medical team, with whom one experienced very genuine and, considering the circumstances, very moving communication.

He was seven years old, with the miniature body of a dying man. He was suffering from tuberculosis and spent his days hidden underneath a blanket, his little face sticking out. He didn't move because he was too weak. But after he had watched you for a moment or two and established in his mind

that you were a beneficial influence in his life, he smiled, and the darkness around him went away. And when his real friend, Agostino, the Italian doctor, came around, he really smiled and then, without any provocation, broke the ghostly silence in the tent with an energetic "ciao." That got to me and I felt like taking him home with me. He was a beautiful little person. God only knows what was going through that mind of his.

Rescuing people from the horrors of the famine was never easy, and for those of us who were there, there was the unending worry that we were never doing enough, that in so many places the problems were beyond us, and that in many ways we didn't understand enough about the deeper problems to be able to correct them.

But there were moments when things seemed to work. When the blankets donated by the Japanese at the end of 1984 arrived in Ethiopia around Christmastime, I flew up with one of the relief flights to Mekele, accompanied by a guide and a group of Japanese. The next morning we visited the camps to watch the distribution. At one of them, thousands of people, huddled in filthy rags, waited patiently in long rows stretching into the distance. Sheer numbers were often overwhelming in Ethiopia, and the Japanese representative of Rissho Kosei-Kai (a Buddhist nongovernmental organization) who was with me was deeply disturbed. He wandered through the crowds, repeating, "Oh, I'm so sorry, I'm so sorry." Later that morning, hundreds waited patiently in an open lot. Some people were exhausted and lay on the ground. When the blankets were handed out in an extraordinary kaleidoscope of bright pinks, greens, yellows, and blues, women smiled. Many of them broke out in loud ululations, an obvious show of pleasure and thanks. Everybody seemed happy then, and somehow the blankets, which were just one of the many props they would need to get through the horrible nights of cold and freezing winds, lent a bit of dignity to people who had been pushed about as far as it is possible to go without losing it all.

There was another time when whatever doubts I had about UNICEF's ability to respond quickly in a crisis were eased. Agencies in Ethiopia feared a cholera outbreak in the camps, and Save the Children U.K. asked UNICEF to requisition some intravenous-feeding units from its warehouse in Copenhagen. The request was put in on a Friday, and by Monday morning ten thousand of them were already in the country.

The director of Save the Children was flabbergasted and said he had never seen anyone, let alone a UN agency, move so quickly.

While all of the high-tension drama of the relief effort went on, few had time to think through and act on long-term solutions. UNICEF would always claim that if children had been immunized in many of the famine-stricken countries, many would never have died from measles and the cluster of other diseases that attack malnourished bodies. So it seemed particularly meaningful that UNICEF was immunizing children in Addis Ababa early in 1985, and that one of the responses to the situation in the Sudan was a national immunization campaign. This was necessary, of course, but only those who have been there can recognize it for the gamble it is—against nearly impossible odds, in a country where moving a sack of grain from one spot to another is about as difficult as anything can be.

It is hard to imagine Africa without children. They are everywhere. They are working, running, playing, teasing, laughing, and crying. Little girls do housework and care for their younger siblings. Little boys run errands and play with everything from pieces of coat hangers to elaborately constructed cars, which they make themselves from wood. But it is equally difficult to contemplate a future for them. The problems that came as such a shock to the world in late 1984 will not go away. The Herculean efforts of certain individuals and the generosity of the world have saved lives and may help stem the tide of future catastrophes. But there are no comfortable solutions to Africa's dilemmas. Countries will continue to be poor; wars will continue to take lives and mutilate societies; and drought and famine will never be far from the lives of many Africans.

Despite the gloomy prophecies, a lot of people will make it, and do so with pride and dignity. Many will be children, who will use their wits and curiosity and whatever help they can get from others. UNICEF is a part of that survival. No matter how many times I despair over the obstacles of bureaucracy, over the terrible limitations placed on our abilities to help by our ignorance of other people's lives, over the breakdowns in communication and the failures of modern technology to get things right, I know that thousands of people owe their lives to the efforts of UNICEF and other organizations like it committed to rescuing humanity.

All is not lost.

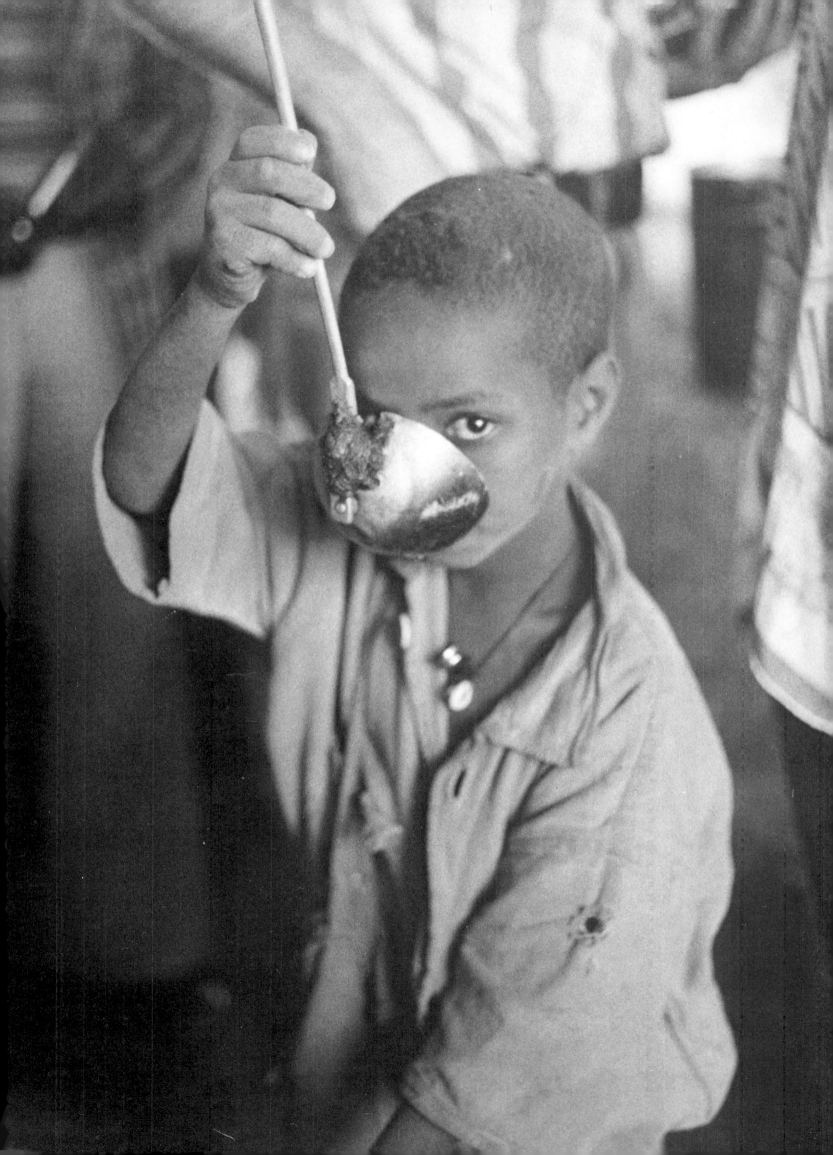

The warehouse

Hard hat, soft heart: Filip Sauerberg, a packer at UNICEF Procurement and Assembly Center—UNIPAC warehouse—in Copenhagen, sits surrounded by thirty-nine key items UNICEF ships to children around the world. Every hour of every day, 365 days a year, UNIPAC staff remain on emergency alert with an ear to the phone and an eye to the telex. When disasters strike children, UNICEF can ship relief supplies within hours, including blankets, tents, medicine, vaccine, and water purification tablets. This, however, represents only a tenth of UNIPAC's work.

Out of Copenhagen, UNICEF ships everything from A (aspirin) to Z (zinc oxide ointment, which relieves minor skin conditions). Ninety percent of its supplies build up long-term services that enable children to survive and thrive. Special kits are made up for midwives, nurses, health workers, teachers, and others who run children's services. Kits containing essential drugs are carefully tailored so that a village health worker can treat everything from minor accidents to diseases prevalent in each country. All kits are made up from five thousand items kept in UNIPAC's stock. UNICEF is also the largest single buyer and supplier of vaccines and oral rehydration salt packets in the world, which makes UNIPAC warehouse a nerve center for child survival.

The UNIPAC warehouse began functioning in 1953 out of the basement of the United Nations building. Twelve years later, it moved to Copenhagen. In 1983, to meet the growing demand for its program supplies, UNICEF's entire supply operation, including its warehouse, was revamped and reorganized. Today a staff of two hundred is responsible for procuring, warehousing, and packing supplies and equipment from some fifty countries worldwide. Valued at about $163 million a year, the supply side of UNICEF's aid reaches children in 118 countries.

Tools and Teaching Aids for Midwives and Health Workers: 1. Bicycle for health worker or midwife 2. Model of female pelvic organs 3. Birth atlas flip book 4. Fetal doll with placenta 5. Newborn doll, Asiatic 6. Newborn doll, African 7. Midwife kit 8. Sterilizer 9. Weighing trousers (one size fits all) 10. Infant scale 11. Weight/height chart 12. Vaccine carrier 13. Bag for health worker

Play and Learning Equipment for Day-Care Centers: 14. Treasure basket with six various-shaped pieces 15. Tricycle 16. Pounding bench 17. Pencil 18. Nontoxic crayons 19. Building blocks

Supplies for Health Centers, Clinics, and Hospitals: 20. ORT (oral rehydration therapy packets) 21. Breast pump 22. Nipple shield 23. Kerosene stove 24. Halazone water purification tablets 25. High-potency vitamin A capsules to prevent and cure nutritionally caused blindness 26. Ergometrine tablets for obstetrical use 27. Microscope 28. Kerosene hurricane lantern 29. Vegetable oil (to be added to K-Mix-2—#34) 30. Bag for surgical kit 31. Water filter 32. Wool blanket 33. Folding stretcher 34. Therapeutic food: K-Mix-2 for severely malnourished children 35. Plastic jerrycan for water 36. Obstetric stethoscope 37. Contents of major surgical instrument kit 38. Syringes for immunization 39. Ferrous sulphate tablets to prevent or treat anemia in pregnant women

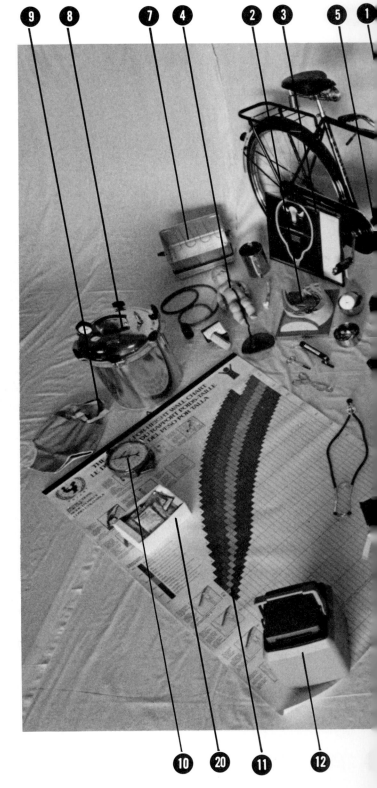

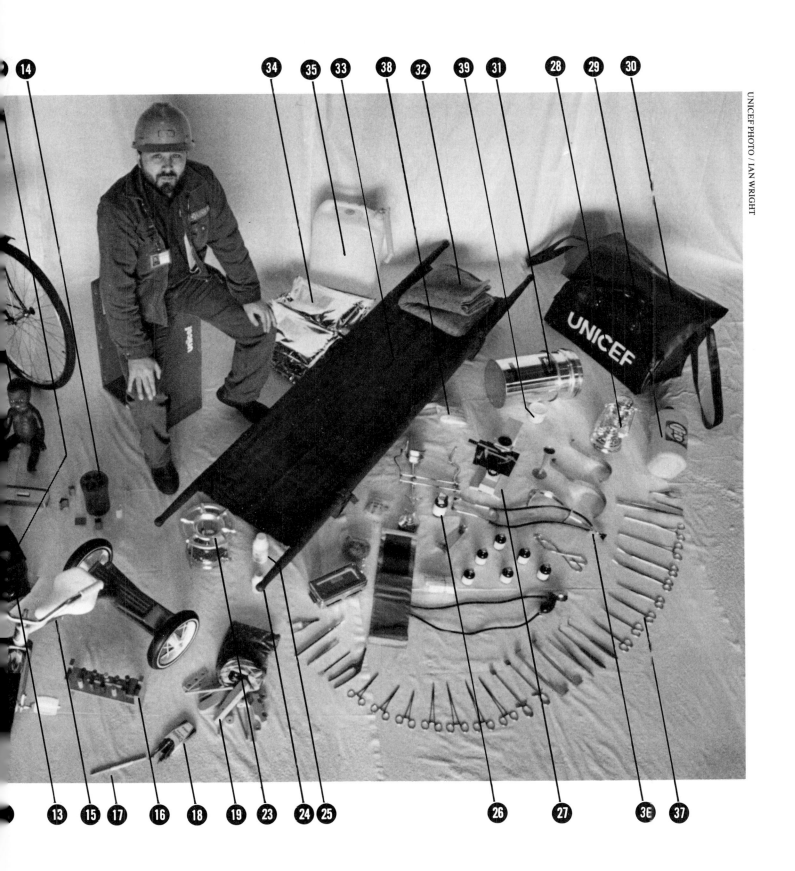

UNICEF PHOTO / IAN WRIGHT

XII. Water

More precious than gold

Fetching water home from ponds, lakes, rivers, and ravines in the Third World is considered "women's work." Girls begin lives of servitude as young as eight. Whether in Pakistan's burning Sind desert, on Bolivia's high Andean plateau, or across India's hard-rock Andhra Pradesh state, women and girls may walk up to sixteen miles a day to and from a water source. They carry pots weighing up to forty pounds on their heads or tied to their backs. In Nepal, women trek up and down mountains all day long in search of water. When their jugs are full, they set them into a backpack basket, absorbing part of the weight through broad cloth straps slung across their foreheads. Hauling water can take as many as six hours a day. In the process, spines and pelvises often become deformed.

RICHARDSON & CRUDDAS

Above: During an impromptu visit to Maruthadi village in Tamilnadu state in 1981, the late Prime Minister Indira Gandhi tried the new India Mark-II deep-well hand-pump. Designed and developed by UNICEF, the pump is manufactured in India. The little girl watching Mrs. Gandhi is one of 120 million villagers who now have access to clean water under the nationwide Rural Water Supply program.

Opposite: For these young girls in an Afghan village, a newly installed UNICEF pump means not having to haul water long distances, leaving more time for education and, perhaps, play.

"Women are 'water slaves,' domestic beasts of burden," says Martin Beyer, UNICEF's senior adviser for water and sanitation. Beyer, a Swedish geologist and water engineer who has directed UNICEF's water and sanitation aid around the world since 1974, knows this firsthand from his own years in the bush.

Water brought home at such a sacrifice is used strictly for the family's daily drinking and cooking needs. Washing babies or children is a luxury almost no mother in water-short villages can afford. Ironically, the water is almost invariably polluted, and it is responsible for many deaths and illnesses. Gastrointestinal infections, cholera, typhoid, and diarrhea lead the list of serious sicknesses. Through the exposure to feces, dirt, and polluted water, children also become hosts to worms and other parasites. These lodge in the skin, stomach, intestines, or other organs. For instance, in a country like Bangladesh, eight out of ten five-year-olds have a medium-to-heavy worm load in their bodies. That is expected to change for the better as a national water program brings clean water to some ninety-eight million people. Meanwhile, unless children are de-wormed, are taught elementary hygiene, and use only safe water to drink, parasites will continue to rob them of health and happiness. As Martin Beyer points out, "You can't do anything about improving child health until there is safe drinking water. Otherwise children keep on getting reinfected."

Until about twenty years ago, the water-scarcity problem seemed overwhelming, its magnitude and cost daunting. The outlook changed dramatically when a technological revolution swept the well-drilling world. Powerful high-speed air-driven drills were developed. Within hours, the new rigs could cut through hundreds of feet of solid rock to find safe water hidden deep in the earth.

That development coincided with one of the worst droughts of the century, which hit the state of Bihar, India, in 1967. Thirty million of the world's poorest people then faced starvation. The first models of high-speed air-percussion well-drilling rigs air-shipped by UNICEF from England to India proved to be lifesavers for Indian villagers.

The combination of drought and high-speed drills propelled UNICEF into well-drilling and safe-water programs on a grander scale than ever before. From the early fifties, it had helped bring safe water to rural health centers and schools, but had left the wider picture—entire villages without clean water—to others. The Indian drought and Bangladesh emergencies of the early 1970s marked a new era in UNICEF's aid to village water programs.

During the past fifteen years, more than 250 million people in rural parts of the world have gained access to safe water, due to direct UNICEF assistance. At least one hundred million are children under age fifteen.

Since 1981, the United Nations has put a gigantic thrust behind efforts to provide safe drinking water and sanitation to vast numbers. At a meeting of the United Nations General Assembly, on November 10, 1980, the world's governments

UNICEF PHOTO / T. S. SATYAN

Opposite: Transporting water is a daily task for the underprivileged slum-dwellers of Cartagena, Colombia. Invariably, the burden falls on the women and girls, who carry buckets weighing as much as forty pounds many miles every day.

Below: Before UNICEF helped to construct a new water system in Mersa, Ethiopia, the only nearby source was this miserable water hole.

As Ugandan youngsters so happily show, the quality of water—disease-free—is just as important to them as the quantity.

Below: Sri Lankan children in the Anuradhapura area fetch water from an India Mark-II hand-pump. Designed, with UNICEF's help, especially for heavy use, the steel pump has a solid bar instead of a pipe handle. This makes it able to withstand great impact—a water buffalo, for instance, rubbing its sides against it—yet makes it easy enough for children to operate.

Opposite: Women in Chad draw water from a hand-dug well. About one-third of all dehydration cases result from the unholy combination of dirt, exposed excreta, and lack of personal hygiene.

UNICEF PHOTO / VIVIANNE HOLBROOKE

jointly launched the International Drinking Water Supply and Sanitation Decade (1981–1990) with the aim of "Water and Sanitation for all by 1990." UNICEF is an active partner, focusing its aid on low-cost systems.

Nothing matches the excitement of a UNICEF-supported drilling team driving a high-speed rig into a bone-dry village. Men, women, and children cluster around, for everyone is curious—most of all the children. A rig is a strange piece of machinery, unlike anything most villagers have ever seen before. In India, village priests come to give their official blessing. They deck the rig with garlands of fresh flowers, sprinkling reddish powder on the ground where the drilling is to begin. Only then can the drill team begin its work. As they hammer the rig down deep into the hard rock, it sounds as if machine guns are being fired. The rat-a-tat-tat-tat of the bit hitting solid rock pierces the air hour after hour, until the moment everyone is hoping for arrives. Out of the depths of the earth, water spurts up, showering drillers and bystanders. Soaked to the skin, everyone yells and claps and revels in the miracle.

Everyone helps—men, women, and children. There are often miles of trenches to dig and pipes to lay down. A concrete platform must be set down over the well to protect it

and hold the hand-pump in place. When the well is capped and the new hand-pump attached securely to its concrete platform, the village priests return to burn incense and bless the pump. Then a villager steps forward to pump up the first potable water for that village. One local chief in Nigeria's Imo state, a water-scarce area where a model program in drinking water and sanitation is under way, described the first drilling: "Good water was struck from the rock to the surprise of all, and people were jubilating that UNICEF had come."

New wells are usually placed no more than two hundred yards from people's houses, making them the instruments of "women's and children's liberation." Having a water pump nearby frees young girls to return to school. It also waters the soil in which the four main techniques of the Child Survival Revolution can grow. No longer exhausted by water-hauling, a mother is able to breast-feed her baby longer and more effectively. Should diarrhea still strike, she would have time and patience to treat it with oral rehydration fluid early on, before dehydration threatens its young life. There would be time and energy for her to carry infants or walk toddlers to the nearest health post for their "shots" and regular weigh-ins.

UNICEF's aid started with the hardware: the all-important

high-speed drilling rigs, pipes, hand-pumps, water-testing kits, and simple maintenance tools. Soon the organization found itself involved in the process—helping to develop plans, supplying experienced mechanics, engineers, sanitarians, master drillers, and health educators—who, with on-the-job training, motivate and educate their national counterparts.

A village hand-pump is only as good as its caretaker, who, until recently, has been male. Many men are out working in the fields and are unable to fulfill this volunteer task. Therefore, more and more women—especially in India and Bangladesh—are being trained to successfully manage pumps and wells. The fact that women are given such responsibilities in the village greatly improves their status and is a first step toward freeing their time. Hindu and Buddhist women believe that acting as caretakers could favorably affect their next reincarnation, because helping others collects "merit."

Those who care for the remarkable India Mark-II hand-pump have less to worry about than with the old cast-iron pumps. This sturdy steel instrument has been designed by UNICEF to operate for years without breaking down. It has several special features: Children can't easily damage the handle or block the spout. It needs little or no oiling. And it is easy for a woman to keep in working order.

A great beginning has been made in providing safe water for millions. But there is the tremendous task ahead of bringing safe water and sanitation to the many still unserved.

"People love Vlado in Ethiopia," a colleague said, "because he is a man of action. He drives where people don't want to go. He flies in shaky planes, lives in campsites alone, drills for water where there doesn't seem to be any. . . . Even the guerrillas know who he is and why he is there. They never attack him." In his own words, Vlado Zakula tells what it means to be a master driller in one of the driest landscapes of the world.

A master driller's story

I am Vlado Zakula, master water-driller for UNICEF in Ethiopia since 1974. I came here in 1962, when the Yugoslavian government sent me as a mining expert to help the Ethiopian government mine for gold, copper, and other minerals. But in 1973, if you remember, the drought was very bad. And Haile Selassie was deposed in a coup d'état. Since I was working for his government, I resigned. UNICEF asked me to join their staff because the people needed someone to help drill for water. Drilling for water is not very different from drilling for gold, but water is more precious than gold for the people of Ethiopia.

Since 1974, we have drilled perhaps four hundred wells. Many people died because of drought, you know. Even in shelters, sometimes one hundred twenty people died in a day. This was one of the problems in Korem, in the north. In 1982

and 1983, there were only two or three days of rain a year. I went there in 1983 to make a well that would give people water on the spot in most of these shelters. You provide water for ten thousand people and sixty to seventy thousand come to the camp.

In Korem, we discovered two springs. In my report I recommended that the government "cap" these. That meant excavating natural water sources and installing pipes with filters. UNICEF immediately ordered the pumps, and the job was finished in a few months. Water was pumped from the springs, at a rate of three liters per second, to the reservoir, and from the reservoir to the shelter.

Mostly no one bothers us in the field. But sometimes the situation can be dangerous. Once I visited some UNICEF-installed wells in Ogaden in 1981–1982 and got caught in cross-shooting. I had to hide in the bush all night. The next day my vehicle had three bullet holes in it.

Wollo and Tigre were within my drilling territory. They were two of the worst drought-stricken provinces in the north, and they had guerrilla fighting too. I was told not to go to Tigre because of the political situation, but I went anyway. First, I took my small car to inspect the villages and the water situation. It was indeed critical. In one village called Korbota, there were four thousand people going eight kilometers for dirty water.

Because I had no driver, I drove the rig myself to Korbota. The roads were in terrible condition, but we got there nonetheless. We worked from morning to night for three days, drilling a well for these people, because I felt so sorry for them. "The well will probably only work for one year," I said. But it is still working.

People were so happy, you know. They killed two sheep for us, brought some local beer called *tala*, and had a big celebration. They were very satisfied.

While working on a project, I prefer to live on the site. I frequently stay alone there. This is because in the daytime I usually work far from the road. People question my not staying in camp. But I think it is better to stay where I drill. There are times at night when lions will come through the camp. But they do not bother us and we are not afraid of them.

Maybe my early life prepared me for Ethiopia. I was fourteen years old in 1944, when the Nazis occupied Yugoslavia. I joined the partisans and lived with them in the forests of Bosnia. Ten of us went on a mission. I went first since I was the leader. I was shot and lost a lot of blood. The bullet went through my chest and came out the other side. I played dead. I was the only one to live; my nine compatriots were all killed.

On the average, we drive our rigs twenty-five miles a day to get to one place. Sometimes there are two hundred miles between places. I must visit all the areas where we have wells. I have driven perhaps thirty-seven thousand miles myself by car.

I always take somebody with me who can translate. I can't say I know the Amharic language very well, but I can ask people what the problem is, why they are not taking water from somewhere, and tell them that the water they are using is not healthy.

In areas where there is enough wind, we put in a windmill. It's a wonderful thing: You get water without having to pump. We installed two in the Wollo. In most places, UNICEF is trying to put in more hand-pumps, like the India Mark-II, because they cost nothing to operate. It is quite a good pump, and is very useful. But then, we must put in more wells.

Sometimes the pumps or wells do break down. I always go myself to see which pump has gone wrong. Sometimes I ask another driller to go repair or install a pump. I never wait for the government because the government has too much work to attend to.

It is very difficult to find water and very hot between Assabot and the Red Sea. We drill a lot of wells in that area and they are usually dry. Sometimes I refuse to drill if I don't agree with the expert. The expert is the hydrogeologist. I am not a hydrogeologist, but I have located several wells. (I am trained in mining and engineering from a technical school in Yugoslavia.) Sometimes I have air photographs at my disposal in which I can see where there is drainage and the possibility of water. Drilling is so expensive that it is essential to work only where there is the greatest possibility of finding water. I have suggested that we try near underground dams because we can close them, allow a lot of water to pass during rainy season, and hand-dig wells so people can use this water.

We did start some hand-dug wells in Hararge in the southeast. You can put them in as long as the ground is not too hard and there is water close to the surface—about three hundred feet down or less. Some 250,000 people have hand-dug about five hundred fifty wells in the whole country.

My job is not only to drill wells and cut down the distance people go for water, but also to train Ethiopians to drill and maintain the wells themselves. When I joined UNICEF in 1973, we didn't have drilling rigs. Modern rigs had never been seen here. Then, in October of 1975, we received rigs and began to teach local people how to use the new equipment.

First, the government sent us older drillers who had had experience with another system. It was difficult to teach them. They didn't even know that modern drills used air or water to clean out the shaft during drilling. So we asked the government to please send us only young people who knew nothing about drilling. Then we could teach them from the beginning. The government responded by sending us people with at least twelve grades of education. We spent time with them in the field and sent them to training courses for six months. We now have a base of good people prepared for water drilling. It is very important for a country to have its own drillers. Hundreds and thousands of people need water. I am happy as long as I can be there to see the exultation on people's faces when they receive it.

YOHANNES BISSRAT

Master water-driller Vlado Zakula is beloved in Ethiopia because he is seen as the provider of precious newly drilled wells and hand-pumps. He is shown demonstrating a new system near Mekki, south of the capital.

XIII. Abandoned children

Nobody's children

by Peter Taçon

For the past thirty years, Canadian-born Peter Taçon has been an ardent spokesman on behalf of abused, exploited, and abandoned children. During the past ten years, his work has concentrated on bringing dignity and a future into their lives, first in Latin America, and later in Asia and Africa. The father of three, Taçon has also raised six youngsters whom he adopted while he was living and working in Latin America and to whom he dedicates the following piece. Today, Taçon's life and work are one. As UNICEF's senior adviser for child development, he continues to work for the millions who are called "nobody's children."

"What do you want to be when you grow up, Alberto?"

"Somebody."

There was anger in that one word—and determination. In a flash Alberto was on his feet, throwing off his T-shirt to expose a long, ugly scar.

"That," he choked out through his tears, "is what you get for being an *hijo de nadie*. That's what happens when you belong to no one. That's what the hospital does when you don't matter." He had been trembling with rage as he recalled what should have been a routine appendectomy, but now he pulled himself together—and up to his full height. "No, I am going to be somebody—maybe a doctor. Somebody."

Thereupon ended the first of many encounters I would have with twelve-year-old Alberto concerning the real world of poor children. During the months that followed, as my work took me to other Latin American countries, Alberto was always at my side, helping me to listen to, speak with, and understand the children we found on city streets. Alberto led me into their lives, and into their sufferings. More than anything else, he showed me that, despite all these youngsters had lost in their neglect and abandonment, they had also acquired an amazing inner strength simply by having had to survive so much. In doing nothing to help them, we were denying our own human family. By not accepting these street children as our own sons and daughters, we were missing out on one of life's great adventures.

This exhausted Filipino street boy has been
working since sunup in the Olongapo city marketplace,
carrying fruits and vegetables to help support his family.

As Alberto became my adopted son, he also became my guide and my teacher—a sort of adviser's adviser. From his own determination and character, I took the strength to abandon my quest upward in Canadian society—a back-home ambition that had been schooled into me ever since I could remember. From his vision of the profound worth of these young *abandonados* (abandoned ones), I came to see them, just like Alberto himself, as members of my own family. This child showed me his brothers and sisters, from whom I could not hide, and their world of suffering, from which I could not escape.

In these past five years, as my travels with UNICEF have taken me increasingly farther afield, new voices have joined my youthful advisory chorus of six adopted children. Some special moments with those other children of the world's streets have left particularly vivid memories:

"Chinche" Benjamín, of Bogotá, telling me, at nine years of age, that his greatest wish in life was to work; Gonzalo, of Guadalajara, after a lifetime of living in bus and train stations, saying he wanted to become a carpenter so he could build houses; María, in downtown San José, ordering me to "buzz off" with my offer of a children's village, because she preferred her twenty minutes of *work* a day (as a streetwalker, I presume); Nelson, in Managua, announcing that the dead are the lucky ones because the living have to go on suffering; Luis Carlos, in Porto Alegre, confusedly wandering about the city center at midnight, looking for a father he knew was out there somewhere; John, of Nairobi, amid the trash of a devastating shantytown, calmly outlining his step-by-step education plan and his faith in the future; Subhan, in a Bombay orphanage, reciting a lifetime of city adventure that would have stirred the imagination of an urbanized Kipling; Giulia, of Naples, observing that cleaning car windshields in the street easily beat the overcrowded anonymity of her home; and Sergio, in his "tin-town" Lisbon slum, taking me under his wing with particular compassion, upon learning that I had to live in a hotel.

Individually, each street child beckons us to look into his or her eyes, and, for at least an instant, not turn the soul behind those eyes into a statistic. Each face draws us bureaucrats away from our paper fortresses and causes us to look upon a single life—as it is, not just as it has been written. Each voice reminds us that, when we can no longer recall a child's image, remember a child's name, or reflect upon a child's personality, we have lost touch with the reality we seek to serve. Each of these boys and girls shows us that, if we are ever to reach the lives of those millions of street children in our world today, we must first acquire the understanding that comes from touching one life at a time.

The number of little people living, playing, and working on city streets increases daily, and the problems facing these children of ours become more and more dramatic. Whatever challenge their young lives present to us today, the fight on their behalf will assuredly be more bitter ten years hence.

Each thin, exhausted frame laid down to sleep upon the sidewalk, even as I write, cries out that survival is not enough. What is needed is human life—vibrant, singing, dancing, rejoicing, human life—for every child everywhere. If we offer less than that to anyone, we sacrifice our own humanity.

The large numbers of abandoned and street children in both developing and industrialized countries today represent a serious social challenge to UNICEF and its partners. While the presence of most of these youngsters is unobtrusive and

PEETER TAÇON

often taken for granted as part of the daily street work scene, the dramatic sight of a smaller number who roam city centers in bands or gangs evokes defensiveness and causes alarm amongst citizens and the media. Day centers as well as full-time institutions have become overcrowded with boys and girls who lack adequate family support. From all accounts they have been left to drift, have been cast off, or forced out by violence, at what appears to be an increasingly young age. Collectively, these often-forgotten children represent a tragic loss to this generation and an even more severe handicap for

the next. Some have estimated that these children of want number as many as one hundred million in our world today, with approximately half living in Latin America alone. Others calculate that if we take no action now to defend the rights and meet the needs of this growing multitude, we may easily have as many as two hundred or even three hundred million street children in our world by the year 2010. While it is true that to date no means of truly determining such global statistics has been developed, it is also true that these boys and girls who work and often live on city streets in virtually

In Latin America,
abandoned children
call the street
"Mama Calle"—
"Mother Street."

every country of our world number in the millions—and are on the increase.

The severe economic crisis now affecting many of the world's countries has placed even greater financial and emotional strains upon families—in a very real sense robbing increasing numbers of children within them of their childhoods. These children are forced into city streets, marketplaces, and factories to earn whatever little they can as their contributions to the survival of their homes. All too often in such circumstances, one witnesses the increasing separation among family members, the ever-growing vulnerability of the children and the constantly increasing risk of their eventual loss and abandonment. Girls, who are these days more and more evident in the street, are particularly vulnerable and unprotected in such situations—more often disenfranchised and more susceptible to exploitation than their brothers, and less included in community or government initiatives taken on behalf of street children in general.

Many of the youngsters who work on or who have become part of the street are the products of what others call "industrial miracles," the progeny of burgeoning urban slums, whose inhabitants have come to the city with a dream inspired by the advertisements of "progress" and "prosperity." Since UNICEF's birth forty years ago, the size and distribution of many Third World country populations have changed markedly as the so-called "revolution of economic development" has touched their societies. Increasingly, rural families have scurried to the city in search of new hope for their sons and daughters. The urban populations of Brazil, Colombia, and Mexico have increased from 30 percent to 70 percent since 1945. In that same period, the population of Manila has grown five times, and Bangkok has multiplied seven times over. Large city slums such as Nairobi's Mathere Valley (population 120,000) and Rio de Janeiro's Rocinha (population 130,000) have become as cities unto themselves—but with few of the basic services and little of the human cohesion that new residents from the countryside envisioned as the urban gift. Indeed, great cities in Mexico, where approximately fifteen hundred new rural immigrants put down new roots daily, find their capacities to serve new residents taxed well beyond their limits. In all of this, the children, of course, are the greatest losers—and none are more vulnerable and less defended in their vulnerability than the children on and off the street.

Since it started supporting initiatives that would effectively protect the lives of street children, UNICEF has, along with other governmental and nongovernmental organizations, learned some valuable lessons. In the past, helpful groups have focused on community-based action, which prevents family separation and abandonment and respects the integrity of the child. While acknowledging that, in the final analysis, the problems of street children are structural in nature and woven into the very fabric of society, UNICEF and its partners have realized that together we can make a difference here and now in the quality of these youngsters' lives, at least at the neighborhood level. On the other hand, while acknowledging that, given the realities of today's world, many children of the urban poor must continue to work, we have understood that "work" can and must be supervised, that it must be limited and dignifying to the children's lives—complementary to, rather than exploitative of, young lives.

As teams working hand in hand, we have found that we do not have to invent solutions for street children ourselves—that in fact a grass-roots army of local leaders has been doing this for years, quietly serving the young without expectation of reward or recognition. We have discovered that by systematically documenting their experiences (on paper and audiovisually) and sharing them with other communities, we can prompt a community's concern. That community will then reach out into the street where the children are—and initiate activities to support sound income generation, alternative education, vocational training, recreation and relaxation, health and nutrition—and also work to heal each child's self-image and his or her image of others, building self-esteem and a belief in the value of life itself. UNICEF has accepted this advocacy as its principal thrust—the changing of minds and attitudes; the development, especially amongst governmental leaders, of greater concern and priority for these children, their needs, and their rights.

UNICEF's own grass-roots experience began in 1981 in just three local communities in Brazil. Five years later, the work has not only grown a hundredfold within Brazil itself; it has also extended within Latin America to four departments and the capital of Colombia, to thirteen cities in Mexico, and to younger but growing national projects in Ecuador, Argentina, the Dominican Republic, Haiti, Peru, and Venezuela. The movement has taken firm hold in the Philippines, while increasing interest is being expressed in such countries as Thailand, India, Pakistan, and Indonesia. Solid proposals for street children have also been submitted by a number of African countries including Ethiopia, Kenya, and Zambia, while serious studies of the lives of street children are being carried out in Mozambique, Madagascar, Lesotho, and on the Ivory Coast. Recently, a number of international nongovernmental organizations have banded together to found a new global networking body on behalf of street-children initiatives. Called "Childhope," it began its activities in the latter part of 1986, in close cooperation with UNICEF.

Since 1981, UNICEF has helped to show that there is hope in a host of local community projects that offer support and protection to these children and their families. A growing international movement, led by nongovernmental organizations, UNICEF, and an increasing number of governments, promises that the suffering and sacrifice need not continue—that what could have become a galloping dilemma by the 1990s can be brought under control within our lifetime and eventually become a problem of the past.

Salamawit: a child alive

What Would You Like to be When You Grow Up?

ALIVE!

More than 12,000 children die each day from diarrhoeal diseases, the biggest single cause of death among the developing world's children. Two-thirds of these deaths result from dehydration and could be prevented by teaching parents how to prepare simple home remedies, such as fluids containing a little salt, plus starchy vegetables or cereals or some kind of sugar.

unicef

When she saw herself on this UNICEF poster for the first time, Salamawit Gebreyes, who lives in Addis Ababa, asked "Is that me?" The poster, initially used in 1984 to promote greeting-card sales and child survival, has evoked an extraordinary response worldwide.

Her name is Salamawit Gebreyes. She is nine and desperately poor. Infection nearly robbed her of the sight in one eye, and when she is ten her mother may no longer be able to afford to send her to school. This is the girl in the poster (left). Her face is seen all over the world, looking out on us with a friendly curiosity—and an extraordinary sense of hope. "Salamawit" means "peaceful" in the Amharic language, and she has understandably become a symbol of what the Child Survival Revolution is all about. That is why we end this book with Salamawit.

There are hundreds of thousands of children like Salamawit in the slums of Addis Ababa. She lives with her mother, grandmother, and three older brothers. Her mother, Almaz, is a widow who somehow has to feed four children and two adults on a government pension of thirty-three dollars a month. Her husband, a soldier, died when Salamawit was only two months old. The family came to Addis from the Ethiopian countryside stricken by drought and famine. They hoped to find work and food and made a home in two rooms behind a bigger house in a shantytown area. The kitchen has mud walls; there are no windows and no running water.

Salamawit and her brothers, Alim, twelve, Mamoosh, fourteen, and Agucho, ten, earn money watching parked cars in the street for foreigners, or running errands for apartment-house dwellers who are better off than they are. To make ends meet, Salamawit's mother and grandmother have set up a little stall made of wood and cardboard in the local market. Every day they sell spices and vegetables to neighbors. Whatever vegetables are not sold during the day go into a soup for the family's supper. Once a month, the family can afford to eat chicken or meat. Once every two weeks, the children drink milk. On Sundays, Salamawit's mother buys water from the local authorities at twenty-five cents a gallon to sponge-bathe the children. She collects the bath water and reuses it to wash the one good set of clothes each child has.

A year ago Salamawit's eye became badly infected. Her mother was persuaded to take her to the Black Lion Hospital so that a qualified doctor could examine it. (Addis has a free health clinic, but the doctors there aren't specialized.) The cost of the hospital visit, the antibiotic ointment, and the tetanus injection the doctor prescribed would have eaten up almost a third of the family's monthly budget. If UNICEF hadn't helped to foot the bill, Salamawit might have lost an eye.

When the picture was taken for the poster, Salamawit had just started kindergarten. Before that, her family couldn't afford the five-dollar monthly school fee. The government

LOUISE GUBB

pays for two children from each family to have free schooling, which means the money for Salamawit and her third brother Agucho has to be found by the family. Although Salamawit is one of the brightest in her kindergarten class, she may not be able to continue studying if her mother cannot find the money next year. Her mother values education. When she married Salamawit's father, she was only twelve years old and had just finished the fifth grade. Now, under the government's literacy campaign, she goes to night school at six o'clock after closing her little vegetable stall. And Almaz encourages all her children to study hard because the competition for jobs is keen.

Not long ago Almaz held a surprise party for Salamawit's ninth birthday. She invited not only the child's playmates but also the local priest. He blessed Salamawit with his ancient cross, asking God to keep her in good grace during the year and to safeguard her health and safety. Every Sunday the whole family goes to nearby St. Giorgis Church to pray. Salamawit belongs to the Orthodox creed, one of the world's oldest forms of Christianity. Custom calls for women and girls to cover their heads in church. Salamawit loves to twist a printed turban around her head—that's the one in the poster. She had just come back from church. When she saw herself in the poster for the first time, Salamawit was stunned and delighted. "Is that me?" she asked. Soon everyone in the neighborhood came to see it. Many international organizations began using it.

The welfare of Salamawit and her family, like that of so many other poor people in the capital, is of the utmost concern to the Ministry of Health and the City Council for Addis. They have committed themselves to halving the city's infant and child death rate in the next five years. A campaign to immunize all youngsters under two in the city is already well under way.

UNICEF is working closely with Addis leaders to assure that Salamawit, and others like her, enjoy the right to grow up in good health—not just to survive, but to be fully and vibrantly "a child alive."

Acknowledgments

Our warmest thanks to the many good people at UNICEF's headquarters, in field offices and national committees, on the staff of the History Project, and especially to all those so willing to be interviewed, searching their memory banks for half-forgotten experiences. All your help has enriched this book immeasurably.

UNICEF and the author deeply appreciate the goodwill and patience of Goodwill Ambassadors Danny Kaye, Liv Ullmann, Peter Ustinov, and Tetsuko Kuroyanagi as well as Prince Talal Bin Abdul Aziz in helping meet the publisher's story needs as well as providing us with personal photographs and memorabilia.

It was a privilege to work with Harold Evans, editor in chief of the Atlantic Monthly Press, during the development of this book.

Special thanks to Tarzie Vittachi, without whose vision and daring this book would never have come to pass, and to James P. Grant for his fine support. Jack Charnow was the good shepherd and tireless editorial administrator who oversaw every stage from egg to chick.

Laura Lopez-Lising and Alex Allard did yeoman service in handling heavy editorial research, photo permissions, and liaison work. Joan Dydo also gave top research help, as did Roy Moyer and Jack Mayer in their area of expertise.

Grateful thanks to: Tsutomo Mizota and Sharon Meager of UNICEF-Tokyo, Maie Ayoub in UNICEF-Addis Ababa, Bituin Gonzales and Loretta Medina in UNICEF-Manila, Bente Lerche at UNIPAC-Copenhagen, for going those extra miles and for producing fine results; Peter Lawrence and Jim Breetveld for their timely editorial help; Louise Gubb, around whose photos and interview with Salamawit's family the book's last story was developed; Martin Stone, UNICEF's good friend, for his invaluable efforts; Dwight Miller, senior archivist, Herbert Hoover Library, and Neil M. Johnson, archivist, the Truman Library, for special research provided; David Miller for summoning up remembrance of making *Seeds of Destiny* forty years ago and for finding photos of his film crew; Jean "Pres" Bowles, whose editorial savvy and early encouragement were pivotal in launching this book on its way; Nikolle Solomone and Dorothy Lewis for typing and other kind help.

Special thanks also to dear friends Rebecca Kalusky, Fred Ephraim, and my mother, Dora, whose encouragement meant so very much.

Judith M. Spiegelman
New York
August 15, 1986

Grateful acknowledgment is made to the following publishers and individuals for permission to reprint previously published material:

Joan Daves for permission to publish lines from "Piececitos" ("Little Feet") published in *Selected Poems* of Gabriela Mistral, Johns Hopkins Press, copyright 1961, 1964, 1970, 1971 by Doris Dana.

Franklin D. Roosevelt, Jr., for permission to quote from *On My Own* by Eleanor Roosevelt, Harper & Row Publishers, Inc.

Francis Cardinal Spellman, "Prayer for Children" from *Prayers and Poems*. Copyright 1946 by Charles Scribner's Sons; copyright renewed 1974. Reprinted with the permission of Charles Scribner's Sons.

Eileen Schneiderman for permission to reprint text by her brother, David Seymour, originally published in *UNESCO Courier*, August 1948.

UNICEF is also thankful to the following organizations and individuals for permission to reproduce photographs and other visuals:

Reverend and Mrs. Clyde Allison (photo, page 113); The American Red Cross (photo, page 45); Irena Rajchman Balinsqa (photo, page 61); Oscar Berger for so generously lending us his caricatures of Fiorello La Guardia (page 56), Eleanor Roosevelt (page 66), and Danny Kaye (page 86); Bettmann Archives, Betsy Gertz and Christine Wiltanger; photographer Yohannes Bissrat for kindly traveling to Mekki to photograph Vlado Zakula (page 213) and for contributing his photo to UNICEF; Rick Brown (photo, page 117); Canapress and Canadian Committee for UNICEF (photo, page 116);

Anders Engman (photo, page 63); The Edward C. Blum Design Laboratory, Fashion Institute of Technology (photo, page 96); Martine Gourbault for her drawing of Peter Ustinov (page 92); The Guinness Book of World Records (photo, page 90); Frantisek Hesik (photo, page 137); The I.H.T. Corporation (cartoon, page 89); Cornell Capa at The International Center for Photography for Robert Capa's photo of Picasso and infant son (page 141); Betty Kelén for cartoon by Emery Kelén (page 60); Magnum Photos, Liz Gallen; The Martha May Eliot Fund for Children, Massachusetts Committee for Children and Youth (photo, page 35); The Pierre Matisse Gallery for kindly allowing us to reproduce the photograph of Henri Matisse in his studio by Helene Adant (page 139); The *New Yorker* magazine for the drawing by William Auerbach-Levy (page 62); the Pate Institute for Human Survival (photos, pages 59 and 64–65); Frank Pennell in Dublin (photo, page 118); Pepsi-Cola International (photo, page 119); Richardson & Cruddas (photo, page 204); Time, Inc. for generously providing photos by Ralph Morse, LIFE (page 31), Co Rentmeester, LIFE (page 74), Bill Ray, LIFE (pages 130 and 131), Gjon Mili, LIFE (page 140), Allan Grant, LIFE (page 143), Loomis Dean, LIFE (page 145); Tropical Medicine Faculty, Mhipol University, Bangkok (photo, pages 76–77); United Features Syndicate, Inc., for permission to reproduce cartoons by Bill Mauldin (pages 24 and 38); Tom Prendergast and the staff of the United Nations Photo Library for 15 historical photos; The White House (photo, page 116); The World Health Organization (photos, pages 73 and 83).